Resilience

Also by R. Michael Medley

How to Teach English: A survival kit for teachers of English at the early stages. (with Carole Doardman, Zakia Sarwar, Ruqulya Jatri, and Joanna Baker). Lahore, Pakistan: Teacher Friendly Publications, 1994.

The challenge of the dream: Papers from a seminar on education and human growth. Lahore, Pakistan: Dar-ul-Hikmat Publications, 1993.

Resilience
Bouncing Back
Through English

R. Michael Medley

Eastern Mennonite University

WESTBOW
P R E S S®
A DIVISION OF THOMAS NELSON
& ZONDERVAN

WestBow Press books may be ordered through booksellers or by contacting:

WestBow Press
A Division of Thomas Nelson & Zondervan
1663 Liberty Drive
Bloomington, IN 47403
www.westbowpress.com
1 (866) 928-1240

ISBN: 978-1-5127-7340-8 (sc)
ISBN: 978-1-5127-7341-5 (e)

Library of Congress Control Number: 2017901312

Print information available on the last page.

WestBow Press rev. date: 02/01/2017

Dedicated to Willi Hugo, Neris, Jean Claude, Hero, Yunis, and countless others who were not dragged down by tough times, but bounced back through learning English.

"Breaking destructive cycles through acting well in spite of threat is spiritual work of the deepest sort. This is not a solitary journey; we need to be connected to communities of like-minded people as we act, listen, and learn in new ways."

(Carolyn Yoder, *The Little Book of Trauma Healing*, p. 77)

Declarations

1. These course materials are based on the training manual of Eastern Mennonite University's program, Seminars in Trauma Awareness and Resilience (STAR).

2. These course materials are not the equivalent of a STAR training seminar. The contents of STAR have been adapted for this course for the purpose of teaching English while students become aware of trauma and build personal resilience. The contents seek to be faithful to the understandings of the STAR training, but may differ in some particulars.

3. This course does not claim to be a form of therapy for any person who is troubled by past traumas. Such persons should seek assistance from a qualified mental health professional.

4. Teachers of this course should, if possible, enroll in a STAR seminar in order to deepen their understanding of trauma and resilience. Information on the program, upcoming seminars, and the application may be accessed at www.emu.edu/cjp/star/.

5. Requests for special training sessions should be made to STAR (Strategies in Trauma Awareness and Resilience) by writing to star@emu.edu .

Contents

Introduction for the Teacher

A contemporary of Shakespeare, playwright Christopher Marlowe wrote a poem in which a "passionate shepherd" promises to make for his lover "beds of roses." From Marlowe's line may have developed the expression, "Life is not a bed of roses." Modern playwright Samuel Beckett put it more bluntly when he spoke to his biographer about "the awful wretched mess of life." At some point in their lives, most people can resonate with that honest assessment. Life is not always good. Some people face many more challenges and difficulties than others. And yet, psychologists tell us, human beings remain optimistic. We find reasons to hope in the midst of trials and tragedies.

Though I personally find language learning enjoyable, for many of my fellow humans it is an arduous but necessary undertaking to obtain a better life for themselves. International students may not have calculated how hard it would be to attain the language proficiency needed to succeed in academic work. Other young adults, determined to lift themselves from poverty, have enrolled in English classes because the job market in their country demands that they use this language. Refugees and some immigrants to English-speaking countries, after enduring all the hardships involved in leaving their beloved homelands, now face the hurdles of acculturating in a land where not everyone welcomes them and where they are expected to know English to survive. In other words, many adult/young adult English language learners have indeed experienced "the awful wretched mess of life" and learning a new language is a part of that mess.

Text Overview

This textbook has been especially prepared for young adult and adult learners who have faced difficulties and challenges in life but who are ready to bounce back through learning English. Its purpose is to bring hope to language learners by integrating the study of English language with information and activities to increase personal resilience in the face of life's difficulties. No other English course gives sustained attention to building resilience and coping in healthy ways with traumatic stress as *Resilience* does.

Resilience is an appropriate textbook for all adult/young adult learners at the high intermediate and advanced level because it provides high-interest, sustained content. Activities and materials are designed to reach all types of learners, providing multiple pathways for them to access the language & content. Even low-literate native speakers of English will benefit from this text. The book guides teachers and learners to create community, which is a powerful resource for language and literacy learning

Resilience is based on the tried and tested materials developed for Eastern Mennonite University's STAR program (Strategies in Trauma Awareness and Resilience) which have been used in training programs around the world (Burundi, Colombia, Croatia, Haiti, Liberia, Mexico, Myanmar, Nicaragua, Palestine, Sudan, Kenya, Thailand, Uganda, and with multi-cultural audiences in the USA). See http://www.emu.edu/cjp/star/ for more information.

Resilience focuses on *reading*, *vocabulary development*, and *development of life skills* that foster personal resilience. The course also provides practice in *grammar study*, *speaking*, *listening*, and *informal writing*. *Sustained focus on coherent content* promotes interest and motivation, develops a strong network of vocabulary, and increases learners' self-efficacy as they become experts in the subject matter. Every chapter of *Resilience* presents two readings of 600 to 1000 words, representing an international range of experiences. Some of the contents of each chapter are adapted from the STAR training manual. Other content was developed and selected for this text to represent conflicts and cultures from around the world in ways that amplify concepts taught in the STAR manual.

Resilience follows a whole-person philosophy of teaching and learning through lesson materials and activities that appeal to diverse human intelligences and build community in the classroom. Every chapter incorporates art, music, and movement, and gives opportunities for learners to develop their interpersonal and intrapersonal intelligence as they learn English. The "whole person" philosophy is also implemented by teaching life skills for coping with trauma and conflict: self-examination, realization of personal strengths or weaknesses, interpersonal communication, active listening skills, stress reduction, sensitivity to mind-body connections, awakening of empathy, awareness of choices in healing the bruises of life, and healthy styles of conflict management. These life skills strengthen learners' ability to bounce back from tough times.

Resilience is an especially appropriate text for trauma-affected learners. These learners need a safe and trusted community; multiple pathways of expression (not just linguistic & logical); space to share their stories; and awareness of the choices they can make in life. Being part of the human family, we all live with the psychological aftermath of traumatic events. All of our lives have been touched or shaped in some way by trauma—whether those were childhood accidents that sent us to the emergency room; or the loss of loved ones who died or disappeared from our lives; or even the traumas of elders and ancestors who endured wars, natural disasters, great depressions, and terrifying migrations. Teachers will become learners with their students as they consider ways in which their present behavior may have sprung from the way their parents or the hard knocks of life have taught them to cope with difficulty.

Structure of a Typical Chapter

Each chapter in the book is divided into three main sections:
1. **Introduction** to the lesson
2. **The first reading**, along with text comprehension, word study & grammar activities and
3. **Life skills**, including a second reading passage and a variety of activities to extend and assess learning

INTRODUCTION to the lesson. Each lesson opens with three sections to get the class prepared for the theme of the chapter and its main reading.

Get to know each other better provides an activity for the class to do that deepens community by helping all class members (including the teacher) to know each other better. The activity is always connected to the topic of the chapter. These activities also stimulate the use of learners' interpersonal, visual/spatial, or bodily/kinesthetic intelligences, and hence are important for reaching all types of learners in the class. Because a healthy community is such a powerful resource for both language learning and personal resilience, it is not advisable to skip these activities. Community-building does not just happen in the first days of class; it needs to be sustained through the entire course.

Connect to the topic is a short paragraph or set of questions that help learners to reflect on how the "Get to know each other" activity prepares them for the lesson.

Picture(s) for discussion. This section of the text regularly provides visual stimulation to learners and provides a natural way to build and activate learners' background knowledge to prepare them for vocabulary and concepts that will appear in the reading.

THE FIRST READING of each chapter represents an adaptation of material from the STAR manual. The chapter titles reflect the main theme of each first reading passage. There are several sections associated with **the first reading**. Each time a reading passage appears in the text, it will be preceded by a box entitled **Develop your reading skills**, which directs learners to practice specific reading skills in the text that follows. A complete list of reading skills can be found in the Scope and Sequence table. Many of the skills are repeated in later chapters since research shows that students need to practice skills several times in order to adopt them for use in their everyday reading.

Following the **Reading** is the section **Understand what you read**, which consists of (a) a set of objective questions about the passage, using a variety of formats throughout the book and (b) some discussion questions that encourage learners to share their own experiences, ideas, and opinions.

Word study *follows* the reading and comprehension activities, but the teacher may want to do some work with the words before students begin the reading. All of the words in the **Word study** section appear in bold type in the reading passage; over 300 words are featured. Generally, the vocabulary featured in this section is to be learned for active use. Texts were carefully edited and vocabulary selected based in part on an analysis of each text with vocabulary profiler software (www.lextutor.ca/vp/eng/), which is very easy for teachers to use in order to survey a text's vocabulary. A significant proportion of these words appear on Coxhill's Academic Word List (see www.victoria.ac.nz/lals/resources/academicwordlist/), but many more of them are specialized words related to the study of trauma and resilience. Students will receive repeated exposure to this specialized vocabulary as they advance through the text and as the concepts build on each other in a sustained way.

Word study consists of four different sections: (1) **You define it** gives students repeated practice in working out the definitions of a few words from cues in the reading passage. (2) In a variety of formats (from one chapter to the next) learners get a chance to *manipulate* the new words. (3) An additional activity follows that pushes students to make the new words their *own* through production in meaningful contexts. (4) Finally, **related words** are presented and (5) one or more **expressions** (or idioms) from the passage are highlighted and practiced.

Grammar study. Like the vocabulary encountered in **Word study**, the choice of grammar structures is driven by the main reading passages. It is, therefore, not systematic. The emphasis is on functional grammar—or grammar for making meaning. Featured grammar is briefly explained and activities are provided for students to practice the grammar as a way of facilitating their discussion of the readings. Through attention to grammar in use, especially at the level of genre and discourse, students will deepen their comprehension of the readings. A complete list of grammar functions and structures appears in the Scope and Sequence chart.

LIFE SKILLS. At this point a second reading appears, representing personal **Stories of Resilience.** These personal stories further illustrate the main concepts taught in the first reading. **Comprehension & discussion questions** follow the stories. Generally, the reading level of these stories is somewhat easier than the first reading passage, but to facilitate comprehension, many new words are highlighted using a degree symbol (°) and a simple definition for each word is provided at the bottom of the page. Each personal story also comes with tips for **Developing reading skills.** Occasionally, the **story of resilience** is followed by a prompt for the teacher to share a personal story with the class.

Building on the chapter's main theme and the personal story of resilience, an **Extend your learning** section offers opportunities to integrate language production and the practice of resilient life skills using modes that appeal to diverse intelligences. Life skills are listed in the Scope and Sequence chart.

These activities are **not** intended to be optional. It is important for students to consolidate their language skills and their understanding of the course content through extended practice. Some language teaching programs, however, have less time than others and instructors will have to pick and choose carefully which extension activities they can implement. Based on their understanding of students' multiple intelligences, teachers may decide to emphasize certain types of extension activities and avoid others.

Every chapter suggests a **journal prompt** for cultivating intrapersonal intelligence. With the students' consent, the teacher may choose to **dialogue** with students by writing responses and questions in these journals. Other learning activities vary from chapter to chapter but most chapters include both **movement** and **music** related to the chapter theme. **Visual art, drama,** and **other forms of interpersonal interaction** appear in some of the chapters. A **self-assessment of learning** ends each chapter.

Advice for Working with Trauma-affected Learners

The lessons in this textbook are devised to support you in helping students who have been dragged through tough times to bounce back if you follow these four basic principles.

Meet learners' needs for safety and community. Persons who are the victims of violence perpetrated by either nature or humans often feel deeply betrayed and distrustful. Many persons who are the victims of crime, rape, torture or other atrocities are embarrassed by what happened to them and ashamed for others to know. They feel cut off from others. Only when they feel safe, accepted, and connected can they begin to release their traumatic experiences and move in a healing direction.

Make room for stories so that learners can acknowledge the trauma in their lives. In accord with the STAR approach on which this course is based, some way of *acknowledging* what has happened is an important part of moving toward healing. This can happen through talking with trusted others about the traumatic experience, or in non-verbal ways through the arts, music, or physical exercise. People sense when they are ready to talk about their tough times and when they are in the presence of others who care about them. Teachers who genuinely care about their learners as whole persons can create the kind of trust and space that learners need to take steps forward. But teachers should also be aware that for a variety of reasons trauma-affected learners may show no inclination to deal openly with others about their situation: they may just not be comfortable with others or may not know how to handle strong emotions and so do all they can to avoid them. *Pay close attention the movement activities* at the end of each chapter and use them to intervene if you sense emotions beginning to overwhelm anyone.

In using this curriculum, it is important to remember that this is a classroom, not a counseling center. You should observe carefully how each learner is doing in understanding the concepts and developing the various language and life skills that are taught. The lessons are designed to raise awareness and provide information. The lessons are not crafted to force or purposely elicit stories that make the learners vulnerable. *A key principle to observe* is that participants should be free to "pass" at any time---to participate or not participate in activities that (from their perspective) render them too vulnerable.

It is also important, however, that the classroom be a space where, if a student shares a personal story *the teacher will neither brush it off nor awkwardly try to move the class quickly past such a story.* Such moments can be moving, even sacred and transformational for all. Briefly, one of the things you as the teacher may do is to thank the person for trusting the group with the story. If the story is painful, it is an opportunity to use some of the movement activities (end of chapter 1) and self-care exercises (described in chapter 7), as well as the principles of compassionate listening (chapter 8). Fellow students can also be invited to offer words of support to the person who shared.

This kind of caring classroom is a humble space of respect and dignity because the teacher recognizes that the students' life-stories are so much bigger than the resources that the class has to offer. The students have other resources to draw on. In the second chapter of the book, learners reflect on their resources. You can keep a record of resources the students have named and remind them of those resources from time to time. As you and the students acquire new awareness and resources in other chapters of the book, you can highlight those for students. These resources will help to carry everyone through moments of vulnerability. While remembering that our role is a humble one in the lives of our learners, ESOL teachers also know that English language learners, especially those outside their home cultures or away from their homes, can be very deeply and positively affected by classrooms that open up this kind of space, providing multiple ways for enhancing their personal dignity.

Not all ESOL teachers will agree with this advice given here because it may make them and the rest of the class feel uncomfortable. They may also believe that ignoring the trauma is the kindest thing they can do for the victims—with the idea that "these people need to move on with life and leave their painful memories behind." As you read through the materials in the textbook, you will learn why this seemingly benign approach may do more harm than good (especially chapter 9). Even when you studiously avoid discussing topics that may bring up the person's trauma, you still cannot be sure whether something you say, do, or wear, or whether some color, shape, or odor in the classroom will trigger a traumatic memory that sets off one of your learners.

Following the suggestions in *Resilience*, caring teachers can create a welcoming space in which learners feel safe and supported sharing their stories when they choose to do so. Teachers should also be familiar with advice given in the following chapters about reducing stress and helping persons to calm themselves when traumatic memories are triggered or when sharing a story begins to overwhelm them: at the ends of chapters 1, 2, and 4 (various tools, including deep breathing), chapter 5 (relaxing music & muscle relaxation), and chapter 7 (tapping acupressure points). Most important, as the instructor you must model for the rest of the class what it means to be a "compassionate listener" (chapter 8).

Make use of multiple intelligences in the ways that we teach. As mentioned in the introduction to the course (above), activities appealing to multiple intelligences (MI) have already been built in to the course for you.

Trauma-affected learners may feel limited in their ability to talk about the pain they experienced, but an MI approach opens up other channels of expression for them. I have included activities like deep breathing, muscle relaxation, tapping, journaling, singing, art, role playing, and drama in this course because experts verify that these are helpful for the trauma affected (Yoder, 2005). One of the common effects of trauma on people is emotional numbing, which involves the loss of connection between feelings and the body. The MI-oriented teaching strategies represented in this textbook "help trauma-affected learners increase awareness of their bodies, maintain concentration on the lesson, and manage their emotions better, thus addressing some of the behaviour issues and mental/emotional obstacles that trauma puts in the way of classroom language learning" (Medley 2010).

Finally, use **lesson content that includes direct teaching about conflict, trauma, and resilience.** This principle is part of the very fiber of *Resilience*. The more learners are aware of what trauma is and how it affects them, the better they will be able to bounce back from the tough challenges ahead on life's path. By guiding learners through this course and taking full advantage of the activities suggested, you are investing yourself in a project to shape more resilient persons. Both their new communication skills in English and increased awareness of trauma will contribute to your students' personal resilience.

I have not supposed that teachers using this book would be working with learners who are *currently* living through severe trauma or diagnosed with a high level of post-traumatic stress disorder (PTSD). If you suspect that a student is very low-functioning because of PTSD, you might want to talk to your supervisor and your student about getting professional medical and psychological help and perhaps dropping the class. Of course, you should be sensitive to the cultural norms of the student if you make any effort to connect him or her with resources to address such problems.

For additional guidance in working with trauma-affected learners, see the references below. I am willing to share copies of my presentations or articles at your request. I also encourage you to consider signing up for a STAR seminar. Information on the program, upcoming seminars, and the application may be accessed at www.emu.edu/cjp/star/.

References

Canadian Centre for Victims of Torture. (2000). Torture and second language acquisition. Available at http://atwork.settlement.org/downloads/linc/torture.pdf

International Institute of Boston, (2000). Mental health and the ESL classroom: A guide for teachers working with refugees. Boston: International Institute of Boston and Immigration and Refugee Services in America. Accessible at www.eric.ed.gov/PDFS/ED467256.pdf

Medley, R.M. (2009a). Nurturing in-service language teachers affected by trauma. Presented at the 44th annual convention for Teachers of English to Speakers of Others Languages, Denver, CO, March 26-29.

-------- (2009b). Hope for the English language teachers of Kosovo. *Global Issues in Language Education*, 72.

-------- (2010a). Teaching trauma-affected learners: Exploring unmapped territory. Presented at the Society of Pakistan English Language Teachers 26th International Conference, Karachi, Lahore, and Islamabad, October 15-24.

-------- (2010b). Meeting the needs of trauma-affected learners. Washington Area Teachers of English as a Second Language (WATESOL) annual fall conference, University of Maryland, College Park, November 13.

-------- (2010c). Serving trauma-affected learners in Pakistan. *SPELT Journal*, 25.4, pp. 2-12.

---------(2012, March). A role for English language teachers in trauma healing. *TESOL Journal* 3.1.

---------(2014, December). Promoting peace by practicing forgiveness in the classroom. *SPELT Journal* 29.4.

----------(2015). Tension and harmony: Language teaching as a peacebuilding endeavor. In C. Hastings & L. Jacob (Eds.) *Social Justice and English Language Teaching*. Arlington, VA:TESOL Press.

Yoder, C. (2005). *The Little Book of Trauma Healing: When violence strikes and community security is threatened.* Intercourse, PA: Good Books.

Permissions and Acknowledgements

The first reading in every chapter preserves the main content and some of the language of the STAR training manual and is used with permission of Eastern Mennonite University's STAR Program.

The personal stories of resilience have been gifted to this book by the authors. The stories of Rasheed Qambari, Elena Zook Barge, Edson Arango, and Vesna Hart (in chapters 2, 3, 4 and 11) are based on oral versions that were recorded by me, transcribed, and carefully edited. The story of David Works (chapter 12) comes from a recording of his address in university chapel at Eastern Mennonite University on September 18, 2009; it was transcribed and edited by me and is used with his permission. I am grateful to have received written versions of personal stories from Neris Gonzalez (ch. 15), Carlos Mendoza (pseudonym – 5), Ruxsana Arshad (6), Carolyn Yoder (7 & 9), Charito Calvachi-Mateyko (8 & 14), and Brian Gumm (13). These stories were extensively edited by me for inclusion in their respective chapters. The story in chapter 11 by me entitled "Truth Comes Out in Bisho" includes excerpts with alterations from *No Future Without Forgiveness* by Archbishop Desmond Tutu copyright © 1999 by Desmond Tutu, used by permission of Doubleday, an imprint of the Knopf Doubleday Publishing Group, a division of Penguin Random House LLC. All rights reserved.

Those images within the text that are labeled as belonging to Eastern Mennonite University are used with permission from the STAR program or with permission from the students and faculty who appear in the photos. I have commissioned and therefore own the drawings by Jon Gehman. Photos in chapter 15 were purchased by me and are used according to the terms set by Shutterstock.

All of the reading skills, vocabulary and grammar activities and explanations in the book are original works of the author. I gratefully acknowledge the inspiration provided by Laurel Pollard and Laurie Martin as I revised my vocabulary teaching exercises. Many of the **Get to know you** activities were inspired by Vesna Hart's collection of activities for Youth STAR, ESL materials developed by the US Institute of Peace, and the website "Experiential Learning Games" www.experiential-learning-games.com/icebreakers.html. Some of the movement activities were inspired by *Making the Brain/Body Connection: A playful guide to releasing mental, emotional and physical blocks to success* by Sharon Promislow and Catherine Levan (Vancouver, BC, Enhanced Learning and Integration, Inc., Kinetic Publishing Corporation, 2005)

I am thankful to the administration of Eastern Mennonite University for granting me a Sabbatical during the 2010-11 academic year in order to work on this book. I am extremely grateful to EMU's STAR Program, its past director Elaine Zook Barge, and its founder Carolyn Yoder for their encouragement, support, and guidance as I undertook this project. I take full responsibility for the final shape of the materials and the perspectives that I introduced into the materials. Not all of the views and opinions expressed in this book are necessarily those of Eastern Mennonite University and the STAR Program.

SCOPE and SEQUENCE CHART

Topics	Reading skills	Language functions	Language structures	Resilient life-skills
1. Success in Language Learning	Survey the text Relate the text to yourself Relate the text to other texts	Define Describe Generalize	Simple present tense	Develop language skills through content, a hopeful outlook & techniques to reduce stress
2. Resilience	Look for definitions Keep reading Make connections	Make statements about one's own and others' personal traits Ask questions about others' personal traits	*be* + adjective *be* + nominal group *have* + nominal group	Think about your personal traits, your level of resilience & your community's resilience
3. Violence and Trauma	Re-read Connect/survey/ predict Learn from different types of texts Read with a purpose	Talk about things as members of categories	Use of *kind* and *type* with verbs *be, have,* and *involve* Use *there + be* to introduce new topics	Reflect on your life story, highlighting the good and bad times
4. What is Trauma?	Make your own graphic organizers Learn from different kinds of texts Use a timeline Read with a purpose	Talk about similar but slightly different things	Use of *both...and* *...but...* *...different from...*	Develop empathy for trauma-affected persons Find strength within to share experiences with trauma
5. Responding to Threat	Use what you know Make predictions Get meaning from examples Skim	Express causes and effects	Use of *when ....* *...because...* *because of* *cause*	Be aware of cross-cultural differences
6. How Trauma Affects Us	Find the main ideas Re-read Pay attention to how events are ordered	Understand links among sentences; understand writer's level of certainty	Pronoun reference Demonstrative determiners Modal *may* & no modal	Develop sensitivity to the effects of stress on the body and mood
7. First Aid for Trauma	Look for signal words to understand text organization Distinguish background from main actions	Give advice and directions	Imperative sentence mood & modals for advising & suggesting (*can, could, might, should*)	Practice techniques of stress reduction
8. The Healing Act of Listening	Practice skimming Read interactively Distinguish background from main actions Activate your knowledge of topic	Elicit stories of others while interacting supportively	Question types Polite requests	Practice supportive listening with classmates, family, and friends who face difficulties
9. The Dangers of Ignoring Trauma	Make connections between texts Learn from different kinds of texts Re-read Find main ideas Pay attention to characters and how events are ordered	Explain behaviors with varying degrees of certainty	Real conditionals and modals	Practice self-examination for effects of trauma; understand sympathetically the behavior of others

SCOPE and SEQUENCE CHART

Topics	Reading skills	Language functions	Language structures	Resilient life-skills
10. The Cycle of Violence	Make connections between texts Use visuals Use/invent examples Think about the title Identify & track participants	Use technical terms to focus on processes, or actions as things	Nominalizations Using the verb, adjective, and noun forms of words	Learn to calm feelings of aggression and discuss controversial subjects calmly
11. Breaking Free through Truth	Use subheadings Skim Make predictions	State opinions and perspectives	Use of "I" language *think/feel* + complement clauses *feel like* + clause *understand* + nominal clause *it's hard/important* + nonfinite clause	Learn healthy ways to remember, grieve, and tell stories
12. Daring to Show Mercy	Use title & subheadings to predict Read first & last paragraph Scan for important facts Re-read Make critical comparisons	Express purpose and express certainty or uncertainty	Clauses of purpose with *to + verb* and *so that + sentence* Modals *will, may might, can, could, & should*	Learn to look for the humanness of people who hurt others, to slow down, to re-gather energy
13. Seeking Justice	Survey, question & predict Summarize as you read Notice connecting words in the text Scan Activate your background knowledge	Talk about processes as things Describe persons, places & things more precisely	Verb+*ing* (gerunds) Relative & reduced relative clauses	Learn to practice restorative justice
14. Building Peace	Keep on reading Make predictions Re-read Use story elements Make a graphic organizer	Understand the purpose of different parts of a text Talk about processes as things	Tense and mood as signals of purpose Review gerunds [verb + *ing* in nominal groups]	Recognize your preferred way of handling conflict; stretch yourself to use a healthier style
15. The Journey toward Greater Resilience	Review before you read & while you read strategies	Understand a writer's point of view Connect ideas within and across sentences	Pronouns *you, they & we* Introductory clauses – finite & nonfinite	Build on your strengths as you reflect on what has made you resilient

Chapter 1 Success in Language Learning

At the beginning of each chapter an activity like this one will help you know your classmates better. It is important in this class for you to know each other well. The deeper your knowledge of each other, the greater understanding you will achieve. Personal knowledge is a good basis for building trust. Personal knowledge will also help your teacher find the best ways of teaching you.

Get to Know Each Other Better
1. Begin by playing a name game. Sit in a circle. The first person will begin by saying
     "My name is _____ and I like _____."
The thing that you like should begin with the same sound as your name. *Example: My name is Tomoko and I like television.* Go all around the circle and let each person say their own sentence.

2. Now go back a second time. The first person will repeat his or her sentence. For example, *My name is Tomoko and I like television.* The next person in the circle will say, *Tomoko likes television. My name is Karina and I like cars.* The third person in the circle will repeat *Tomoko likes television. Karina likes cars.* Then he or she will go on to say *My name is _____ and I like _____.* This will continue all around the circle until you come back to the first person. The first person will repeat all the sentences for the group. ***Feel free to give help to anyone who has problems remembering. Laugh and have some fun with this activity!***

Each chapter begins with some comments or questions that help you connect with the main theme of the chapter.

Connect to the Topic
1. Tell the other class members and the teacher about your past language learning experiences. Where did you study English? What methods of teaching did the teacher use? How did you feel about your English classes?
2. Think about <u>why</u> you have been a successful language learner. What personal qualities do you have that helped you learn English at an advanced level?

In every chapter, either here or before the section "Connect to the topic" you will see some pictures to look at and use for a learning activity. Some learners have high visual intelligence. We can all grow in our ability to understand what pictures are communicating. We can all use our visual intelligence to support our language learning.

Look at the pictures
1. Do any of the pictures on the next page remind you of language learning experiences you have had?
2. Do any of the pictures suggest something about the purposes for language learning? Do any suggest that specific subjects can be part of language learning?
3. Use the Internet (or magazines) to find more pictures that represent ways of language learning, purposes for language learning, or subjects that can be part of language learning.

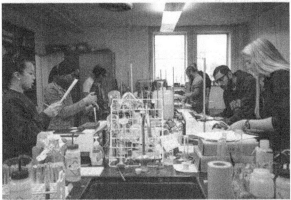

Eastern Mennonite University, 2016

There are two readings in every chapter of *Resilience*. Before each reading is presented, there is a box like this that asks you to practice specific reading skills. An important goal of this course is learning and practicing reading skills in English. You may be a good reader already in your native language. You will discover that you can use many of the same strategies to read more effectively in English. In order to excel at using these skills, you will need to practice them many more times.

You also need to read <u>more</u> than the materials in this textbook. To excel in reading, you need to spend a lot of time reading. Choose materials that you feel comfortable reading. Read about subjects that you enjoy. Whenever you read something outside of class, whether in English or your native language, try practicing the skills described in boxes like this one.

READ

> **Develop your reading skills:**
> **Survey the text**
> Before reading the text, look at it. Think about the title. Look at the bold headings marking each section. What do the headings mean?
> **Relate the reading to yourself**
> As you read the text below, relate it to your own language learning experiences. Interact with the text as much as you can. Look at the second section of the text. The text asks you to do something. Do it!

Learning Both Content and Language

People have different reasons for learning new languages. They may want to use the new language to gather information. Scientists need to find out about research happening all around the world. Knowing a language like English can give those scientists a way to get the information they want. Businesses may want to sell their products in other parts of the world. Or they may need materials and workers from other parts of the world. Knowing other languages can help business people reach their goals. Some people are eager to meet and talk with others. They want to learn their opinions and share ideas that might help to create a more peaceful world. Learning other languages gives people the power to work together.

Why have you been studying English?
Put a check beside all the different reasons that you want to use English:
___ to get a new job or improve your **performance** in your present job
___ to manage your day-to-day life more easily
___ to get more information about a subject of interest to you
___ to get some benefits from a government office or social agency
___ to get further education
___ to do business with people and businesses in other parts of the world
___ to travel to other parts of the world
___ to meet and talk with other people using English
___ to share your opinions and learn ideas from people in other parts of the world
___ (any other reason) _____

Ways of learning languages
        People learn other languages because they want to **communicate**. Language teachers around the world work on helping people to communicate. This was not always the case. Language courses used to begin with the study of grammar and lists of new words. But language courses today emphasize practical communication. We call this ***communicative language teaching***. It is becoming more common around the world.
        Have you experienced communicative language teaching? When you walk into a communicative language classroom you will often see students working in pairs or small groups. They are talking with each other in the new language. They may be sharing information with each other. They might be doing role plays. They may be solving a problem together. They may be giving a presentation to the class about their country. The new language is an important tool that they are using to make meaning together.

Content-Based Instruction
        Not all communicative language teaching is the same. Language courses that emphasize communication proceed in different ways. One way is ***content-based instruction***. A content-based language course presents a specific subject. This subject is studied for a short time or for the whole course. The course writer first selects the content, not the grammar and vocabulary. The vocabulary and grammar come from the content. Because we use language to share meanings with others, the content has first place. But the language is important, too. There are many chances to learn and practice new words and grammar. Students spend a lot of time listening, speaking, reading and writing the new language.
        Resilience is a content-based language course. It has been especially prepared for people who have faced difficulties and challenges in life. Its purpose is to bring hope to language learners by combining the study of English language with information and activities to help people handle life's difficulties. As you will find out in the first few chapters, a special focus of the book is ***trauma*** and ***resilience***. Having knowledge about trauma can give you more resources to help yourself. You can use these resources to help your family, friends, and neighbors handle difficult situations in life.
        Improving your knowledge of English gives you another helpful resource in facing difficulties. Increased ability to read, understand, and use English can provide you with more knowledge. You can use English to communicate with people who may be able to help you. Along with the tools and information you get from *Resilience*, your ability to use English may one day help you in a difficult situation.

After each reading are some questions to check your understanding of the reading. You will deepen your understanding when you compare your answers with others in the class and share your answers to the discussion questions.

UNDERSTAND WHAT YOU READ:
Circle the best answers from the choices given.

1. Very few people learn a new language because they want to _____
   a. do international business
   b. give their brain exercise
   c. travel, meet, and talk with people from other countries
   d. learn about new developments in science and technology

2. Most language courses today emphasize
   a. grammar   b. vocabulary   c. specific content   d. communication

3. All the methods below, except for one, are examples of *communicative language instruction*. Circle all of those methods, leaving one of the items uncircled.
   a. studying a specific subject in the new language
   b. doing a role play
   c. writing sentences according to a grammatical pattern
   d. working in pairs or small groups with other students

4. Which <u>one</u> of the following endings makes a true statement about content-based instruction?
   Content-based instruction _____
   a. pays attention only to specific content from science or business
   b. doesn't pay much attention to grammar and vocabulary
   c. teaches language skills by paying attention to a specific subject

5. Circle <u>all</u> of the endings that make true statements about your textbook, *Resilience*.
   Resilience _____
   a. is a content-based language course
   b. gives learners information about handling difficult situations in life
   c. teaches English grammar and vocabulary related to the specific themes of trauma and resilience
   d. gives learners practice with speaking, listening, reading, and writing skills

For discussion:
1. Collect everyone's answers to the question in paragraph 2. Make a graph that shows the number of check marks for each of the answers.
2. In some countries, like Malaysia, India, or Kenya certain subjects or even the entire school curriculum is taught in English rather than in the native languages of the students. University courses are taught in English in several European countries as well as many countries in Africa and Asia. In English speaking countries, immigrant children learn the language at the same time they are learning their various subjects. What experiences do you have with this kind of language learning? What is your opinion about it?
3. Does the content in *Resilience* seem relevant to members of this class or not? Why?
4. Make a list of the resources you have that can support you in learning English. Make a second list of resources that you can draw on to help you through tough times in your life.

Every chapter of *Resilience* contains some vocabulary for you to work on. Some of the vocabulary items are special words related to the topic of trauma and resilience. Many other words are general academic words that you will find useful in many different subject areas. These words are **bolded** in the text.

The first part of the vocabulary work helps you understand the meaning of selected words. The next part provides ways for you to practice. There are not many difficult words in this first text, so the following exercises are only an example.

WORD STUDY
Define it yourself!
A. *Look at these words in the text above. Can you find a definition for these special terms already given in the text? Write the definitions here:*

communicative language teaching (l. 25) _____

content-based instruction (l. 34) _____

B. *Try to match these words with their definitions. Then use these words to fill in the blank spaces below to complete the sentences. The line number from the text has been given to help you find the word quickly.*

		line #		
1	___**performance** (noun)	10	a	teaching
2	___**communicate** (verb)	21	b	the behavior of someone or operation of some machine
3	___**instruction** (noun)	33	c	ideas, meaning or subject matter
4	___**content** (noun)	33	d	give and receive information

C. *Fill in the blank of each sentence using the most appropriate word from the list above.*

1. I am not satisfied with the _____ of this cell phone. It drops too many calls.

2. Jasmine tried to _____ with me by cell phone. She left a voice message.

3. I can't tell you the _____ of her message because it is a private matter.

4. Jasmine is very happy with the quality of _____ in her English class.

D. *Work with a partner to ask and answer the following questions. The questions ask you to share your <u>opinions</u> about the pictures on the second page of this chapter. Make complete sentences. Try to use the new words in your answers. Be prepared to share some of the best answers with the rest of the class.*

1. Which students seem satisfied with the **performance** of their teacher?
   Example answer: The students in picture #3 seem satisfied with the <u>performance</u> of their teacher because she is helping them with their writing.
2. Which students seem satisfied with the **performance** of their laptop?
3. Which kind of language **instruction** seems most helpful to the students?
4. Which students have the best chance to **communicate** with each other?
5. Which students find the **content** of the class most interesting?
6. Tell about anything you have bought whose **performance** you are satisfied with or not satisfied with.
7. What kind of language **instruction** do you prefer?
8. What is your favorite way to **communicate** with others?
9. When you read magazines, newspapers, or the Internet, what kind of **content** do you prefer to read?
   Example answer: I prefer to read <u>content</u> related to the politics of my country.

Every chapter of *Resilience* gives you a chance to work on important grammar related to the text you have just read. The purpose of the grammar practice is to help you notice how the grammar helps you to create certain meanings.

GRAMMAR STUDY
Uses of the simple present tense
In the first text of each chapter, you will find the simple present tense used a lot. Why is this? The first text in each chapter presents some important ideas about how humans respond to difficulties in life. These texts define important terms. They discuss the qualities of people, things, and ideas. They state general truths about human experiences; these statements are true for many people in many different places and times. Let's look at some examples of how the present tense is used in the first text of this chapter "Learning Both Content and Language."

1. **We use the simple present tense to <u>define</u> special terms:**
Communicative language teaching **is** a common approach to language teaching.
In communicative language teaching, students **learn** a new language by giving and receiving information in the new language.

Write a definition of <u>content-based instruction</u> using the sentences above as a model.

Content-based instruction_____

_____

2. **We use the simple present tense to <u>describe the qualities</u> of people, things, or ideas**
People **have** different reasons for learning new languages.
Communicative language courses **proceed** in different ways.

Write two sentences to describe qualities of your textbook.

Resilience _____

The grammar and vocabulary in Resilience _____

_____

3. **We often use the simple present tense to talk about people *needing, wanting, or knowing*.**
Scientists **need to know** about research happening all around the world.
Businesses **want** to sell more products around the world.
Language teachers **know** that communicative language teaching works well for most students.

*Write sentences using **need, want,** and **know** in the present tense with **students** as the subject.*

Students_____

_____

4. **We use the simple present tense to make general statements about human experience.**
Communicative language teaching **works** well for most students.
We **use** language to share meanings with other people.

Give as many different answers as you can to the question: Why do people learn new languages?
Verbs that you can use are *learn, study, use,* or *need.*

People_____

_____

More grammar practice:
1. Return to the first discussion question following the text above. You made a graph to show everyone's purposes for learning English. Write or practice speaking sentences that describe the results. Try to use the simple present tense.
2. Compare the first paragraph of the text with the two paragraphs in the section headed **Ways of learning languages**. Which paragraph has the most instances of simple present tense? Why? Why do the other paragraphs use a mixture of tenses?

The second reading in every chapter is a personal story. These stories provide examples to help you understand better the ideas from the first text of the chapter. There are no vocabulary exercises following these stories. Some difficult words (marked with °) are defined below the story. Following the story are some questions to help you deepen your understanding of the reading.

LIFE SKILLS
Story of Resilience

> **Develop your reading skills:**
> **Relate new texts to texts you have already read.** The first text of this chapter was about reasons for learning new languages and ways of learning new languages. There was a special emphasis on *communicative language teaching* and *content-based instruction*. When you read this text, think about how you can connect the ideas from the first reading to this one.

From Zero English to Graduate School in 12 Months

When Willi came to our intensive English program,° he could barely speak a word of English. He was 26 years old. He came with the goal of earning a master's degree in theology° from our university. For years he had been involved in peacebuilding° and church work in his home country Guatemala. He began his studies in our program at the lowest level. Willi worked hard and made unusually fast progress. By the end of twelve
5   months, Willi was speaking, reading, and writing English at a very advanced level. Even though we believed he would struggle in his MA program, we allowed him to begin that program. Willi got extra help from tutors during his theological studies. And at the end of his two-year MA program, he received an award for academic excellence.

If you knew more of Willi's story, you might be surprised at the difficulties he has faced in life. When
10 he was just 10 years old, his father was murdered and his home was burned. His father was a poor, hard-working farmer. But he was killed by soldiers for the "crime" of organizing the farmers in his small village into an agricultural cooperative.°

One night shortly after his father's death, he awoke crying. Suddenly, he realized his mother was there, and she embraced° him. She took him outside to a small hill, and said "Look up." It was a wonderful night. The
15 stars were shining brilliantly, lighting up the night sky. And his mother said to him, "Don't be afraid. The light still shines in the darkness." When he looked at her, his mother's face was filled with peace, even in the midst of great suffering. Willi has never forgotten that night or his mother's words.

Despite many struggles in life, Willi successfully learned English. He earned his master's degree. And he is now the academic dean° of a theological school in Guatemala. He is preparing leaders to work for justice
20 and peace in a country that faces many problems.

I think there are several things that account for° Willi's success as a learner of English. First, Willi learned from a young age how to face difficult situations in life. Willi gained strength and hope from his mother. Like her, he found peace even in the midst of suffering. He entered his first stage of English studies with strong goals. He worked hard learning the basics of English in the intensive English program. The
25 program also offered him some content-based instruction. He was learning about interesting and meaningful things while studying English. Then when he reached an advanced level, all of his studies were centered on the theological content. He was very eager to study theology. While learning this content, he had tutors to help him. They helped him improve his reading and writing.

30 Not all of you will learn English as fast as Willi did. But you have strengths that will help you be successful. Your strengths may be different from Willi's. But like Willi, you can reach success by setting your goals and working hard.

Some material in this text comes from an article by Ron Copeland, available at http://www.emu.edu/seminary/features/pcrcz.

°intensive English program (noun phrase) – a language school or institute in which students study English full-time
°peacebuilding (n.) – activities that help people and societies live in peace
°agricultural cooperative (noun phrase) – a farmers group that works together, sharing the costs and profits of farming
°embraced – (v.) hugged
°academic dean (noun phrase) – the leader of the program of studies in a college or university
°account for (v.) - explain

Understand what you read

Below are five opinions about the text. Mark the following sentences A *for agree and* D *for disagree. Be prepared to discuss your answers with the class.*

1. ___ Willi's experience doing peacebuilding and church work did not play an important part in his language learning.

2. ___ Willi's mother played only a very small role in his success.

3. ___ The opportunity for him to study theology may have helped Willi to learn English faster.

4. ___ Willi would not have needed extra help to succeed in his theological studies if he had spent another 6 months in the intensive English program.

5. ___ Willi's fast progress in learning English is normal; anyone can learn that fast.

Discuss

As you think about your own language learning, answer these questions.
1. How could your work experiences in the past help your language learning?
2. What relation could there be between studying English and difficult situations in your life?

At the end of each chapter are some activities to give you extra practice with the new language and information from the chapter. If you do all or most of them, you will extend and deepen your understanding of resilience and trauma. And you will grow in your ability to communicate in English.

Most chapters include
- some kind of activity involving motion
- activities involving cooperative work in small groups
- a musical activity
- activities requiring imagination, drama and art
- a journal assignment so that you can think quietly by yourself about what you are learning

Why are these kinds of activities needed? Learners have different kinds of intelligences. In one small class, there may be people who are very good at
- using their bodies to communicate
- relating to other people
- enjoying or creating music
- appreciating or producing art
- learning from quiet self-reflection

These activities give every kind of person a chance to learn in ways most helpful to him or her. These activities give you a way to express your ideas and feelings that may be better than just talking.

Although these activities are not optional, you and your teacher may select to do some of them and not do others. Suppose that no one in your class likes drawing, and the teacher has learned this from working with you. She/he may choose not to do any activity that uses drawing because she/he knows that you may not learn much from doing the exercise. Ideally, the teacher will discuss with you to find out which activities are most likely to be successful with at least some of the class members.

However, remember, it is not bad to feel a little bit uncomfortable with a new activity. When you were growing up, your family sometimes served you food that was new to you. You didn't know if you would like it, but you tried it anyway. At first, you didn't like it very much. But after a while, you started to like it a lot. Maybe now it is one of your favorite foods. The same thing applies to language learning activities. An activity you don't like today may become one of your favorites by the fourth week!

EXTEND YOUR LEARNING

1. **Keep a journal:** What dreams do you have for learning and using English?
What dreams do you have for your life?

2.**Music:** Listen to "I Have a Dream" by Westlife   http://www.youtube.com/watch?v=c_PoDIiGFqg
The Irish boy band Westlife performed from 1998 to 2012. In 1999 their recording of the ABBA song "I Have a Dream" was number 1 in Ireland and the United Kingdom.

In 2011, Voice of America Special English broadcasted a report about using songs to learn English. English language learners from around the world suggested songs that were helpful to them. Aurelio Lourenco Costa Gusmao wrote that he began to like English when his teacher played this song by Westlife "I Have a Dream." From that moment, the dream of improving his English stuck with him.

You can view the VOA Special English broadcast "Are you learning English? These songs may help" here: http://www.youtube.com/watch?v=33qbMCuJ5XI. This broadcast can give you more suggestions of good songs for learning English.

Suggestions for using this song:
1. Just listen and follow the words.
2. Listen again. This time, after the singer sings each phrase, the whole class says the phrase.
3. The third time through, everyone can join together and sing along.

Discuss
Which words in the song suggest that the singer faces changes or difficulties in his life? What things mentioned in the song give the singer hope?

3. **Drawing**: For some people, a good way to express ideas or feelings is through drawing. Throughout the book you will find drawings of cartoon characters by artist **Jon Gehman**.

Jon grew up in South Texas where he spent most of his time drawing pictures and riding his bike. Later he attended Eastern Mennonite College where he spent some of his time taking a few drawing classes and riding his bike around the rest of the time. Now he lives in Linville, Virginia with his wife and daughters, two Border Collies and some goats. He still spends a lot of time drawing and riding around on his bike.

Jon Gehman

The illustrations in this text are based on characters Jon has been drawing for over 20 years. They have appeared on blackboards, the margins of church bulletins, dirty car windows, and hundreds of pages in dozens of sketchbooks. The three characters he feels the closest to are Loomis the Crow, and Lala and Squib, the Girl Mouse and Boy Mouse.

Jon says, "They really have become friends to me, but all the various birds, mice, dogs and other animals in this little universe are kind and pleasant to be around. When I asked them to act out some of the scenes where they're not being very nice to each other, I had to convince them this textbook would be a worthwhile project that could help all sorts of people from all over the world learn English. In the end they were all very happy to co-operate. They wish success and prosperity to everyone using this book."

Jon's picture (above) shows that some people learn better by using music and movement. Now you try it. Draw a picture of the most enjoyable and effective way for you to learn anything.

4. **Movement:** Language learning can be stressful. One way to deal with stress in life is movement. The dancers in the picture above are moving to the music, working out their stress, and having fun. Because movement is a very good way of dealing with stress, you should try doing all of the movement activities suggested in the book. Remember to use these activities later on in the course, along with the other movements taught in the various chapters.

A. **Touch your head, touch your toes**
Listen to the teacher's commands and follow her/his example. After a short time of warm-up, the teacher will speed up the commands. After speeding up, the teacher will also mix up the commands. The exercise will help you release some energy and create some laughter.

Touch your head (with both hands)
Touch your hips
Touch your knees
Touch your toes

You can add the following commands to the commands above and then mix them all up!
Shake your head
Shake your arms/ hands/fingers
Shake your hips
Shake your legs/feet

B. **Exercise after class**
One of the best ways of staying healthy in body and mind is regular exercise. Try to do some kind of vigorous exercise two or three times a week. Jog, run, walk, cycle, or play a sport. If you feel stressed before or after class, do some kind of physical exercise.

C. **Tactical breathing:**
David Grossman is an expert in training soldiers to manage stress in dangerous situations. You can learn to manage stress using his tactical (or four count) breathing exercise. If English class ever makes you feel stressed, you may want to try tactical breathing (end of Chap. 1). You might want to do this exercise <u>before</u> you speak in class.

1. Breathe in through your nose and count slowly to four (1, 2, 3, 4). Let your stomach expand when you breathe in. Count silently--in your head.

2. Hold your breath and count to four (1, 2, 3, 4).

3 Slowly let your breath out through puckered lips and count to four (1, 2, 3, 4).

4 With empty lungs, count to four (1, 2, 3, 4).

5. Begin the cycle again by breathing in while you count to four.
You should repeat this cycle at least 3 times.

Once you have learned this routine, the teacher will say, Do tactical breathing *and you should do the activity by yourself.*

[See Grossman and Christensen (2004) *On Combat: The Psychology and Physiology of Deadly Conflict in War and in Peace.*]

D. **Self-massage**

Massages are very relaxing. Not everyone can afford a professional massage. Giving yourself a relaxing massage costs nothing but a little time.

Use your fingertips.
Rub your forehead in slow circular motions.
Rub your jaws the same way.
Rub the sides of your neck the same way. (also try knees and feet)

Use your hand.
Squeeze your neck.
Squeeze your shoulders.
Squeeze your arms from the shoulder to the wrist.

Use your hand. Make a loose fist.
Tap on your sides.
Tap on your lower back.
Tap on your legs

Each chapter ends with self-assessment. Self-assessment is important for three reasons.
1. The action of assessing yourself reminds you that you are responsible for your language learning
2. It helps you think about what works best for you so that you can use that knowledge to help you 'soar with your strengths'
3. It will help your teacher know how to adjust the instruction to help you and your classmates. For this reason, it is important for you to be honest in your assessment.

SELF-ASSESSMENT

Think about your learning. Complete this assessment. Discuss your answers with the rest of the class. When you discuss your answers, notice how yours are like or different from your classmates' answers.

A. Read the choices in the sentence frame below. Then write two sentences that are *true* for you.

Example: *I liked listening to music because I learn a lot by using music.* OR
I liked listening to music because it made me feel happy and hopeful.

I liked or I didn't like	<ul><li>discussing the pictures</li><li>reading the texts in this chapter</li><li>discussing the questions with the class</li><li>writing in my journal</li><li>listening to music</li><li>singing</li><li>doing the _____ exercise</li><li>(add your own)</li></ul> _____ _____	because I learn best by or because I don't learn well by	<ul><li>reading and writing</li><li>working with other people</li><li>understanding myself</li><li>using pictures</li><li>working with my body</li><li>organizing things logically</li><li>using music</li></ul>

True sentence 1. _____

_____

True sentence 2. _____

_____

B. Now answer these questions:

The most helpful thing I learned from this lesson was _____

One thing that I want to practice more is _____

My goals for this course are _____

_____

_____

MUSIC SURVEY

During this class period or for homework, complete a music survey. Share the answers with your teacher or discuss them in the class.

1. Do you enjoy listening to music?   Yes, a lot Yes, a little   Not very much   Not at all

2. How do you like music <u>without</u> words?
        Like it a lot   Like it sometimes   Seldom like it   Don't like it at all

3. How do you like music <u>with</u> words?
        Like it a lot   Like it sometimes   Seldom like it   Don't like it at all

4. What kinds of music do you listen to? (check as many as you like)

___pop	___folk	___Latin
___hip-hop	___country-western	___world music
___reggae	___jazz	___new age
___rock'n'roll	___blues	___spirituals
___alternative rock	___techno	___classical
___ other _____	___ other _____	___ other _____

5. What kind of music gives you energy? _____

6. What kind of music makes you feel happy? _____

7. What kind of music calms and relaxes you? _____

8. What is your favorite kind of music? _____

9. Who is your favorite singer? _____

10. Do you enjoy singing?   Yes, a lot Yes, a little   Not very much   Not at all

11. When and where do you sing? _____

12. Do you play any musical instrument? Which one? _____

> *Learning Tip: As you begin this course, set some personal learning goals. What do you want to be able to do better by the time you finish this course? As the course goes on, think about how you are doing in reaching your goals. Review your goals about every 2 to 4 weeks.*

Chapter 2: Resilience

Get to Know Each Other Better

Play Bingo

1. Read the phrases in the boxes below. If you have any questions about their meaning, ask your teacher.
2. You want to find out which persons in your class have the abilities described in each box.
3. Get up from your seat so that you can walk around the class and find someone who can sign their name in one of the boxes.
4. A class member can only sign your page one time. This means you need to talk to at least nine other people in the class.
5. When your card is filled with names in every box, you can yell out "Bingo!"

_____ reads something for enjoyment almost every day.	_____ likes to do work with his/her hands or play sports.	_____ can sing or play a musical instrument.
_____ easily does math problems in his/her head.	_____ likes to meet and talk with new people.	_____ likes to be outdoors and knows the names of many plants or animals.
_____ always notices the fashion and colors of others' clothing	_____ plans to have a quiet time to think every day	_____ likes to think about big questions like "Why are we here on earth?"

Connect to the Topic

You are a person with many strengths and abilities. You have had hard times in your life. But now you are stronger. You are beginning this English class. You are moving forward to the next stage of your life.
What gives you strength in your life? What makes you a strong person? Think also about your past. Who or what gave you strength?

Look at the picture

Look at the cover of this book and then discuss the questions below.

Discuss

What do you see in this picture?

What do you feel when you look at this picture?

How can you compare this picture to a person's tough times in life?

READ

> **Develop your reading skills:**
>
> **Look for definitions**
>
> In the title and in the first line of the reading, you probably see a new word: *resilience*. Sometimes you can find the definition of a new word in the text. Look at the sentence in which the word appears. Look in the surrounding sentences. After you find the definition of *resilience*, see if you can do the same thing to another new word: *flexible.*
>
> **Keep reading**
>
> Some parts of a text may be more difficult than others. Perhaps the vocabulary, the grammar or the ideas in some parts of the text are more difficult than in other parts. Don't let the difficult parts stop you. Take the list in the middle of this reading. You may not understand every line in the list. Don't worry. Put a question mark (?) by the line you don't understand. Go on reading and then at the end go back and think about the lines with the question marks. Use a dictionary or look ahead to the vocabulary exercises to learn the meanings of new words.

What Is Resilience?

Resilience is the ability to bend without breaking. A **resilient** person can **bounce back** after **hardship**. A resilient person can suffer through hard times and **recover**. Resilience is like a tree in strong wind. The tree is **flexible**; it bends and **sways** but does not break. Like a flexible tree, people and societies can go through difficult situations without being destroyed.

5 **How can we build resilience?**

There are several ways that we can build resilience. As you read the list below, put a check [√] in front of any statement that is true for you. Remember, you can put a question mark (?) next to any line that you don't understand.

____ You live in a place where your basic needs for food, clothing and housing are met.

10 ____ You have good health care, education, and social services.

____ You have a caring group of family and friends to support you.

____ You believe good things about yourself.

____ You have **confidence** and **motivation** to face life's difficult situations.

____ You have the knowledge to help you act wisely in some kinds of difficult situations.

15 ____ You can find **creative** solutions to life's difficult problems.

____ You are interested in new ideas and willing to **explore** them.

____ Other people can trust you to behave wisely and well.

____ You have a good understanding of your own feelings and the feelings of others, and you know how to talk about feelings.

20 ____ You know when your body feels **stressed** and you can make yourself feel **calm.**

____ You have a good sense of humor; you can laugh at yourself or your situation.

____ You belong to a religious community or have a philosophical outlook° that gives you meaning and hope even in life's most difficult times.

Think: *Are you a resilient person? How does your community help to make you stronger?*

25 **Building social resilience**

Resilience is not just for individuals. In fact, the society where you live can strengthen or weaken your personal resilience. Whole societies can be more or less resilient as they **respond** to change and difficult situations. This is called **collective resilience.** Resilient societies can respond to changes and emergencies in **healthy** ways. These societies help all people to feel a part of the **community**. They show flexible and
30 **creative** thinking. When new problems come up, they try new solutions. A resilient society uses hardships to grow stronger and become one people living in community. When you live in a resilient society, you can draw on the community's strengths to help you face problems.

°*philosophical outlook*: a view of life based on deep thinking

UNDERSTAND WHAT YOU READ

Choose the best answer for each sentence:

1. A resilient person is like a tree that _____
    (a) breaks in the storm   (b) stands tall in the storm   (c) bends with the storm

2. This reading suggests to us that people _____
    (a) are born without resilience   (b) can become more resilient   (c) easily lose resilience

3. Which answer best completes this sentence about the second section of the reading?
   A resilient person must have_____ of the qualities in the list above.
    (a) all   (b) many   (c) a few

4. Most of the qualities of resilient persons mentioned in the list relate to our bodies, our personal inner qualities and our _____.
    (a) social relationships   (b) material wealth   (c) level of education

5. The reading suggests that resilient societies can be flexible and solve problems in new ways by
    (a) giving higher education to the most intelligent people
    (b) teaching families how to raise children wisely
    (c) including *all* people in the community and using their talents

Discuss
1. Think of 4 or 5 things that give *you* resilience. Share one thing with the class.
2. Think of specific societies or countries. What are specific qualities which make that society or country more resilient?
3. Which of the ways for individual people to build resilience relate in some way to the whole society?
4. What do you think: Can people or societies grow stronger through experiencing hardship? Why or why not?

WORD STUDY
Define it yourself!
A. *Look at these words in the text above. Some of them are used several times. The surrounding words and sentences should help you understand the meaning. Write your own definition. Compare your definition with the dictionary's definition. [Line numbers appear in brackets.]*

Example
flexible (adjective) [3] _____ *something that can bend or move and not break* _____

resilience (noun) [1]_____

31

resilient (adjective) [1] _____

collective resilience (adj. + noun) [28] _____

community (noun) [29] _____

B. *Review the reading above and try to match these words with their definitions. Then use these words to fill in the blank spaces below to complete the sentences. The line number from the text has been given to help you find the word quickly.*

		line #		
1	___**calm** (adjective)	20	a	get better, get back one's health
2	___**confidence** (noun)	13	b	bend or move back and forth
3	___**creative** (adjective)	15	c	leading to physical, emotional, or social wellness
4	___**explore** (verb)	16	d	new and different or unusual
5	___**healthy** (adjective)	29	e	quiet, peaceful
6	___**hardship** (noun)	2	f	belief in your own strength and ability to do something
7	___**motivation** (noun)	13	g	pressured, strained, tense; often felt by one's body
8	___**recover** (verb)	2	h	a difficult situation or happening in life
9	___**respond** (verb)	27	i	a desire, a good attitude
10	___**stressed** (participle of the verb *stress*)	20	j	think about and study
11	___**sway** (verb)	3	k	to do something or change because of something else

C. Sentences for completion:

Fill in the gaps with one of the words from list B above:

1. Jamal had a clothing shop. A few years ago, he suffered a great _____. A fire destroyed his shop.

2. After the fire, he could not sleep and did not feel like eating. He felt _____ because he had to feed his family and pay bills. Since he lost his business, he had very little money.

3. Of course, Jamal was upset at first. But he did not lose hope. He stayed _____ and was at peace about the future.

4. Jamal had good relationships with his extended family and with community members. They knew he had great abilities. They supported him and gave him the _____ to move forward.

5. Jamal had a strong desire to rebuild his life. He had the _____ to start his business again.

6. He _____ many _____ ideas about how to build a better shop. He studied many different building plans and was happy with new and unusual things that he learned.

7. Jamal was flexible like a tree. He _____ in the storm; he bent but did not break.

8. He _____ in a _____ way to this difficult situation. He took positive actions. These actions also helped him to stay well during those difficult times.

9. His philosophical outlook helped him to _____ from this shock. Jamal feels very well again. He is a good example of a resilient person.

Now listen to your teacher or partner read the sentences and check your answers.

D. Look again at the picture on the cover: How many of the following words can you use to make a sentence about the picture? *flexible, calm, healthy, hardship, recover, respond, stressed, resilient, creative.* Work in pairs or groups with each pair or group taking some of the words. Work together so that every class member can say one sentence.

E. Turn to a partner to ask and answer the following questions. Be prepared to share some of the best answers with the rest of the class.
1. What is your **motivation** for taking this class?
   You can start your answer by saying: My **motivation** for taking this class is….
2. What will give you more **confidence** to use English?
   You can start your answer by saying: I will get more **confidence** in using English if….
3. How can we build a stronger **community** in this class?
   You can start your answer by saying: We can build a stronger **community** by….

Expression:
bounce back: when you throw a ball to the floor, it comes back to you: it bounces back. When a person is sick, injured, or discouraged, they are like a ball thrown down. If they are resilient, one day they will get better. Like the ball, they will "bounce back."

Can you make sentences like this one? Work with a partner to make as many different sentences as you can. Then share your answers with the class.

Nadia was sad because she did not do well on the test, but she bounced back.

_____, but she/he/they bounced back.

Try it a different way: Make your sentences *silly*! See who can make the class laugh the most.
   Example Javier sat on a hamburger at lunch, but he bounced back.

GRAMMAR STUDY
Practice language functions and structures
Talk about yourself and other people using forms of the verbs BE and HAVE.
When you talk about yourself or others, the verb BE can be followed by a noun or adjective. But the verb HAVE must be followed by a noun. Notice also how questions and negatives are made.

(Pronoun + BE + Adjective)		(Pronoun + HAVE + Noun)	
I am creative…	Are you creative?	She has confidence.	Does she have confidence?
She is flexible…	Is she flexible?	I have creative ideas.	
He is calm…		He does not have confidence.	
She is not calm…		We have a strong community.	
They are resilient…		They have resilience.	Do they have resilience?

(Pronoun + BE + Noun)	
I am a flexible person… He is a calm person… Is he a calm person…? We are a community. We are not a flexible community.	

Can you use the vocabulary lists and the reading about resilience to say or write more expressions like the ones above? Add them in the correct box below according their structure.

(Pronoun + BE + Adjective)	(Pronoun + HAVE + Noun)
(Pronoun + BE + Noun)	

Practice speaking about yourself and others
Read the questions in the first column. Add any questions that you would like to ask other class members. Work with a partner. Take turns asking each other questions and noting the answers. Then be ready to report your answers to the class. Hint: Look at lines 9-23 of the reading to get some ideas of questions you might ask.

Questions	choose one phrase	Yes / No	Example reports
Are you calm…? *Example: Are you calm before a test?*	before a test during English class during a storm	Yes (or No)	Rosalinda is calm during a storm. (or Rosalinda is **not** calm during a storm.)
Are you creative…?	in your job in the way you dress with language		
Do you have confidence…?	about speaking English during a test at work		She has confidence. (or She does **not** have confidence.)
Do you have resilience…?	in the event of a flood or earthquake in the event of sickness because of a strong family		

Now you add some of your own questions following the pattern of the table above.

You can collect your answers and make a bingo game (like the activity at the beginning of this lesson) for a later class session.

LIFE SKILLS
Story of Resilience
Read *this story about a person who* ***bounced back*** *after difficult experiences.*

> **Develop your reading skills:**
> **Make connections**
> You can improve your understanding by making connections between this reading and what you read earlier.
> Before you read this story of resilience, review the first reading in this chapter and your class discussion about
> what makes a person resilient. Did you make a list of resilient qualities? As you read this story, look for the
> ways in which Rasheed Qambari was resilient.

What Gives Me Strength
by Rasheed Qambari

In 1996 at the age of 27, Rasheed Qambari fled from his native Iraq and left behind his Kurdish° family members because he was accused of being a traitor° to Iraq for working with a foreign-sponsored humanitarian° group. When he arrived in the United States as a refugee, he didn't have a dollar in his pocket. Now he owns his own small business and works in a management position in another company.

I will never forget the tragedies° I experienced growing up in Iraq because whatever tragedies happened will remain part of my life. But I have needed to learn how to get over what happened and reach for the good in life here. Combining the good here in the United States and the good from my past has made me a stronger person.

5 **The terrors of my life in Iraq**
Growing up in Iraq, I saw a lot of terrible things. Almost all of it was out of my control. During the 8-year war between Iraq and Iran, I was very young. Aircraft came and bombed our city. On the street I saw lots of dead people and body parts—legs, hands, heads. Whenever I close my eyes and remember it, the tears start falling.

10 Whenever I would see an intelligence officer° or policeman in our neighborhood, I would be frightened. I remember visiting a neighbor who was taken away by the police because he said something against the Iraqi government. When I went to visit him with my father, he couldn't speak a thing to us. We learned later from his wife that the police had cut out his tongue. I knew many people who disappeared forever when an intelligence officer visited their house. This is the way the government instilled° fear in people of my 15 generation°.

My struggle for education
Even though my father did not know how to write his own name, he was very pro-education. He always said, "Don't be a blind person like me. I am blind to books because I can't read." My father didn't let me work and help him in his shop because he was afraid my grades might drop if I spent time working. All my elders encouraged me, saying, "You are the future of the country. You need to get your education because you 20 are the one who is going to be a leader of the country. The generation after you is going to be lost unless you get your education."

My older brother is an assistant medical doctor. He could have been a medical doctor. But at the time when he was doing his training, the economy was weak and he had to work to help my father support our family. So he couldn't go as far in his education as he wanted to. He has often told me, "Because of you, I 25 couldn't finish college. I sacrificed° my life for you, so please don't disappoint me. You got a bachelor's degree in physics. Now maybe your children will get a master's or PhD."

The challenges of life in a new country
When I came to the US as a refugee, I knew a little bit of English. Those who came not knowing English had tougher challenges. To get into any house, you need to have the key. The key to coming to a 30 country like the United States is English.

35

Nobody in this country encouraged me to forget my language or my religion. Actually, I experienced the positive side. People told me, "Please talk to your children in Kurdish. We want them to be bilingual° when they grow up in this country. Teach them your culture. Practice your religion because this is a free country." For me these were very strong points. I took the good things from my Kurdish background and combined them with the good things I learned here, and the negative stuff I threw away. This made me stronger to survive, and not just survive,° but become very active in the community.

When I was in college, I dreamed of going on for graduate studies in physics. But if I study now, it would take a lot of time and money. I would not be able to provide for the family like I do now. So I sacrifice myself for them. The kids are always making straight A's because I provide everything they need. I focus on those kids because they are the future. I come home from my job at the poultry plant° tired and sometimes frustrated. But I take a shower and get refreshed. My kids show me their report cards, and I see that they have received all A's. I am afraid they might see the tears starting to fall from my eyes.

Conclusion

When I come home from the late shift, I go down to the basement and look at my children sleeping. They are all snoring.° I look at them, and then I put my head down on my own pillow, and I feel safe. If I don't get any other benefit from being in the United States, I am not afraid that I will wake up in a bombing or that somebody will knock down my house with a bulldozer.° I am not worried when my children leave for school in the morning that somebody will attack them. All that is over.

What happened in our past life, we can't completely forget. It's part of who we are. It's our history. But like a computer we can reboot° ourselves. We can keep the files we need and remove the files we don't want. If we keep dwelling on° the bad things that happened in our lives, we might be controlled by them and led into the wrong paths. We need to notice the good things in the world and keep moving forward to grasp new opportunities.

°Kurdish (adj.) – one of the ethnic groups living in northern Iraq are the Kurds; the adjective form is *Kurdish*
°traitor (n.) – a person who is not loyal to his/her group or nation, who may put the group in danger
°humanitarian (adj.) – a person or organization that tries to improve living conditions for people
°tragedies (n.) - sad events
°intelligence officer (n. + n.) – a spy who works for a government agency
°generation (n.) - group of people who are the same age
°instilled (v.) – taught, planted in the mind
°sacrificed (v.) – gave up something valuable for a specific purpose
°bilingual (adj.) – speaking two languages
°survive (v.) – to continue living even under hard conditions
°poultry plant (n.+ n.) – a factory where chickens or turkeys are killed and their meat is processed
°snoring (v.) – making sounds from the nose and mouth while sleeping
°bulldozer (n.) – a big machine used to move earth or to knock down buildings
°reboot (v.) – to start again the operating system of a computer
°dwelling on (v.) – thinking or talking about something all the time

Understand what you read

There are 20 blank spaces in these sentences that summarize Rasheed Qambari's story. If you need them, use the 17 words in the box below to fill in the blanks (three words will be used twice). But first try filling in the blanks without using the words in the box.

1. Rasheed Qambari's story takes place in (1) _____ and (2) _____.

2. Some of the bad things that he experienced in Iraq were (3) _____ and (4) _____.

3. People mentioned the most in Rasheed's story are his (5) _____, (6) _____ and (7) _____.

4. His (8) _____ and (9) _____ put a lot of pressure on Rasheed to get a good education.

5. Now Rasheed strongly supports his (10) _____ so that they get a good education.

6. Rasheed had an easier time adjusting to life in the US than some immigrants because he already knew a little (11)_____.

7. Rasheed grew stronger by combining his (12)_____, (13)_____, and (14)_____ with the good things he found in the US.

8. One thing that Rasheed could not get in the US was (15)_____ because he had to give priority to his family.

9. If Rasheed kept focusing on the bad things that happened to him, he would not be able to take (16)_____ for his family.

10. One of the greatest benefits of living in the US that he feels is (17)_____.

11. He believes that people can never (18)_____ their (19)_____, but they don't have to be controlled by the (20)_____ that happened to them.

history	evil things	abuse by police	older brother
safety	father	culture	language
responsibility	Iraq	children	more education
English	bombings	forget	religion
United States			

Discuss
1. What are some of the Kurdish values that Rasheed has made a part of his life in the United States?
2. How does Rasheed's experience with education compare with his children's experience?
3. What is your opinion on the role of language learning in meeting difficult challenges in your life? (review what Rasheed said about English in lines 30-32)
4. What lessons about growing stronger do you take from Rasheed's story? What has made him more resilient?

Teacher Story
Listen to your teacher tell a story about a time when he or she bounced back from a difficult experience.
   Discuss: What helped Rasheed and your teacher to **bounce back** from their hardships? Where did Rasheed and your teacher find strength? What makes them resilient persons?

EXTEND YOUR LEARNING

1. **Keep a journal** that you can share with your teacher. For this lesson answer questions like these in your journal:
   a. Are you a resilient person?
   b. What makes you resilient? What personal strengths do you have? What strengths do you find in your community?
   b. Share a story about how you bounced back from a difficult experience in your life.

2. **Music:** *Listen to "My Roots Go Down" by Sarah Pirtle. Pirtle is an American writer of literature for young adults and an expert on teaching social skills through the arts.* http://www.youtube.com/watch?v=s1_cJ--kxYc .

After listening once, sing along and do the motions as shown in the video.

My roots go down, down to the earth
My roots go down, down to the earth
My roots go down, down to the earth
My roots go down. (refrain)

I am a pine tree standing on a hill (3 times)
My roots go down...

I am a willow swaying in the storm (3 times)
My roots go down...

I am a wildflower reaching for the sun (3 times)
My roots go down...

I am a waterfall flowing free (3 times)
My roots go down...

[Lyrics used by permission of Sarah Pirtle http://sarahpirtle.com/Lyrics/LyricsSFT.htm]

Discuss: How do the words of this song relate to the idea of resilience?

What are your roots, which keep you living and standing up even when the storms blow?

3. **Drawing:** How do you picture a resilient community?
   a. For this activity, you may work by yourself or with a small group as directed by your teacher.
   b. Draw a picture of a resilient community. What does it look like? What are people doing? What colors do you see in a resilient community? What does it smell like? What sounds do you hear there? You can use words with your picture if you want.
   c. Get in a circle and share your picture with the class. Let them ask questions. You answer their questions.
   d. Talk about your circle sharing.
      How did you feel when you saw and heard about the other pictures?
      What things were the same and what things were different in everyone's pictures?

4. **Movement:**

Resilient people have healthy feelings, minds, and bodies. We know that our feelings and mind can affect our body. If we feel sad or worried, our bodies may feel weak or tired. And our bodies can affect our thinking and feeling. If our bodies are tired or sick, we can't think clearly. We may feel stressed. Movement is one way of getting free from stress and gaining strength. Throughout this course, you will learn to be more aware of your body. You will notice connections between your mind, feelings, and body. And you will learn ways to make your body feel better. Listen carefully to your teacher's instructions for this activity.

Deep breathing
Breathe in.
Breathe out.
Breathe in through your nose.
Breathe out through your mouth.
Let the air out fast.
Pucker your lips.
Relax your lips.
Breathe in through your nose.
Pucker your lips.
Let the air out slowly through your puckered lips.

Once you have learned this routine, the teacher will say, Breathe deeply, *and you should do the activity.*
When can deep breathing help you? Deep breathing can relax you when you feel stressed. It can also wake you up when feel tired by sending more oxygen to your brain. You can use deep breathing whenever...
   • you feel nervous about speaking in class
   • you feel upset because you can't understand what others are saying
   • you feel uncomfortable with the class activity
   • you are a little angry with your teacher or classmates

- you are upset by the topic of the discussion
- you feel tired or sleepy in class

Discuss: Are there special ways of breathing used by people from your culture to help them become calm?

SELF-ASSESSMENT

Think about your learning. Complete this assessment. Discuss your answers with the rest of the class. When you discuss your answers, notice how yours are like or different from your classmates' answers.

A. Read the choices in the sentence frame below. Then write two sentences that are *true* for you.

Example: *I liked thinking about my own resilience and writing in my journal because I learn best by understanding myself.*

I liked or I didn't like	<ul><li>reading the texts in this chapter</li><li>discussing the questions with the class</li><li>thinking about my own resilience and writing in my journal</li><li>drawing the picture of a resilient community</li><li>doing the deep breathing exercise</li><li>(add your own) _____ _____</li></ul>	**because I learn best by** **or** **because I don't learn well by**	<ul><li>reading and writing</li><li>working with other people</li><li>understanding myself</li><li>using pictures</li><li>working with my body</li><li>organizing things logically</li><li>using music</li><li>observing nature</li></ul>

True sentence 1. _____

_____

True sentence 2. _____

_____

B. Now answer these questions about the lesson:

d. The most interesting thing I learned about myself was _____

e. The most interesting thing I learned about a classmate was _____

f. The most helpful thing I learned from this lesson was _____

g. One thing that I want to practice more is _____

h. An idea that I want to explore more is _____

Learning Tip: Make yourself flash cards or keep a notebook so that you can add more words to your vocabulary beyond those words taught to you by the textbook. You can also make flashcards for reviewing important grammar points.

Chapter 3 Types of Violence

Get to Know Each Other Better
Common Ground
This activity will help you see what you have in common with the other class members.
1. The teacher will read some sentences. These sentences are going to describe some or all of the students in this class.
2. When the teacher says a sentence that is true for you, you should stand up. If the sentence is not true for you, then do not stand up.
3. Look around and see who else is standing for each sentence.

Example sentences: You like math.
Those who are quiet people should stand up.
If anyone has ever mispronounced your name, stand up.

Discuss this activity:
What did you notice as you and other students were standing up?
What surprised you?
What was comfortable or uncomfortable for you?
What is the value of sharing similarities and differences?
What did you learn about your classmates?

Connect to the topic
This activity is an example of *classification.* When we group things together according to qualities that they share, we are *classifying* them. The verb *classify* and its noun form *classification* both have in them a word that you know already: *class.* In a class, people are grouped according to their age, or their goals, or the subject they are studying. In the lessons ahead, you will learn about two classes of things: *violence* and *trauma.*

Look at the pictures
1. What two kinds (or classes) of violence do you see?
2. What do you see in each of the pictures? What words can you give for each picture?
3. What pictures could you add to these?

What is trauma? Trauma is a wound in the body, mind or emotions.
What kinds of violence cause trauma?

What kinds of violence are caused by humans?

What kinds of violence are caused by nature?

Jon Gehman

READ

Develop your reading skills:
Re-read. Remember that you will not deeply understand a reading on your first try. You have already read and discussed two texts about resilience in chapter 2. Before trying to read this text, you may want to quickly re-read the texts from chapter 2. Also review any notes that you made about the texts in chapter 2. When you are ready to read the text below, you will want to survey it first (see the advice below) or read it quickly once to get the main ideas. Then read it a second time more slowly. Reading a text more quickly twice is usually better than reading it very slowly just once.

Connect → Survey → Predict
In chapter 2, we studied about **resilience**. Now, suddenly, the topic has changed to **violence**. Before you read this text, first **think** about this question: What is the *connection* between violence and resilience?
Then **survey** the text by reading **the title** and **the headings** for each paragraph. **Predict** what you think the text will say about the connection between violence and resilience.

Violence—A Test for Resilient People

[1] **Causes of violence**
     There are many different kinds of **violence.** Nature can be **violent.** People can also be violent to each other. One person, a group, or a whole society can *be the target of* violence.
     Here are some examples of different kinds of violence. Put a check [√] in the blank if this kind of
[5] violence ever happened to you or someone you know.
     ___Natural **disasters**: floods, **hurricanes, tornados, tsunamis or earthquakes**
     ___Violent words: *name-calling*, **insults, threats,** or **shaming**

___**Physical** violence: hurting the bodies of others in some way by pushing, hitting or kicking; using guns and other weapons to destroy people or things

10 ___**Structural** violence: Structural violence happens because of the social situation. One group **harms** another group. For example, people of one skin color feel **prejudice** from people of another skin color. Or rich people allow their neighbors to stay poor, hungry, and homeless. Or a government makes unfair laws. People in these situations suffer structural violence.

___War: War affects everyone in society. It harms social **institutions** like the government and business.
15 It destroys natural **resources**. War causes people to accept violence as a normal part of life.

Violence causes trauma

Trauma comes from the Greek word "traumat", meaning wound. Trauma is a deep wound that causes **extreme shock** or pain. A **traumatic** event leaves you feeling like your life or others' lives are in danger. You feel upset. You are confused. You may lose hope.

20 Violence is a big cause of trauma. All kinds of violence can be traumatic. A terrible kind of trauma comes from sexual **abuse**. A serious illness can also cause trauma. Sudden loss of your home, your job, a family member or friend can cause trauma. When people cause you to feel **shame** all the time, this can cause trauma.

Even seeing violence can cause trauma. Seeing other people hurt on the TV news can have a traumatic
25 effect on you. Seeing violence in your neighborhood or on the streets can cause trauma. If people attack other members of your group, you can suffer trauma. Attackers can also suffer trauma by doing violence to others.

But not all violence causes trauma. Trauma happens when the violence **overwhelms** you in mind, body, or spirit. Everyone has a breaking point. Everyone can be overwhelmed by violence.
30

Bouncing back from a traumatic event

Remember—a resilient person can suffer through hard times and recover. Resilience is the ability to bounce back after hardships, including violence and trauma.

How quickly can individuals or groups recover after a traumatic event? The recovery depends on the answers to several questions. What happened? How long did the traumatic event last? How much support
35 does the person have? How healthy is the community or society? How resilient is the person? Review some ways to build resilience that you learned in chapter 2.

UNDERSTAND WHAT YOU READ

Did you understand these main ideas? Choose the correct words from the box below to fill in the blanks.

recover	groups
overwhelms	nature
individuals	societies
humans	trauma

1. There are two main kinds of violence: violence caused by _____ and violence caused by _____.

2. People suffer _____ when violence _____ them.

3. Violence and trauma affect _____, _____ and whole _____.

4. When resilient persons suffer hardships, violence, and even trauma, they are usually able to _____.

Now look at the details. Match the beginning of the sentences with the best ending:

1 Kicking, insults, hunger, and war are___   a poor people and others without power
2 Trauma is like a wound that makes you_   b cause trauma.
3 Trauma can come from___   c our health, a job, or a loved one.
4 Seeing violence on TV or on the street can___ d feel upset, confused & hopeless.
5 Structural violence often harms ___   e kinds of violence that people cause.
6 We can suffer trauma by losing ___   f sexual abuse, illness, or personal loss.

Discuss
1. We all know many people who have suffered hardships or misfortunes. We may not all know people who have suffered trauma. What is the difference between suffering hardship and having trauma?
2. What are some specific examples of violence around the world that you know about?
3. Would you feel comfortable sharing about someone you know who was deeply wounded by some kind of violence?

WORD STUDY
A. Define it yourself!
Look at these words in the text above. Some of them are used several times. The surrounding words and sentences should help you understand the meaning. Write your own definition. Compare your definition with the dictionary's definition.

violence (noun) and **violent** (adjective) _____

_____
(Hint: Look at all the examples of violence *and* violent *in lines 2-15)*

To help you learn how to use violence *and* violent *correctly, write here some of the words that go before or after* violent *and* violence. *(Two examples have been given to help you get started.)*
violence: *kinds of violence* _____

violent: *can be violent* _____

physical (adjective) _____
(Hint: Look at the examples of *physical violence* in lines 8-9. Notice the difference between *violent words* (line 7) and *physical violence*.)

structural violence (noun phrase) _____
(Look carefully at lines 10-13)

trauma (noun) and **traumatic** (adjective) _____

To help you learn how to use trauma *and* traumatic *correctly, write here some of the words that go before or after* trauma *and* traumatic. *(Do as you did for* violence *and* violent *above.)*
trauma: _____

traumatic: _____

B. Word meanings
Study the definitions of these words. Find the line where the word appears, read it, and then write the line number in the blank in front of the word. Write the plural form of the nouns in the blank after the definition. Write the whole word so you can practice spelling it. Then use the words in the blank spaces below to complete the sentences

section by section. You might have to use the plural of some nouns; and you might have to put a different ending on the verbs. Check your spellings of the plural with your teacher or the help of a dictionary.

Write the noun plurals here

__6_ **disaster** (noun) – an event that causes damage, hardship, or even death   _disasters_

___**earthquake** (noun) – a shaking under the ground by natural causes   _____

___**extreme** (adjective) – very much

___**harm** (verb) – to cause someone or something to be hurt or damaged

___**hurricane** (noun) – a severe storm of wind and rain on the sea; in some   _____
 parts of the world a *cyclone*

___**natural resource** (noun phase) – a thing in nature that is useful to people   _____

___**tornado** – (noun) a severe wind storm on the land   _____

___**tsunami** – (noun) a large ocean wave caused by shaking of the earth   _____
 under the sea

C. Use the words above to complete the sentences 1 to 4. *Some words will be used more than once.*

1. _____ and _____ are natural _____ that involve wind and weather.

2. _____ and _____ are natural _____ that involve the earth and the sea.

3. War _____ important _____ _____ like water, land, trees, and animals.

4. Even resilient persons will be frightened and shaken by _____ natural _____ like the
_____ and _____ that occurred in 2011 in Japan or the ones in 2004 in the Indian Ocean
that affected Indonesia, Thailand, Sri Lanka and India.

D. More word meanings

Write the noun plurals here

___**abuse** (noun) – bad treatment, violent treatment   _____

___**insult** (noun) – words that make a person feel bad or that attack a   _____
 person's honor

___**overwhelm** (verb) – to beat down, to defeat, to overpower, to crush

___**prejudice** (noun) – an opinion based on feelings, usually feelings of   _____
 not liking someone or some group of people

___**shock** (noun) – a hard blow (or hit) to the mind or feelings   _____

___**shame** (noun) – a bad feeling because others think you are a bad person   _shame_ cannot be plural; it is
 or others think you did something bad   not countable

___**shaming** (present participle of the verb *to shame*) – making people have
 bad feelings because you think they are bad persons or did bad
 things

___**target** (noun) – an object that people aim at and try to hit   _____

___**threat** (noun) – words that frighten someone or promise to hurt someone   _____

E. Use the definitions above to help you decide which sentence is the best example for each word. The first example has been done for you (see the checked answer)

1. abuse
a. ___√__ The angry mother locked her son in his room for two days without food.
b. ___My overwhelmed roommate forgot about the food in the oven and burned our dinner.

2. insult
a. ___The teacher said to me, "Your work on the last essay disappointed me very much."
b. ___The teacher said to me, "You are one of the dumbest students I have ever taught."

3. overwhelm
a. ___After I heard the bad news, all I could do was go into my room and cry.
b. ___After we heard the bad news, we had a long discussion about what happened.

4. prejudice
a. ___When we called on the phone, the owner said the apartment was for rent. But when we went to see the apartment, she saw that we were Africans, and she told us it was already rented.
b. ___By accident we broke the bathroom window in our apartment. Even though we told the owner that we didn't have the money to fix it, he said we had to pay for the damage.

5. shock
a. ___There was a big forest fire near our house. Our home and some of our neighbors' homes were damaged, but we were glad that no people were harmed in the fire.
b. ___We left the rescue shelter and went back to our home. It was a huge surprise to find that the flood had completely washed away our house and everything in it.

6. shame
a. ___I caused an accident because I was in a hurry. A bicyclist was injured. My picture was in the paper, and I felt very bad because all the people in our small town knew what a bad thing I did.
b. ___I was in an accident last week. It was my fault. I went through a stop sign and crashed into another car. I went home shaking like a leaf. It was a scary experience.

7. shaming
a. ___My father always made me feel bad when I made mistakes during our school soccer matches, especially if our team lost.
b. ___I appreciated the advice my mother used to give me on how to avoid mistakes in important soccer matches.

8. target
a. ___The teacher often smiles when the students say the correct answer.
b. ___The students in Jack's class always make jokes about him.

9. threat
a. ___I was worried by my neighbor's words: "You need to trim that tree. Too many falling leaves are coming into my yard."
b. ___My neighbor's words frightened me: "If you don't keep your dog out of my yard, I will shoot it."

Nouns and verbs:
Three words above can be used as both nouns and verbs. The right side of the table below shows the verb use. Notice the differences in pronunciation. Repeat the words with your teacher.

You supply sentences showing the noun use. If you need help, use sentences from the reading above as your model.

45

Nouns	Verbs
abuse (a-BYOOS)	**abuse** (a-BYOOZ) Sadly, some adults sexually **abuse** children.
insult (IN-sult)	**insult** (in-SULT) The shopkeeper **insulted** me because he doesn't like people who speak other languages in his shop.
shame	**shame** The parents said, "Our son **shamed** us because he would not marry the girl we chose for him."

Word families:

In this chapter you have learned words that belong to the same family. This chart will help you remember how to use each word correctly. Write your own sentence for each word in the right hand column.

violence (noun)
Violence causes many people to suffer all around the world.

If we work closely with teachers, we can end *violence* in schools.

violent (adjective)

Violent crime seems to keep increasing in our cities.

The earthquake that shook Japan was the most *violent* in a century.

trauma (noun)
Trauma affects our ability to live healthy and happy lives.

Healing from *trauma* is possible, but it takes time.

traumatic (adjective)
The *traumatic* event ended in only a few minutes, but it had an effect on me that has lasted for years.

Her experiences on the first day of school were *traumatic*.

Expressions

be a/the target of – people use **targets** like the one pictured here to shoot at with arrows or guns; but we can also say that anything or any person can become a target: a building can **be the target of** a bomb; a person can **be the target of** violence.

name-calling – this idiom comes from the expression "to call someone names." A little child might cry to his mother, "Mommy, she called me a liar!" Or a student might say to her teacher, "Sir, he called me a pig!" **Name-calling** is one way that people insult other people. *Have you ever been the target of name-calling?*

What are some ways to complete this sentence? Work with a partner to find as many different answers as you can. Then share your answers with the class.

    No one likes to be a target of _____.

GRAMMAR STUDY
The language of classification
Complete the chart by looking again at the reading above. The words in bold in the top row of the chart are category terms or classes. These words show the general class. You fill the words in the row below to show all the members of this class. Some examples have been done for you.

Types of violence	Kinds of natural disasters	Kinds of physical violence	Causes of trauma
Natural disasters Human-caused violence	floods		

Look again at the reading. Are there any other classes? Could you add another column to this chart with another category term?

Some ways of talking about classes and their members

1. **There are** many **types of** violence: violent words, physical violence, war, and natural disasters.
2. **There are** different **kinds of** violent language, **including** threats, insults, and name-calling.
3. We learned about all **kinds of** natural disasters, **including** _____.
   (you fill in the blank with a list)

4. One **type of** _____ is _____ (no list here).
5. This **kind of** _____ includes _____ (one or more items in a list)

6. Trauma **has** many **causes**, including _____ (one or more items in a list)

7. War causes trauma **and so does** sexual abuse.
   This sentence is the way that we express the following meaning:
   7a. War <u>causes trauma</u>, **and** sexual abuse <u>causes trauma</u>.
   *Notice how "causes trauma" is repeated twice in this sentence. We can make the sentence shorter and better by putting "so does" before "sexual abuse, and deleting the second "causes trauma." Notice that we need to keep the word **and** in order to join the two parts of the sentence.*

Practice speaking about classification
Round Robin Memory Game
1. Move into a circle so you can see everyone else in the class.
2. The game starts out by practicing sentences #4 and #5.
3. The first person to go says, "One type of violence is_____" (fill in the blank with her/his choice)
4. The next person in the circle *repeats that sentence* and adds "This kind of violence includes _____ (naming one item).
5. The next person repeats everything said so far and adds one more item to the list started by the previous person, "One type of violence is _____. This kind of violence includes ____ and ____."

If a class member forgets a word, the rest of the group may help out by reminding her or him of the word.
Try the game again using a different sentence pattern from the examples above.

Story of resilience

Read this story of a person who faced the test of violence.

> **Develop your reading skills:**
> **Learn from different kinds of texts.**
> Notice the difference between the earlier text "Violence: A Test for Resilient People" and this reading "Rocket Attack!" The first text is organized by *classification*. It explains different kinds of violence and different causes of trauma. That type of text starts clearly with the main point: *There are many different kinds of violence....* But "Rocket Attack" is a story that one person tells about an experience in her life. Notice how different the first line of this story is: *On April 15, 1985....* In stories, the main point is not openly explained.
> **Read with a purpose.**
> Think about the purpose of this story. Why is it a part of this chapter on violence and trauma? You can apply your knowledge of violence and trauma to this reading. As you read this story, you can create *a purpose for reading*: for example, *look in the story for the different kinds of violence and the different causes of trauma.* By reading with this purpose in mind, you are also practicing the skill of *making connections*.

Rocket Attack!
by Elena Zook Barge

In 1985 El Salvador was in the middle of a civil war. Elena Zook Barge and her husband Nathan were living in a small village about two hours from the capital city. They were helping people who had to flee° from their homes because of the war. Many people in their village were very poor. According to Elena, the main cause of the war in El Salvador was the inequality° between the very rich and the majority of people, who were very poor. Here is Elena's story.

On April 15, 1985, Nathan and I were on a bus full of people. We were returning to the village where we lived, San Jose Guayabal, El Salvador. We were with friends from the United States who were visiting us. We had not lived long in El Salvador and knew only a little bit of Spanish.

5 All of a sudden a rocket exploded behind the bus. We came to a stop in front of a big farm house. We found ourselves underneath ten helicopters that were firing at the area. And the national guard° immediately surrounded us. We got down on the floor of the bus. Everybody was down on the floor just hoping and praying that we were not going to get hit by these bullets. I wasn't able to think clearly what to do. I was holding two melons in my lap. When I fell on the floor, I put them between my head and the side of the bus, thinking they would protect me from the flying bullets.

10 We were terribly° afraid for our own lives, but the national guardsmen were afraid, too. We heard them radioing up to the helicopters, "Stop shooting." The firing finally stopped after about 15 or 20 minutes when the helicopters left. The man who lived at the farm house came out. He was wounded and bleeding. One of the rockets from the helicopter hit the place where he and his family were hiding. He was walking back and forth saying over and over again, "You killed my wife and my two sons; kill me too." I felt great sadness for the man.

15 They put the bleeding farmer and a wounded soldier on the bus with us. There were soldiers lining both sides of the road all the way to our village. When we got there, it looked like a scene in a war zone°. A helicopter was landing and they were taking out dead soldiers.

The next day we went to the funeral for the farmer's wife and two sons. That is when we really felt terrible° because we were US citizens. We knew that all those helicopters and weapons came from the US.
20 We were connected to the harm that the Salvadoran military did to this man and his family.

° *flee (v.) – run away*
° *inequality (n.) – differences, often unfair differences*
° *national guard (adj. + n.) – soldiers, the army*
° *terribly (adv.) – very, with great fear*

∘*zone (n.) – area*
∘*funeral (n.) – ceremony for burying the dead*
∘*felt terrible (v. + adj.) – felt very bad*

Understand what you read
Give short answers to these questions.
1. Which persons in the story were physically harmed?
2. Which persons in the story seemed overwhelmed by the violence?
3. Were Nathan and Elena wounded in any way? Explain your answer.
4. Why did Elena and Nathan feel terrible about the death of the farmer's wife and sons?
5. What kinds of violence did you find in the story?
6. What <u>kind of text</u> is "Rocket Attack"? (circle the best answer)
    a. an explanation
    b. a personal story
    c. a description
    d. a historical account
7. Which sentence below best states the reason why the story "Rocket Attack!" is included in this chapter? (circle the best answer)
    a. The story shows different kinds of violence and the effects of violence.
    b. A war zone is full of confusion because people & soldiers are dead or wounded.
    c. Violence happens because of inequality between the rich & poor.
    d. The story shows that violence is not the right solution to any problem.

C. *Discuss*
1. What emotions did you have while reading this story? Did you feel sad, angry, or upset?
2. What parts of the reading present the events of Elena's experience and what parts present her feelings?
3. If you know anything about the civil war in El Salvador, how do your feelings compare with Elena's?

EXTEND YOUR LEARNING
1. Music: *Listen to "Fragile" by Sting*
Sting is a British singer, song writer and social activist whose real name is Gordon Matthew Thomas Sumner. He has made 25 albums and won 16 Grammy awards. He has also acted on television and in film. He is a member of the Rock'n'Roll Hall of Fame and the Songwriters' Hall of Fame. He first became a popular solo singer in the 1980s. He is still presenting concerts around the world today. In March 2010 he performed for a crowd of 16,000 in Dubai, United Arab Emirates. His song "Fragile" came out in 1987 on his album Nothing Like the Sun.

Here is a version of the song with the words: https://www.youtube.com/watch?v=EmDQFWNjHpA

1. First, listen to the song and just enjoy the music. If it helps you, close your eyes and listen.
2. Discuss the music. How did the music make you feel?
3. Now listen again and follow the words. The words are poetry, so they are not very easy to understand. That's all right. You can enjoy the song without understanding all of the words. The most important word to understand is *fragile*. *Fragile* means *easily broken or able to break easily.* The repeated line *How fragile we are* means *We are very fragile.*
4. Pronunciation note: Because Sting is from Britain, he pronounces *fragile* [fræ-jayl]. English speakers in the North America tend to say [fræ-jəl].
5. 5. Listen to the song one more time and this time try singing the refrain "On and on the rain will fall" etc.

Discuss
a. What do you think the song means when it says "something in our mind will always stay"?
b. When the song says "that nothing comes from violence and nothing ever could," do you agree with that or not?

c. Songs often paint pictures for us. What picture is painted by these words: "On and on the rain will fall, like tears from a star." What does this picture mean to you?
d. How would you connect the song with the story "Rocket Attack"?
e. How does the idea of being fragile connect with trauma?

2. Drawing
River of Life
Think of your life as a river. The beginning of the river is like the early years of your life with your family. As the river flows, it moves through the different years of your life to the present. Draw a river to show the story of your life. Sometimes a river is calm, like the peaceful times in your life. Other times the river is violent and noisy, like the hard times in your life. As you draw the river of your life, show the calm and peaceful time as well as the difficult times. You can also show the important influences that come into your life, like small streams that come into a river. You can draw important people and events of your life along the banks of the river or in the river. Include in your river anything that made you a stronger person.

Sharing: When you are finished drawing, find another person and show him or her river of life. Share whatever you are comfortable sharing about your river of life.

Talk about your sharing with the class
a. Seat yourselves in a circle
b. How did you feel when you were talking about your river of life to the class?
c. How did you feel when you listened to others talking?
d. What did you learn about our group?
e. What surprised you?

3. Journal
Write a few lines about your "river of life" in your journal.

4. Movement
You are going to play a game. As you experience this game, think about how the game can be like some parts of life. Just like life, there will be some surprises in this game. And surprises are sometimes good and sometimes not.
Creating Chaos
a. Stand up and form a wide circle
b. Hold your hands out in front of you until you have received the ball
c. The first student takes the ball, calls out a person's name, and throws the ball to that person.
d. Remember two important things: the name of the person to whom you threw the ball and the name of the person who threw the ball to you.
e. After you receive and throw the ball to the next person, put your hands down.
f. Listen to the teacher. When she/he calls "freeze," stop throwing the ball. When she/he calls "reverse," then throw the ball to the person who originally threw the ball to you.
g. It's no big problem if you drop the ball. Just pick it up and throw it to your partner.

Discuss *Creating Chaos*
a. How did you feel during this activity? How did you cope with the situation?
b. Did you see any patterns of behavior occurring?
c. How did you respond to the crisis? Were you in the center of things? Did you stay on the outside? What did you learn about yourself?
d. How is this activity like a real crisis or traumatic event?
e. How would you complete these sentences using just one word:

Trauma is _____.   Trauma is like a (an) _____.

50

SELF-ASSESSMENT

Think about your learning. Complete a self-assessment for this chapter by using the template at the end of the textbook (p. 194).

> *Learning Tip:* Remember to review your new words every day. Find 10 minutes to flip through your flashcards. Try to find some topic of conversation in which you can use of your new words with another speaker of English. Using is the most powerful form of remembering. .

Chapter 4 What Is Trauma?

Get to Know Each Other Better

1. Look at the labeled color chart that your teacher shows you; choose the color that you like the best.*

2. Think of a reason why you like this color. Prepare to share your reason with the whole class. Use a sentence like

   a) I like _____ because it reminds me of _____ . OR

   b) I like _____ because it is like _____ . OR

   c) I like _____ because _____ .

3. Share your color and your reason with a partner.

4. Now share your color and reason with the whole class and listen carefully to every class member.

5. As you listen, notice what color they chose, and notice the reason they give.

6. Now get into groups based on colors that you think are similar. Discuss with your group members what makes these colors similar and different. Discuss also the difference and similarities of your reasons.

7. Be prepared if your teacher asks you to give a short report to the whole class about your group.

*Alternate method: Select a color from a large box of crayons. Note the name of the color on the side of the crayon. Take a 3x5 inch index card and use that crayon to color one side of the card. Fold the card in half and place it in front you on the table. Then do step #2 through 7 above.

Connect to the Topic

In this activity, you again practiced classification as you gathered in groups with similar colors. As you discussed the small differences in colors and your different reasons for choosing those colors, you were making comparisons. Things that belong to the same class are not always exactly alike. There are small differences among members of the same class, just as shades of orange or shades of blue are slightly different from each other. Most of you have good memories connected with the colors that you chose. Or you connected those colors with other things that you like.

In the lesson below, you will learn more about trauma. You found out in chapter 3 that trauma is a deep psychological wound. It makes a person feel upset, confused, and hopeless. You will find out, however, that there are different kinds of trauma. They all belong to the larger class, *trauma*, but they have small differences.

If you had to pick a color to represent "trauma" what color would it be?
 In other words, for you which color means "trauma"? Why?

Look at the pictures

1. Notice that the pictures are arranged in columns and rows. In the first column, you see pictures of traumas that occur to individuals. In the second column you see traumas that occur to groups of people (collectively). In the first row, you see traumas that occur from a single dramatic event. In the second row, you see traumas that occur over a longer period of time.
2. Discuss what you see in each picture and explain why the picture fits in that row.
3. Can you think of other pictures that might be added to these? Where would you place those new pictures?

Individual

Collective

Single events

Onging events

Jon Gehman

READ

> **Develop your reading skills:**
> **Create a graphic organizer to help you understand**
>   As you read any text, you can understand it better if you organize the information in the form of a diagram or picture. The pictures above already suggest an organization for you. Divide a page in your notebook into four squares. Label the columns *individual* and *collective*. Label the rows *single event* and *ongoing event*. As you read the text below, look at the <u>underlined key words</u> to help you understand the different kinds of trauma. Write the key words and some examples for each kind of trauma in the different squares of your graphic organizer.

Types of Trauma

1   What is the color of trauma? Or perhaps we should ask, "What are the colors of trauma?" Trauma comes in many forms. This article describes some of the main types of trauma. As you read, keep in mind the definition of trauma (from chapter 3). How are these types of trauma **similar** to each other? How are they different?

5   <u>A single event</u> can cause trauma. This one-time event may be caused by nature or humans. The event is **intense** and threatens to kill or seriously harm people. Earthquakes, floods, robberies, or car accidents are examples of single events that cause trauma.

        Other kinds of trauma arise from <u>ongoing events</u>. These events do not have a clear beginning or end. One example might be bullying at school or work. Other examples include abuse of children or **neglect** of

10   **elderly** people. Illness, disease and war are also **ongoing** causes of trauma.

        <u>Individual people</u> suffer trauma from both single and ongoing events. Sometimes their trauma may be acute. <u>Acute stress reaction</u> is a **technical** term that doctors use. It means that the immediate **reactions** to

traumatic stress are strong; they last for at least two days but go away in thirty days. If the reactions **persist** after that time, the medical name used for this condition is <u>Post Traumatic Stress Disorder</u> (PTSD).* A
person with PTSD suffers great stress and **anxiety**. Reactions to the event create problems with thinking and feeling. These problems cause **distress** and **interfere** with living. The effects of PTSD can be delayed; they can appear days, weeks, months or years after the event

Individuals can suffer two other kinds of trauma. One is called <u>secondary trauma</u>. When we see or hear about someone else having a traumatic experience, we can suffer secondary trauma. Those who **rescue** suffering people in a disaster can experience trauma. And **counselors** who listen to the stories of traumatized people can have secondary trauma. Another kind of trauma is called <u>participatory trauma</u> . We don't often think about it, but those who harm others can also suffer trauma by abusing, torturing, or killing others. Police officers may suffer Post Traumatic Stress Disorder from harming others.

When large numbers of people in a society share a traumatic experience, we call this <u>collective or shared trauma</u>. Whole nations can experience collective trauma from natural disasters, wars, or loss of a leader. On a smaller level, communities suffer collective trauma from violence. People in whole neighborhoods may suffer trauma from long-term poverty and wrong done to them.

When collective trauma extends across **generations**, we call this <u>historical trauma</u> . An important example of historical trauma is slavery in the United States. European Americans enslaved African people in North America between 1501 and 1865. The traumas of these 364 years of slavery still affect people today both Black and White. We see other examples of historical trauma in Northern Ireland in the conflict between Catholic and Protestant Christians and in the conflict between Hindus and Muslims in Pakistan and India.

When one group tries to destroy part or all of a culture or people, we call this <u>cultural trauma</u>. The **original** peoples of the Americas and Australia have suffered cultural trauma. During World War II, the Nazis tried to destroy the Jewish culture and people in Europe.

Finally, when a community or society lives in unfair political, economic, or social conditions, we call this <u>structural trauma</u>. Structural trauma puts people in a **disadvantaged** position. In South Africa, apartheid was a system that kept black Africans disadvantaged. In many parts of the world poor people, women, and people of different color suffer structural trauma.

Trauma of all kinds can be passed from one generation to another. We can see the effects of trauma over several generations. Have you decided yet what the colors of trauma are?

***Note:** There is wide agreement among doctors and psychologists on the definition of Post-traumatic Stress Disorder but sometimes disagreement in diagnosing individual cases. Experts sometimes make changes in the definition of PTSD as they better understand the experiences of persons responding to trauma. In this course, however, we are <u>not</u> primarily concerned with PTSD but with other types of stress.*

UNDERSTAND WHAT YOU READ

Match the kind of trauma with an example. Write the numbers in the blanks in front of the examples. Do the matching for each group separately. Key words have been underlined to guide you to the intended answer. For some questions, more than one answer might be possible. Discuss your answers with the rest of the class.

Group 1 - An example of…
1. a single event that causes trauma
2. an ongoing event that causes trauma
3. an individual suffering trauma
4. a group suffering trauma

a. <u>a nation</u> is shocked when its popular president dies in a plane
   crash
b. an earthquake <u>suddenly destroys</u> a city
c. <u>an elderly woman</u> living alone is tied up by robbers who broke
   into her home
d. the war <u>has lasted 9 years</u> already

Group 2 - An example of…
5. post traumatic stress disorder
6. secondary trauma
7. participatory trauma
8. historical trauma

e. the present-day effects of <u>Black slavery in North America</u>
f. a rebel group <u>destroys a museum of history</u> for native peoples of
   the land
g. a returned soldier has <u>nightmares</u> about the war and is <u>always
   worried about being attacked</u>   *(see two more items on the next page)*

54

9. example of cultural trauma   __   h. <u>a counselor listens</u> to stories of earthquake victims
10. example of structural trauma   __   i. <u>the government does not allow</u> girls to get education
                                              j. a child soldier is <u>forced to kill people</u> in a village

Discuss

1. What are some events in the world today that are causing people to experience trauma? Look at this week's newspaper and identify specific events.
2. What are some examples of historical trauma from your part of the world?
3. Do you agree that nations and individuals can be affected by traumas that occurred many years ago? What support can you give for your opinion?

WORD STUDY
A. You define it!
Look at these words in the text above. Some of them are used several times. The surrounding words and sentences should help you understand the meaning. Write your own definition.

similar (adjective) _____
(Hint: Notice the question following similar in line 3. If the second question asks about what's different, then what about the question with similar?}

ongoing (adjective) _____
(Hint: Carefully compare the paragraph beginning with line 5 about single events with the next paragraph that discusses ongoing events.)

*The next six words are **technical** words defined for you in the reading. Find the definitions and write them here.*

acute stress reaction (noun phrase) _____

post traumatic stress disorder (noun phrase) _____

secondary trauma (noun phrase) _____

participatory trauma (noun phrase) _____

collective trauma (noun phrase) _____

historical trauma (noun phrase) _____

B. Which of the words below can replace the underlined words in the following sentences? *(Line numbers give you a clue to help you choose the right word; the symbols before each word are for activity C below.)*

@	anxiety (noun)	&	neglect (noun or verb)
%	counselor (noun)	@	original (adjective)
&	disadvantaged (adjective)	%	persist (verb)
@	distress (noun or verb)	&	reaction (noun)
%	elderly(adjective)	@	rescue (verb)
&	generation (noun)	%	similar (adjective)
@	intense (adjective)	&	technical (adjective)
%	interfere (with) (verb)		

1. _____ The many forms of trauma are <u>alike</u>, but they also are slightly different from each other. (3)

2. _____ A single <u>strong</u> event, like a natural disaster, threatens the lives of many people. (6)

3. _____ _____ <u>Old</u> people can suffer trauma if their children <u>never visit them or help</u> them. (10, 9)

4. _____ PTSD is a special term used by experts to describe the most severe kind of trauma. [*one word*] (12)

5, ___ Severe trauma lasts longer than three months. (13)

6. _____ Traumatized people live in a state of worry or nervousness. (15)

7. _____ A person with PTSD experiences psychological suffering. (16)

8. _____   _____ Responses to traumatic events may hinder normal living. (16)

9. _____ If you help to save people who are caught in a natural disaster, you can experience trauma, too. (19)

10. _____ It is often important for people who experience trauma to speak with a trained psychological adviser because they know how to help people cope with their feelings and thoughts. (20)

11. _____ In many parts of the world, the first people who lived on the land have suffered many wrongs and hardships. (35)

12. _____ The effects of trauma can be passed from one age group to the next. (28)

13. _____ People who are poor, who don't have good education and don't have jobs, or who suffer from prejudice may be the ones who need the most help after a natural disaster has happened. (38)

C. Practice your new words:
1. You will have noticed that some words in the new vocabulary are marked with the symbols @, some with %, and some with &
2. Choose one symbol @, %, or &) and make your own sentences using the words with that symbol.
3. Make one sentence for each of the five words (for example, the @ words—*anxiety, distress, intense, original,* and *rescue*)
4. Cooperate as a class to make sure that there are students writing sentences for all the words.
5. After you write your sentences, do the "Give One/Get One Activity."
   ### *Give One/Get One*
   a. In the next 10 minutes, talk with as many different class members as you can. Give one of your sentences to each person that you talk with. Then get a new sentence from each class member that you talk with.
   b. After giving and getting sentences, share one of your favorite sentences with the whole class. The sentence could be one that you gave or one that you got.

Word family:
In this chapter and chapter 3 you have learned two words that belong to the same family. This family has a third member that can be useful to you also. Write your own sentence for each word in the right hand column.

trauma (noun) - this form of the word means "a severe shock or upsetting experience that a person suffers"	
*The people bounced back from the **trauma** they suffered in the earthquake.*	
traumatic (adjective) – this form is used to describe events or experiences that are upsetting	
*The family suffered a **traumatic** loss when their house burned down.*	
traumatize (verb) – this form of the word describes the action of causing trauma	
*The accident **traumatized** her so badly that she could not sleep for three days.*	

Expression

keep in mind – means to remember and think about. Usually this idiom is used in relation to ideas about the world, principles, questions, etc: *You need to keep in mind your level of fitness and choose goals that are realistic. This is an important thing to keep in mind. The government should keep in mind some first principles.* Sometimes it is used to talk about persons – for example, *Keep me in mind if any job opens up.*

Use the expression as you answer these one of more of these questions:
What should you *keep in mind* about trauma?   **Example:** *I should keep in mind that* _____.
When you face difficulties in life, what should you *keep in mind*?
What words do you want to *keep in mind* for later use?
What reading strategies should you *keep in mind* to be a stronger reader of English?

GRAMMAR STUDY
Making comparisons in English
A comparison shows how two or more things are alike or similar. There are two very easy ways of making a comparison in English. One way is to use *both...and....* By using *both...and...* we group together two things and then make a comment about this group in the rest of the sentence. The order *group + what makes them similar* can be switched to *what makes them similar + group.*

1. *Both acute stress reaction and PTSD are technical terms.*
Group (*acute stress reaction, PTSD*) **What makes them similar** (*are technical terms*)

2. *Single events that cause trauma include both natural disasters and human violence.*
What makes them similar (*Single events that cause trauma include*) **Group** (*natural disasters, human violence*)

Another way to make a comparison is to (a) use the conjunction *and* to link the members of the group and (b) use the verb *be* + the adjective *similar*. In this sentence, the main statement is that the members of the group are alike; this statement is followed by a reason. (*because...*).

3. *Acute stress reaction and PTSD are similar because they are both technical terms.*
Group (*acute stress reaction, PTSD*) **are similar** **Reason** (*because they are both technical terms*)

Making contrasts in English
A contrast means a difference. We can show differences between two or more different things in two easy ways. The easiest way of contrasting is to use the word *but* between two statements.

4. *Acute stress reaction lasts for less than 3 months, but PTSD persists for more than 3 months.*
Statement 1 (*Acute stress reaction lasts for less than 3 months*) **but** **Statement 2** (*PTSD persists for more than 3 months*)

You should also learn this more complicated way of making constrasts. Notice in the **reason** part of the sentence, you need to use the comparison forms *adjective + er* or *more + adjective* or *verb + more*

5. *PTSD is different from acute stress reaction because in PTSD the effects last longer and interfere more with daily living.*
Item 1 (*PTSD*) **is different from** **Item 2** (*acute stress reaction*) **Reason** (*because in PTSD the effects last longer and interfere more with daily living*)

Sentence Practice:
Complete these sentences with the information you got from the reading.

Comparison
1. Both _____ and _____ are examples of collective trauma.

2. Examples of ongoing events that can cause trauma include both _____ and _____.

3. Both _____ and _____ are examples of _____.

4. Both cultural trauma and _____.

5. Historical and cultural trauma are similar because _____.

Contrast

6. Secondary trauma affects _____, but participatory trauma affects _____.

7. Historical trauma _____, but structural trauma _____.

8. Collective trauma is different from individual trauma because _____.

9. Secondary trauma is different from _____ because _____.

More practice

1. Write your own sentences about the similarities and differences in the kinds of trauma discussed in the reading.

2. Think about the opinions that you and your classmates expressed in answering the discussion questions above or in the questions related to the idiom *keep in mind*. Write some sentences comparing and contrasting these opinions using the patterns above.

3. Use the Give One/Get One activity that you practiced with the new vocabulary to share your sentences with each other; or trade sentences with a partner and make suggestions for improving each other's grammar.

LIFE SKILLS

Story of Resilience

Read this story by someone who helps others in a time of trauma.

Develop your reading skills:
Learn from different kinds of texts
Review the reading skill that you used for the second text of chapter 3. Notice that the first readings in chapter 3 and chapter 4 are similar. They are based on **classification**. Lines 1-2 of the reading in chapter 4 gives you the main idea: "Trauma comes in many forms." You will notice that the reading below is in a style similar to Elena Zook Barge's personal story "Rocket Attack."
Use a timeline
Earlier in the chapter you used a graphic organizer to help you understand a text about the different kinds of trauma. When you have to read a different kind of text, like the story below, you will need to use a different kind of graphic organizer. A good graphic organizer for many stories is a timeline. Draw a line down your page. The top of the line represents the first event in Celeste's story. Note the main events that take place as the story unfolds. Put the last event at the bottom of the line.
Read with a purpose
What would be a good purpose for reading this story? What would you like to learn from reading this story? [*Hint: Think about what you have learned about trauma so far in this chapter. And then suggest a purpose for reading.*]

Celeste's Shocking Experience
by Edson Arango

   Edson Arango worked as a veterinarian° for a pharmaceutical° company in Colombia. But in the 1990s violence related to illegal drugs began to wrack his country. Colombia also experienced a severe economic recession° and the company Edson worked for went out of business. Although his wife worked as a lawyer, she was not paid well. Moreover, the work she did came with a price: twice she received threats,
5   *one time by the military. Both safety and economic needs forced Edson and his wife to consider moving to the US. Getting permission to stay in the US was not an easy process and the couple had to work at very*

common jobs much below their educational levels. Finally, Edson got a job teaching high school Spanish classes. Eventually, he shifted from teaching Spanish to serving as liaison° between the school and the families of the many Spanish-speaking students in his school. In the roles of both teacher and liaison,
10 *Edson has supported many teenaged immigrants going through difficult times. Here he tells the story of how he supported one student.*

When Celeste was one year old, her mother came to the US. She left Celeste in Honduras with her grandmother. Finally, when Celeste was eight years old, her mother brought her to the US. When she arrived at the airport, some relatives went to pick her up, but not her mom. Maybe she had to work that
15 day. When Celeste arrived at the house, she saw several ladies sitting at the table and she had to ask which one was her mother.

At the beginning her life in the US, everything was good because Celeste was the center of attention. But later she realized that her mother was living with a man who was not her father. It was tough for her. She began to feel that her mother really did not love her because she had left her in
20 Honduras. And then when the mother brought her to the US, she left Grandmother back there in Honduras. And Grandmother was the one who had given Celeste attention and love.

Actually, her mother had made a lot of sacrifices° for her and for her family. But at that age Celeste couldn't understand it. It was painful for her.

When I met Celeste, she was in high school in the 9th grade. She was in my Spanish-for-native-
25 speakers class. I gave the students an assignment to write about tough times in their life. It was a kind of autobiographical piece. That's how I found out about Celeste's story. As an immigrant myself, I know that every newcomer to the US goes through tough times. I wanted to help students like Celeste to develop their reading and writing skills and share stories of their tough times.

Celeste was doing well in school. She was really smart. But then she realized that she was
30 undocumented.° And she wanted to go to college. A lot of kids don't know that they are undocumented when they start at the high school level. They begin thinking about going to college, and then they find out that they are undocumented. She became discouraged.

Celeste also took a second Spanish course with me, and a lot of the time in that class she was discouraged. I knew her abilities, but she was not doing well. I tried to encourage her with the hope that
35 there were still a lot of opportunities for her. I told her that there are scholarships for kids like her. If she worked hard, she could still go to college.

She began doing a little better. She was in JROTC° and she got a lot of attention. The director of the program encouraged her a lot. She stayed in JROTC for 3 years and became a leader there. Her grades are really good, and she is what we call 'college material.' She is active in sports and clubs. She loves to
40 volunteer. She volunteers to help with the parking at football games. Through one club she helps in other schools with child care when they have parent-teacher conferences.

Celeste is planning now to go to the local community college and then transfer to a larger state university where she wants to major in business. There are some requirements to go to college—like volunteering and participating in clubs. And since I want the students to have these opportunities, I
45 encourage students like Celeste to become active in all these ways. Not all students have another person in their lives who is leading them to see a brighter future. They have no one just telling them "Hi," telling them "You can do it," and showing them love. I am glad I could do these things for Celeste.

°*veterinarian (n.) – a doctor for animals*
°*pharmaceutical company (n.) – a company that makes medicines*
°*liaison (n.) – a person who works to help communication between two groups, like the school and home*
°*sacrifices (n.) – giving up something valuable for a specific purpose*
°*economic recession (adj. + n.) – a time when the economy is weak, many people lose their job*
°*undocumented (adj.) – not having the legal papers to be in a country*
°*JROTC (n.) – stands for "Junior Reserve Officer Training," a military training program for high school students*

Understand what you read

Put the events of this story in order using the numbers 1, 2, 3, 4, and so on. The first event has been indicated for you.

___ Celeste found out that she was undocumented.

___ Celeste realized the man her mother was living with was not her father.

___ Celeste became active in clubs, sports, and JROTC.

_1_ Celeste's mother came to the US.

___ Celeste planned to attend college.

___ Celeste's relatives picked her up at the airport.

___ Celeste shared the story of her tough time with her teacher

___ Celeste became very discouraged and did not work hard in school.

Discuss

1. What kind of trauma do you think Celeste suffered?
2. What are some actions that Edson took to help Celeste?
3. What are some other things in Celeste's situation that helped her grow more resilient?
4. How did Edson gain the wisdom and strength to encourage Celeste?
5. As a teacher learning about the tough times of so many students, could Edson suffer secondary trauma? Why or why not?

Teacher Story

Listen to your teacher tell a story about how she or he worked with a discouraged student who struggled through tough times at home or at school.

>   *Discuss:* How was this student's discouragement similar to or different from Celeste's? How were your teacher's responses similar to Edson's responses to Celeste? How was your teacher affected by this whole situation?

EXTEND YOUR LEARNING

1. Listen to *"Stand by Me"* by Ben E. King, Jerry Leiber, and Mike Stoller., originally performed by Ben E. King

In 1999 Broadcast Music International named "Stand by Me" the 4th most performed song of the 20th century. The song was first performed in 1961 by Ben E. King, when it was among the top ten songs in the US. In the 1980s it was again in the top ten, showing its enduring appeal to listeners. In 2010 Prince Royce recorded a bilingual (English-Spanish) version of the song. It hit the top of the charts on stations that play Latin music. And in 2009 Playing for Change released a version of "Stand by Me" on their CD/DVD "Songs Around the World." It is performed by a team 35 musicians in about ten countries.

http://www.youtube.com/watch?v=Vbg7YoXiKn0 (with Ben King - the lyrics appear below the video)
https://www.youtube.com/watch?v=foyH-TEs9D0 (with Prince Royce)
http://playingforchange.com/episodes/2/Stand_By_Me (Be sure to watch this fun version by Playing for Change from "Songs Around the World")

Discuss
1. What connections can you make between Edson Arango's actions and the song "Stand by Me"?
2. What are some of the causes of trauma that the song mentions?
3. Is this song just a love song or does it have a deeper meaning about humans supporting one another? What's your opinion?
4. What do you think about the different versions of the song?
5. Why do you think this song has been popular for so many years?

2. Drawing: Make a symbol of resilience
1. First, think of a time when you or someone you know faced a difficult situation. Then think of something that helped you (or them) get through that difficulty.
2. Make a *symbol* for the person, thing, or idea that helped you (or the other person). A symbol is a sign, a mark, a very simple picture, or other object that represents something. You should draw a symbol of something that gave or gives you strength in a difficult situation.
3. Get ready to tell the class what your symbol of resilience means. Why did you choose this symbol?
4. Share your symbol of resilience in a class circle

Example:
   Marco said: *I remember a time when my boss was treating me very harshly. I thought I might lose my job. I had one co-worker, Paloma, and she gave me some very wise advice. This advice gave me courage and strength. Since the name* Paloma *means* dove *in my language, I drew a picture of a dove to symbolize the wise advice of my co-worker.*

Talk about your sharing in the class circle
a. What did you feel when others were sharing their symbols?
b. Where did your class members get help and strength? Can you classify the types of help?
c. Were you surprised by any of the symbols of resilience you heard about?

The Last Word/Shutterstock

3. Journal
Write about your symbol of resilience. Was it difficult for you to think of a symbol? How did you feel about making this symbol and sharing it with the class?

4. Movement: Polarized breathing
An expert in stress management Sharon Promislow says that polarized breathing "can help balance the brain and body for relaxation and better thinking." If sharing about your symbol of resilience, made you feel stressed, you will want to try polarized breathing.

Preparation steps:
Put your tongue tip on the roof of your mouth.
Lower your tongue.
Put your right pointer (finger) on the side of your nose.
Put your hand down
Put your left pointer (finger) on the side of your nose.
Put your hand down.
Close your right nostril with your right pointer.
Breathe in
Take your finger off.
Close your left nostril with your left pointer.
Breathe out.

Polarized breathing:
Put your tongue tip on the roof of your mouth.
Lower it and keep it lowered.
Close your right nostril.
Breathe in.
Close your left nostril.
Breathe out.

Repeat the breathing three times.
Then reverse nostrils. Breathe in through the left and out through the right.

Once you have learned this routine, the teacher will say, Breathe deeply and polarize your breathing, _and you should do the activity by yourself. Do this kind of breathing whenever you need to relax and clear your mind._

SELF-ASSESSMENT

Think about your learning. Complete a self-assessment for this chapter by using the template at the end of the textbook (p. 194).

**Learning Tip:** Pay attention to what kind of activities you enjoy the most and which ones help you to learn the most. Choose to spend more time doing the activities that help you learn the most.

Chapter 5 Responding to Threats

Get to Know Each Other Better
Play "Look down, Look up"
1. Sit in a circle.
2. When your teacher says "Look Down," everybody looks at the floor.
3. Put your eyes on the feet of just <u>one</u> other person in the group.
4. When your teacher says "Look Up," slowly lift up your eyes to look in the face of the person whose feet you were looking at.
5. If that person is looking directly at you and your eyes are meeting, you both must "die."
6. Act out your death dramatically. Give your classmates some fun. Make them laugh!
7. Then leave the circle.
8. Your teacher will continue saying "Look Down " and "Look Up." until the last two students remain in the circle.

Connect to the topic
1. Which members of the class did the best job of acting out their deaths? What made their acting enjoyable?
2. How did you feel as you were slowly lifting your eyes? Did your heart beat faster? Did your breathing change? Did you fear that there might be a pair of eyes looking right back at you? Were you surprised? Were you relieved?
3. During this game, you were facing danger—but the "danger" was fun and not life-threatening. Still you probably felt your body reacting to the pressure of this threat.

Look at the pictures
Describe what you see in each of the pictures. What are different ways that people respond to danger or something that threatens their life?

Trauma Responses

Fight

Flight

 Freeze

EMU STAR Program

63

READ

How do we respond to threat?

Jon Gehman

1   Dr. Peter Levine tells the following story in his book *Waking the Tiger*. In the grasslands of South Africa, a herd of impalas is **grazing**. A hungry cheetah **springs** to attack the herd. The impalas quickly **dash** away to safety, except for one young one. This young one trips and becomes the target of the cheetah. Just before the cheetah makes **contact**, the young impala falls to the ground. It looks dead, but it is not. It is just playing dead. Like other animals, when the impala is **threatened** it freezes. It is protecting itself from the pain of being torn

5   apart by the cheetah. Levine says there is a chance the cheetah will drag the "dead" impala some safe place to eat it later. Meanwhile, the impala could wake back up again. When the impala awakes, it will **literally** shake off the fear that it recently experienced. It will **tremble** and shake away the **energy** that was stored at the time of the attack. Then it will run off to safety.

     When you face a **threat**, you will often be afraid. Being afraid can be a **positive** thing because it helps you

10   protect yourself when in danger. When you face danger, your whole body quickly gets ready for action. Often you don't have control over how you respond. And you may react in one of the following ways: fight, **flight** or freeze. These are three natural ways that our bodies protect us.

     No matter how you respond to threat, your body produces an **enormous** amount of energy. That energy gets used in different ways. If you fight, the energy is used to ***get back at*** the source of threat. You fight back against the attacker. If you **flee**, energy is used up in your flight. You move fast to escape the danger. If you

15   freeze, the energy is not completely used up. The energy is trapped in your body.

     The freeze response does not allow the trauma energy to be completely used up. The body looks **motionless** on the outside, but inside there is a powerful **roar**. Inside your body an intense storm is **roaring**. Energy is produced but cannot be used up. When this happens, trauma is like a storm – fierce and destructive.

20   It *wreaks havoc* on the bodies and minds of the people who experience it. It wreaks havoc on communities and societies as well.

    Shaking, trembling, crying or sweating are normal responses to trauma. They are helpful to the body and mind in the long run. If you allow yourself to shake and tremble, you are helping your body use up traumatic energy. The energy that has built up during the freeze response can be **released**.

    Wild animals like impalas do not seem to **exhibit** long-term trauma responses like humans. This is because they **instinctively** shake and tremble after freezing. They also automatically use deep breathing and
25 panting as ways of releasing trauma energy.

UNDERSTAND WHAT YOU READ

Which of the following sentences are true and which are false?
How would you change the false sentences to make them correct?

1. _____ When impalas are attacked by a cheetah, they usually run away.
2. _____ When an impala plays dead and then wakes up, it immediately runs away quickly.
3. _____ Being afraid is sometimes a good thing because it protects us from danger.
4. _____ We do not usually have control over our reaction to danger.
5. _____ Our bodies are slow to produce energy when we feel in danger.
6. _____ By fighting, fleeing or freezing, our body uses up energy.
7. _____ We are more likely to suffer severe trauma when we freeze.
8. _____ It is normal to cry, shake or sweat when we experience a traumatic event.
9. _____ Wild animals have long-term problems with trauma just like humans.
10. _____ Deep breathing is a good way of using up traumatic energy.

Discuss

1. How did you react when you faced a threat or danger in your life?
2. Do you think it is all right to compare human reactions to threat with animals' reactions?
3. What does your culture teach you to do with your emotions when you are hurting inside?
4. What might be some additional things you might try that would be healthy ways of releasing sadness and painful emotions?

WORD STUDY

A. Define it yourself!

graze (verb) _____
    Hint: Look at the picture. Why is the impala in the grass?

spring (verb) _____
    Hint: Look at the picture. What is the cheetah doing?

dash (verb) _____
    Hint: Look at the underlined words—the impalas quickly dash away to safety.

positive (adjective) _____
    Hint: Look at the underlined words—...a positive thing because it helps you protect yourself

tremble (verb) _____
    Hint: Look at the underlined words—It will tremble and shake ...

threat (noun) _____
    Hint: Compare the word threat in chapter 3 with its meaning in this paragraph.

threaten (verb) _____
    Hint: Think about the situation. The impala is not dead, but it feels threatened. Does the cheetah need to speak?

energy (noun) _____
    Hint: This word is used 11 times between line 12 and the end.

65

Word meanings

B. First do the exercise with the sentences below. Then try to write short definitions here.

contact (noun) _____touch, touching, hit_____

exhibit (verb) _____

enormous (adjective) _____

flee (verb) _____

flight (noun) _____

instinctively (adverb) _____

literally (adverb) _____

motionless (adjective) _____

release (verb) _____

roar (noun) _____

roar (verb) _____

C. For the sentences below, you have been given three choices. Only <u>one</u> choice is not correct; the incorrect choice gives the <u>opposite</u> meaning. Cross out the wrong choice. Then write your definition of the word in the spaces above.

Example: The cheetah was running toward the impala and soon _____ it.

   ~~a. stayed away from~~   b. made contact with   c. was touching

1. Impalas _____ their fear by running away from cheetahs.

    a. show   b. exhibit   c. hide

2. The elephant is not a tiny animal. It is _____.

    a. enormous   b. large   c. small

3. The _____ of the lion may frighten even elephants.

    a. quiet sound   b. loud sound   c. roar

4. When afraid, some people might freeze and others might _____ from the threat.

    a. stand still   b. flee   c. run away

5. Fighting and freezing are ways of responding to threat. Another response is _____.

    a. flight   b. escape   c. waiting

6. Both humans and animals do _____ shake and tremble as a normal response to trauma.

    a. really   b. not actually   c. literally

66

7. Some experts may *think* about shaking as a way to get free from trauma. But some animals and humans _____ tremble and shake.

    a. do not naturally   b. without stopping to think   c. instinctively

8. The attacking cheetah is moving fast. The impala who plays dead is _____.

    a. active   b. motionless   c. still

9. You probably feel unwell if traumatic energy _____ inside of you.

    a. roars   b. whispers softly   c. makes a loud noise

10. If you <u>keep</u> the traumatic energy inside of you, this will cause problems. Instead, you should try to _____ the energy.

    a. let go of   b. hold onto   c. release

D. Picture conversation. Use the new vocabulary to have a conversation about the pictures that go with the reading. You may include the pictures from the beginning of this chapter, too. Here are the steps to follow:

1. Divide up the words and have everyone in the class write some of the words on cards—one word on each card. The class should make 18 cards with 18 different words.

2. Collect the cards, shuffle them, and deal them out to everyone in the class. In a class of 9 people, every student would receive 2 cards. If the class is larger, make a double or triple set of cards and work in two or three groups.

3. You can begin your discussion with a question like this: *What happens when animals or humans sense danger?* In order to take part in the conversation, you need to <u>use the words on the cards</u> that you have. Use those words in a sentence to make your contribution to the conversation. Remember to use the pictures to help you.

Word family. In this chapter and chapter 3 you learned two words that belong to the same family. Write your own sentence for each word in the right hand column.

threat (noun) a person or a thing that is a danger to someone else; also words that promise something dangerous or unpleasant to others	
*Two great **threats** in the desert are the hot sun and the lack of water.*	
*I was afraid because of her **threats** to call the police.*	
threaten (verb) this is action of saying that you will harm someone or showing that someone or something will harm you	
*She **threatened** to call the police if we didn't leave.*	
*The hurricane **threatened** the whole village.*	

Expressions:
in the long run – after a long time   A long run takes a long time. Sometimes, life seems like a long race.

shake off – to get rid of; to get free from something   We can shake off real things.
We shake the dirt off our pants. Dogs shake off water after they have a swim. But we can also shake off things that are not actual objects. A footballer may have a hard fall and hurt his arm, but he can shake off the injury and keep playing. If you have a bad dream in the night, you can shake it off in the morning and have a good day.

get back at – to repay or punish someone for something bad that they did to you. We can get back at other people by physical actions or words. If someone hits me, I can get back at them by hurting them physically. If someone says bad things about me to other people, I can get back at them by threatening them or by saying bad things about them.

wreak havoc –cause a lot of trouble or problems. You will almost always find these two words together. You may see combinations like *cause havoc* or *play havoc* as often as you see *wreak havoc*. They all mean about the same thing. But you will not often see the verb *wreak* with other objects than *havoc*.

Try a little experiment. Type these word combinations into Google using quotation marks and see how many results come up for each combination. Write the number of results in the blank.
"wreak havoc"   _____
"cause havoc"   _____
"play havoc"   _____
"wreak destruction"   _____
"wreak vengeance"   _____
"wreak revenge "   _____
"wreak damage "   _____

Use the expressions as you answer these questions:
1. *In the long run,* what will be the benefits of learning English?
In the long run, what will be the benefits of learning about trauma and resilience?
 In the long run, what will be the benefits of _____ (doing any difficult work or facing any difficult situation)?
Begin your answer: *In the long run,* _____.

2. What would you like to *shake off*? (remember, we normally want to *shake off* bad things)
Begin your answer: *I would like to shake off* _____.

3. People often have disagreements or fights. Sometimes one person insults or harms another person. What are some ways that people *get back at* each other for insults or injuries?
Begin your answer: *People get back at each other by VERB+ing* _____.

GRAMMAR STUDY
Cause and effect sentences tell us why something happened. We can talk about causes and effects in English with the help of several common words and grammar structures. Compare these four structures (1-4) with the example sentences (1a – 4a) below them.

Cause   **Effect**
1. (When + sentence) + Sentence
2. (Because + sentence) + Sentence
3. Noun phrase + *cause* + (noun phrase + *to* + verb)
4. (*Because of* + noun phrase) + Sentence

In the real world, the cause comes first, and then the effect. We can express the real world order of cause and effect in sentences like these:

Cause   **Effect**

1a. When the impala senses a threat, it flees.
2a. Because the impala sensed a threat, it fled.
3a. The cheetah caused the impala to flee.
4a. Because of the cheetah the impala fled.

But in the world of language, we can also reverse the order. We can mention the effect first and then tell the cause.

Effect   **Cause**

1b. The impala flees when it senses a threat.
2b. The impala fled because it sensed a threat.
3b. The impala's flight was caused by the cheetah.
4b. The impala fled because of the cheetah.

Notice that all the example sentences answer the question *Why did the impala flee?* This question mentions the effect and asks about the cause. Questions can also mention the cause and ask about the effect. An example would be *Why is being afraid a positive thing?* Possible answers might be *When we are afraid, our body gets ready to face the danger* or *Because we are afraid, our body gets ready to protect us.*

First practice by putting these sentence parts together in ways that create good sentences of cause and effect. Be ready to read the correct sentence aloud to the class.

1. it wreaks havoc on your body and spirit	trauma energy is trapped in your body	when
2. trembling and shaking after a traumatic event	the trauma energy to be released	causes
3. overwhelming threat	we suffer trauma	because of
4. trauma energy is released	we tremble and shake after a traumatic event	when
5. we must help people shake off trauma energy	we want a healthy and peaceful society	because

A note on punctuation: Carefully compare sentences 1a and 2a with 1b and 2b. What difference in punctuation do you notice? These two pairs of sentences are examples for a rule of comma usage in English. If you begin a sentence with *When + sentence* or *Because* + sentence, you will place a comma at the end of that first sentence (clause), and then continue with the main sentence (clause). Which sentences are examples of this rule? But when you begin with the main clause and end your sentence with *when + clause* or *because + clause*, you don't need any comma between the two. Which sentences are examples of this rule?

Now for each of the questions below, write an answer using one of the patterns above. Use two different patterns for each sentence. Try to use all the different patterns.

1. Why did the impala play dead? (effect)
2. Why is fleeing (or fighting) a good response to trauma? (effect)
3. Why is deep breathing good for you? (cause)

Speaking & listening to each other
Read your sentences to a partner. Listen to the partner's sentences. Help each other improve your sentences. Share example sentences with the whole class. Try to collect examples of all the different cause and effect grammar structures.

Optional practice: Work together in pairs or teams and make questions based on the five sentences above. Some of the questions may ask about the cause, and some may ask about the effect. Then teams can take turns asking their questions while the opposite team provides an appropriate answer.

Example: **Question:** Why do we suffer trauma?
Answer: We suffer trauma because of overwhelming threat.

LIFE SKILLS
Stories of resilience
Read this story about one person who faced a dangerous threat.

> **Develop your reading skills:**
> **Skim.**
>
> You understand a reading better if you first know what kind of text you are reading. You can become aware of the kind of text by *skimming* it before you read it. To skim the text, just read the first sentence of each paragraph. Do it now. Then answer these questions: Is this text describing causes and effects? Is it classifying ways of responding to threat? Or is it telling a story?
>
> You should be able to tell from skimming that this is a story. What helps you to identify this text as a story? Remember, for stories you can use a **time line** to help you understand better the events in the story (see chap. 3).

Facing Threats with Courage

Carlos Mendoza and his family now live in the United States. They are from the country of Honduras in Central America. Honduras is a country that has suffered from natural disasters. It also suffers from high crime and government corruption. Carlos shares his story eagerly. He believes it is very important for others to know the threats that people in his country face.

[Names and other identifying information in the story have been changed to protect the hero of the story.]

1   Carlos Mendoza is a man of courage and convictions. He belongs to the Honduran social movement. Along with other ordinary Hondurans, he has protested corruption in Honduras. He has opposed the strong influence of drug runners, corrupt politicians, and international companies in Honduras. These companies, with the help of politicians, push poor people off their land so that they can extract gold, lead, oil, gas, and wood.

5   In 2008, Carlos discovered that the police were secretly investigating him because of his social actions. Even though he knew his life was in danger, Carlos was not going to give up his important work for social justice. He got help from a private security agency. He began driving different cars. The director of the security company often helped him if there was any emergency.

        On the night of November 23, his family began to suspect that someone was watching them. At first,
10   they found it hard to believe. Then on the night of November 25, Carlos returned from a meeting held in the city at 7:45 p.m. He found a green Nissan parked in front of his house. He parked behind this vehicle instead of parking by the gate of his house. He quickly memorized the license plate number—YZA 5629. Carlos got out his car and walked past the Nissan. At first he did not see the man in the car because the windows had dark tinted glass. But then the man's cell phone came on, which permitted Carlos to see him. He rapidly opened the
15   gate and entered his house.

        Once inside he closely observed the movements of this man through the window of a second-floor bedroom. He made several phone calls. He then went down to the door of his house and turned off the light in order to see the vehicle more closely. The individual became aware of this. He started his vehicle and sped off. Carlos immediately went out to the street to see what direction the car headed. He got in his car and went after
20   him. But he was unable to discover where this suspicious person lived.

        As he returned to his house, he was surprised to find another car already in the same place. It was a blue Honda, but he couldn't see the license number. He quickly turned around and parked some distance away

in order to watch the Honda. He phoned the director of the security company to come and help. After about twenty minutes the Nissan came back and parked. The Honda left, though after 15 minutes it passed by again.
25 In this situation of high danger, he took off in his vehicle and headed toward the house of the security company director. They exchanged cars in order to throw the suspects off track.

They both drove back to Carlos' house. The two vehicles were gone. They drove around the area, trying to find those two vehicles but couldn't find them. It was a night with lots of traffic. Together with his wife, he stayed awake all night, for fear that they would come again.
30 Carlos realized that this was no game. He and his family were in danger. He did some research on the license number of the Nissan. He found that the owner was a major in the army. The military was secretly investigating him. Carlos knew it was more important than ever to continue his work in Honduras. But his family could not keep living in this situation of insecurity and corruption. He decided to take his family to another country for safety. And he made plans to continue his work for social justice in Honduras from this
35 new place.

° convictions (n.) – strong beliefs or principles
° protest (v.) – to say that something is wrong or untrue; to take action that shows disagreement
° investigate (v.) – study, find information about
° social movement (adj. + n.) – groups of people who work together to change society
° corruption (n.) – dishonest actions
° corrupt (adj.) – the adjective form of *corruption* (above) meaning dishonest
° extract (v.) – take out
° security (n.) – safety, protection from danger
° suspect (v.) – believe but not know for certain
° vehicle (n.) – car or anything that can carry something from one place to another
° observe (v.) – look at carefully
° suspicious (adj.) – someone who cannot be trusted
° throw off track (v.) – to cause someone to lose the way, to confuse them so that they won't be able to follow
° major (n.) – an army officer higher than captain but lower than colonel
° military (n.) – army
° insecurity (n.) – opposite of *security* (above) – no safety, no protection from danger

Understand what you read

(1) After skimming the text, you found that it is a <u>story</u> and not a text about causes and effects or classification. There are different kinds of stories, but most stories use phrases about time to help readers understand when the different actions happened.

First, see if you can find any time phrases at the beginning of each paragraph; write the line number and the sentence in the spaces below. Underline the time phrase.

Line	Sentence
5	<u>In 2008</u> Carlos discovered that the police were secretly investigating him because of his social actions.

Did you notice that most of the actions reported in this story take place in a single night? Go back and look at paragraph 3. What night did most of the actions happen? _____

(2) Follow carefully the actions of Carlos in this story. Look for sentences in which *Carlos* or *he* (referring to Carlos) plays the main role. Find the action word that describes what Carlos did.

Line	Actions
2	He protested, he opposed
5	Carlos discovered

(3) What are some adjectives that you could use to describe Carlos and the actions that he took?
Circle some appropriate adjectives from the box below. If you don't know the meaning, look them up in a dictionary or ask your teacher. Then add some of your own adjectives. Be ready to give reasons for your choices.

Some choices: Your own adjectives:
brave   friendly   aware   afraid   dangerous
handsome   intelligent   slow-thinking   persistent

C. *Discussion*
1. How did Carlos respond to the threats that he sensed?
2. What is your opinion about the way Carlos responded?
3. Why didn't Carlos call the police to get protection?
4. How do you think Carlos will feel when he gets to another country with his family?

Teacher Story
Listen to your teacher tell a story about a time when he or she responded to a threat.
   Discuss: How does your teacher's experience compare with the experience of Carlos?

EXTEND YOUR LEARNING
1. Readers theater
Work together to write a drama that follows up on Carlos's story. If you are a large class, your teacher may have you work in two or three smaller groups.

Carlos and his family have been invited by the Human Rights Commission in his new country of residence to answer questions about their experiences.

1) Decide who will be members of the Human Rights Commission & who will represent Carlos and his family.
2) Now decide what questions the Human Rights Commission will ask Carlos. Try to make at least one question for every member of the committee, so that everyone can ask questions.
3) Suggest what kind of answers Carlos and his family members will give.
4) What will members of the Human Rights Commission say in their short speeches after questions and answers?
5) After you have written out each person's lines, practice reading them.
6) Then act out the drama for the whole class. Don't memorize your lines. Just read them.

Discuss: How did you feel when you were watching the drama? If you were playing one of the parts, how did you feel about your character?

2. Journal
Write in your journal about a time when you faced a threat. Describe how you felt. Explain how you responded to the threat.

3. Music
Listen to 2 or 3 of the following relaxation songs. Which one is the most relaxing for you? What makes the music relaxing for you? Give a description of the music in one word.

Cherokee Morning Song, "We n' de ya ho" (I am of the Great Spirit)
            https://www.youtube.com/watch?v=YhcgX1VHsgk
Enya "Long, Long Journey" http://www.youtube.com/watch?v=5A01guT4HL4
Gregorian chant "Da Pacem" (Give us Peace) http://www.youtube.com/watch?v=eC-JKId3SoA
Paul Collier "Air" http://www.youtube.com/watch?v=rUq3tZNJmtw
Secret Garden "Lotus" http://www.youtube.com/watch?v=U66L3t68D5A
Samuel Barber, "Adagio for Strings" http://www.youtube.com/watch?v=KylMqxLzNGo

4. Movement
As you read in the first text in this chapter, animals instinctively shake off trauma energy. You can practice shaking, too. If you feel tense, shaking can help you relax. You shake off the stress in your body.

Shaking

Shake your head very fast.
Leave your mouth open.
Relax your jaw.
Shake your head again and feel your lips shake.
Shake your arms and your shoulders.

Relax your hands
    and let them shake freely with your arms.
Shake your torso
Hold onto a chair for balance.
Lift one foot from the ground at a time.
Shake your legs and feet one at a time.

Another way you can relax your body is to tighten up your muscles and then loosen them.

Tensing & relaxing muscles

Tighten all the muscles in your face.
Keep them tight for a few seconds.
Then let them go loose.
Tighten all the muscles in your arm. Make your
    hands into fists.
Keep your arms and fists tight for a few seconds.

Then let them go loose.
Tighten all the muscles in your legs and feet.
Keep them tight for a few seconds.
Then let them go loose.
Tighten all the muscles in your face, your arms, and
    your legs.
Let them go loose.

Which way of relaxing worked the best for you? Or do you feel relaxed in different ways from doing these two exercises?

SELF-ASSESSMENT

Think about your learning. Complete a self-assessment for this chapter by using the template at the end of the textbook (p. 194).

> *Learning Tip:* Pay attention to the others in your class. What kinds of activities do they seem to enjoy the most? What can you learn from your classmates? If you have questions or problems, which of your classmates can help you because they are good at doing those tasks?

Chapter 6 How Trauma Affects Us

Get to Know Each Other Better

One by one every class member will have a chance to talk for at least 15 seconds on one of the following six topics. You will not know in advance which topic you will talk about. The topic will be decided by the roll of a die or toss of a coin.

TALK ABOUT...

	1. a new idea you recently thought about	
2. something or someone you have strong feelings about	3. an old behavior you want to change or a new one you want to adopt	
4. the health or fitness of your body	5. a belief or value that is important to you	
	6. a memory that is important to you	

Connect to the Topic

You have just talked about six very important aspects of our lives: thoughts, feelings, behavior, body, beliefs, and memories. A person's total well-being depends on the health of these six aspects. Resilient persons have healthy thoughts, feelings, behaviors, bodies, beliefs and memories. But resilient persons also face difficulties in life. Tragedy can strike at anyone. Resilient people can grow wiser and stronger through their experience of trauma if they understand how trauma affects every aspect of their lives.

Discuss

What strengths did you notice in your classmates as you got to know each other better through the "Talk About..." activity?

Look at the pictures

1. Describe what you see in the pictures below. The words in the diagram will help you.
2. Where is the beginning point of the cycle? What kinds of events occur at this beginning point? Review what you learned in earlier chapters about the causes of trauma.
3. Think about how you respond to scary, dangerous, or threatening situations. Discuss with the class what your normal responses are to these kinds of situations.

THE VICTIM EXPERIENCE

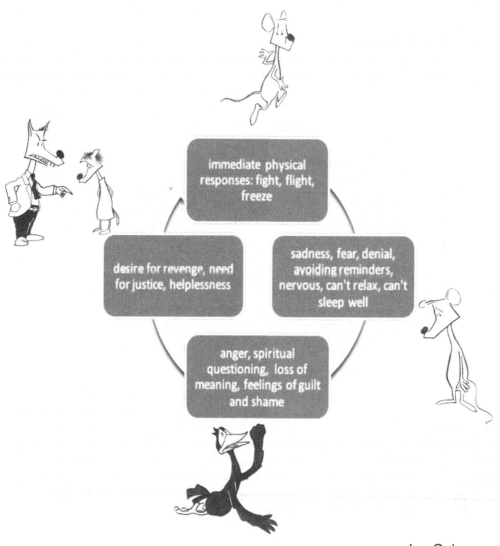

Jon Gehman

READ

Develop your reading skills:

Find the main idea of the reading: In a short text like this one, you will usually find the main idea in the first paragraph. You can also take some help from the title. If you turn the title into a question, what answer does the first paragraph give for that question?

Identify the main topic of each paragraph: Identify the key words or phrases that signal the main topic for each paragraph. The paragraphs have been numbered for you. Number your own paper 2 – 8 and make a note about the main topic for each paragraph.

In many texts, the topic of a body paragraph is found in the <u>first sentence</u>. School textbooks are usually carefully organized in this way to make reading easier. Now what should you look for in the first sentence?

   (a) Look for participants & processes mentioned in the first sentence

   (b) Look later in the sentence for new information because it tends to come at the end.

   (c) Topic sentences from the middle of a text often begin with the old information from earlier paragraphs and go on to introduce the new topics for the current paragraph.

Example: Look at the first sentence of paragraph 2. "After the initial shock of the trauma event, <u>people</u> **may**

76

experience <u>changes</u> in the way <u>they</u> **think, feel**, and **behave**." [<u>underlined</u> = participants and **bold** = processes]
Now skim quickly through the rest of paragraph 2. Do you find more mention of <u>people</u> or <u>they</u> and <u>changes</u>? And what about the process of **thinking, feeling**, or **behaving**? Which of these processes are discussed in para. 2?

Now look at the first sentence of paragraph 3: "*Trauma affects people* both emotionally and spiritually." The *italicized* words are old information (notice that all of those words are in the title). The new information in this sentence is at the end: emotionally and spiritually. Skim quickly the rest of para. 3. Do you find more discussion of emotional and spiritual effects?

Keep using this method to help you understand the main ideas of each paragraph. You can use underlining, draw boxes around words, and use colored pencils to keep track of participants, processes, old information and new information.

How Trauma Affects People

1 (1)　　Fight, flight, and freeze are immediate physical responses to threat. They are normal reactions of the body. But trauma affects more than the body. It also affects our minds and emotions. It **shatters** meaning and creates a need for justice and even **revenge**. The **Victim** Experience (above) shows common trauma responses following a frightening event. These responses do not happen one at a time or in neat **linear** order.

5 (2)　　After the **initial** shock of the trauma event, people may experience changes in the way they think, feel, and behave. Trauma victims find it difficult to **concentrate** and think clearly. They have problems remembering new things they are trying to learn. Their ability to solve problems **diminishes**. Because of this decrease, they get into **frequent** conflicts with others. Their own family members become targets of their anger and violence. They cannot relax or sleep well. Often they choose to withdraw from social

10 relations and **isolate** themselves. Sadly, some traumatized persons become dependent on alcohol or drugs. If they smoke cigarettes, their smoking increases.

(3)　　Trauma affects people both emotionally and spiritually. Emotionally, trauma victims may feel sad, angry, or guilty. They may lose control of their emotions. Sometimes they have **fantasies** of **revenge** against those who harmed them. Spiritually, they feel like the meaning of life has been shattered. They may

15 question whether God cares for them or whether God exists. They have difficulty trusting other people. They can feel empty and lack energy. They may lose their **commitment** to do anything to help themselves or to help others.

(4)　　Victims' emotional and spiritual troubles are exhibited in **chronic** physical problems. They feel weakness. Their appetite and sleep patterns change. They may suffer **vomiting** and headaches. There is one

20 very important point to remember. All these changes in thinking, feeling, and behaving, with their spiritual and physical expressions, are normal reactions to traumatic events. We should expect victims of trauma to **exhibit** some of these responses.

(5)　　Some persons may experience more serious responses to trauma. These victims relive the event. They have **vivid flash backs**. Memories of the event come back suddenly and uninvited. They may be

25 triggered by sights, sounds, or smells in the environment. These memories may show up in bad dreams or nightmares. Sometimes a trauma victim just can't stop thinking about what happened.

(6)　　Trauma victims also **avoid** reminders of the event. Because the event was so horrible, they avoid thinking and talking about it. They avoid sounds, sights and smells that are reminders of the event. Some people who have experienced traumas in their lives have never told their children about these terrible events.

30 They never talk to anyone about the events. Because their trauma has caused emotional pain, these people try not to have any emotions. Their feelings are **numb**. That is why they have a hard time **sympathizing** with the pain that others feel.

(7)　　Finally, the most seriously affected victims are **hypervigilant**. This means they cannot relax. They are always looking for signs of threat. They have once before been caught off guard, and they were seriously

35 harmed. They don't want that to happen again, and so they always stay on guard, watching for some threat to their well being. Their body is working to protect them in case some danger comes near again.

(8)   If these serious responses continue for more than three months or even start long after the trauma has ended, a person probably has Post Traumatic Stress Disorder (PTSD). This person needs additional support and care. He or she should see a counselor or doctor.

UNDERSTAND WHAT YOU READ

A. How does trauma affect people? Look at the table below. In the first column, you will fill in the main ways that trauma affects people. What parts of a person's life can be affected by trauma? In the second column are examples from each way that trauma affects people. You add at least one more example for each effect.

Main ways a person is affected by trauma:	Examples:
1. *thinking*	cannot think clearly,
2.	conflicts with others,
3.	feel sad,
4.	meaning of life destroyed,
5.	feel weakness,

B. What are three responses to trauma that are more serious? Some people suffer more serious trauma. In the first column, write the main topic. In the second column, add other examples.

Main effects of serious trauma:	Examples:
1.	bad dreams,
2. *avoid reminders of the event*	
3.	cannot relax

C. Look at all the topics you identified in the first column of the two tables above. How are those topics arranged in the paragraphs of the text? Compare your answers with the first sentence of each paragraph.

Discuss
1. How do the normal reactions to trauma described in the text compare with the ones that you discussed when viewing the pictures (p. 76)?
2. At the end of paragraph 4, the text says that these reactions to trauma are "normal." How are these normal reactions similar to the more serious reactions explained in paragraphs 5-8? How are the "normal reactions" different from the more serious reactions?
3. The text seems to say that victims of trauma have very little choice. It claims that people naturally react in these ways. Do you agree or not? Can people choose to have different reactions to traumatic events? Share any examples you can think of to support your opinion.
4. How do people in your culture view any of the responses to trauma described here?

WORD STUDY
A. You define it!

victim (noun)_____
Look at the way this word is used in lines 3, 6, 12, 18, 21, 23, 27

flash backs (noun) _____
Look at the following sentence (line 23-24).

numb (adjective) _____
Look at the sentence before (line 30-31)

hypervigilant (adjective) _____
Look at the following sentences (line 33)

B. Word meanings
The words on the left were used in the text above. Match those words with their meanings on the right.
1. ___ **linear** (adjective)
2. ___ **shatter** (verb)
3. ___ **initial** (adjective)
4. ___ **frequent** (adjective)
5. ___ **concentrate** (verb)
6. ___ **isolate** (verb)
7. ___ **fantasy** (noun)
8. ___ **revenge** (noun)
9. ___ **commitment**
10. ___ **diminish** (verb)
11. ___ **chronic** (adjective)
12. ___ **vomiting** (noun)
13. ___ **vivid** (adjective)
14. ___ **avoid** (verb)
15. ___ **sympathize** (verb)
16. ___ **exhibit** (verb)

a. stay away from
b. get smaller, become less
c. regular, repeated
d. dream, imagination
e. break, destroy
f. lively, lifelike, very real
g. remove, separate
h. first
i. firm decision, dedication
j. attacking, fighting, getting even with
k. think about closely, keep attention on
l. throwing up, bringing up from the stomach
m. long lasting
n. feel for, show mercy
o. show
p. moving from one stage to another with a clear beginning and ending point

C. Word practice – Get the context right! The underlined words in the sentences below are your new words for this chapter. But there is something wrong with the sentences. Part of the sentence does not go along meaningfully with the underlined word or words. You need to change the sentence to make its meaning agree with the meaning of the underlined word(s). The first one has been done for you.

1. Her presentation was very <u>linear</u> as it moved from one topic to the next topic without any clear connections or logic.

   Example: Her presentation was very <u>linear</u> as it moved <u>in a very clear and organized way from the beginning to the end</u>.

2. The boss <u>shattered </u>my dreams of success by giving me a better position in the company.

3. In the <u>initial</u> days of a child's life, it is important to send her to school.

4. If you have <u>frequent</u> bad dreams, you probably have a very calm and relaxing life.

79

5. If there is a lot of noise in the classroom during the test, the students will be able to underline{concentrate} very well and earn a high score.

6. Since the children were playing so well with each other, their mother decided to underline{isolate} them in separate rooms of the house.

7. It was no underline{fantasy} when Faheem looked in the mirror and saw tiny little men crawling into his ears.

8. Yesterday the company gave Eduardo a big salary increase so he decided to take underline{revenge} on his boss by not coming to work all week.

9. As time went on, Lola's underline{commitment} to the project underline{diminished}, so she attended every meeting and spent every spare minute working to complete the tasks that were given to her.

10. When the doctor heard about the underline{chronic vomiting}, she told the parents they did not need to buy more medicine because their children were in great health.

11. Because Gloria had underline{vivid} memories of her favorite vacation, she could not tell her friends any details of the hotel where she stayed, the shopping she did, or the restaurants where she ate.

12. He underline{sympathized} with the family that lost their son in the war, so he underline{avoided} meeting and talking with them.

13. The underline{victim} of the robbery is underline{hypervigilant} so she usually forgets to lock all the doors and windows of her house.

14. From all their screaming and crying, we could see that the children were underline{numb} from the terrible hardship they had suffered.

15. Your underline{flash backs} of the hurricane probably help you to feel calm and safe as you think about the sights, sounds, and smells of that big storm.

Expressions

trigger -- A trigger is part of a gun; when you pull the trigger the gun fires. When one thing causes something else, we can say it *triggers* that thing. The reading explains that sights, smells, or sounds *trigger* memories.

show up – This is a two-word verb. It means *appear* or *become clearly seen. The shock of trauma shows up in physical problems that a person has.* It can also be used in an informal way. *He didn't show up for class yesterday.* In this sentence, it means *come.* Someone who is expected but does not show up can be called a *no-show.*

stay on guard – A person who *stays on guard* is always looking out for danger, just like a soldier with a gun or sword who is guarding people or a place. *Some trauma victims stay on guard so they won't be harmed again.*

catch off guard – *Being off guard* means that someone is not looking out for danger or is not ready to face danger. When we *catch people off guard*, it means we do something they did not expect. If you are not ready for something, you can be *caught off guard. Trauma victims don't want to be caught off guard by any threats.*

Discuss these questions with your classmates:
1. What *triggers* laughter in your class? What *triggers* worry? What *triggers* conflict?
2. Are you sometimes *caught off guard* in class? What (or who) catches you off guard?
3. What should you *stay on guard* for in class or in life?
4. Why is it important to *show up* for class?

GRAMMAR STUDY

A. Pronoun reference: Being able to understand pronouns is an important grammar skill that will help your reading. You will understand more and read more fluently if you know what a pronoun is referring to. If you don't understand how pronouns link sentences together, then it will be difficult to understand what a text means. For example, read again these sentences from the first paragraph:

*Fight, flight, and freeze are immediate physical responses to threat. But trauma affects more than the body. **It** also affects our minds and emotions. **It** shatters meaning and creates a need for justice and even revenge.*

You know that pronouns like *it* refer to nouns or stand in the place of nouns and noun phrases. In the sentences above, what does *it* refer to? Look at the sentences before the first *it* appears. Does *it* refer to *the body* or *trauma* or *threat*? What helped you to get the right answer?

The first paragraph shows one of two common patterns in the way pronouns are used. In this example, the pronoun is standing for an important participant whom (or which) the writer wants to keep in focus. To keep this participant in focus, the writer almost always mentions the participant in the beginning of the sentence (or main clause). The word *Trauma* is the focus of the second sentence. The idea of *trauma* stays in focus in the next two sentences, only it is expressed by the pronoun *It*.

Look at paragraph 7 for a second example of the same pattern:
*Finally, the most seriously affected victims are hypervigilant. This means **they** cannot relax. **They** are always looking for signs of threat. **They** have once before been caught off guard, and **they** were seriously harmed. **They** don't want that to happen again, and so **they** always stay on guard, watching for some threat to their well being.*

The focus of this paragraph is *seriously affected victims who are hypervigilant*. **They** stays in first position in each clause of the paragraph to mark the continuing focus on this group.

1. The most common pronoun in this text is *they*. Find two uses of the pronoun *they* near each other. Copy the sentence or sentences with *they* here and note the line number. Write the noun or noun phrase to which *they* refers and note the line number.

<u>Sentence(s) with *they*</u>   <u>Noun/noun phrase</u>

_____   _____ (line   )

_____   _____ (line   )

2. Find the only example in the text where *he* or *she* is used and do the same thing

<u>Sentence with *he* or *she*</u>   <u>Noun/noun phrase</u>

_____   _____ (line   )
Share your answers with a partner or other members of the class. How many different examples did you find?

B. Demonstrative determiners
Because pronouns refer to other words, we can call them ***pointing words***. Other pointing words include ***this, that, these*** and ***those***. Like pronouns, these words help us to understand a text by linking one sentence with a previous one.

*The Victim Cycle (above) shows <u>common responses</u> following a frightening event. **These** responses do not happen one at a time or in neat linear order.*

In the second sentence, the word *these* in the phrase *these responses* is pointing back to *common responses* in the sentence before. In this way, the pointing words help to create connections between sentences.

You will notice from this example that determiners like ***these*** can also be in the first position in the sentence and, thus, mark the focus, just like pronouns. But like pronouns, the demonstrative determiners can come later in the sentence. In every case, though, the determiner is pointing backward and linking with a topic that has already been discussed. In the reading above, we see more variety in the pattern for using demonstrative determiners than in the use of pronouns.

1. Find two more examples of sentences with *these*. Copy the sentence with *these*. Write the noun or noun phrase that *these* is pointing to.

Sentence(s) with *these*   Noun/noun phrase

_____   _____ (line   )

_____   _____ (line   )

2. Find one example of a sentence with *this*.

_____   _____ (line   )

Share your answers with a partner or other members of the class. How many different examples did you find?

C. Possibility
Sometimes the small words are the most important. Look at the two sentences below. What is the difference? And what is the difference in meaning?

   (a) *Emotionally, trauma victims feel sad, angry, or guilty.*
   (b) *Emotionally, trauma victims may feel sad, angry, or guilty.*

Sentence (a) says, "This is always or usually true: trauma victims feel sad, angry or guilty."
Sentence (b) says, "This is not always true, but it is possible that trauma victims feel sad, angry or guilty."

Find two other sentences with *may* and copy them here.

_____

_____

There are many sentences in the text that do not use the word *may*. Look at the second paragraph for examples. If the author does not use *may*, does he mean that the statement is always true for all people? Take, for example, the sentence in lines 6-7:

   They have problems remembering new things they are trying to learn.

Is this statement true all the time for all trauma victims? Is your interpretation affected because the first sentence in the paragraph uses *may* in making a general statement about the thinking and behavior of trauma victims? What is the effect of the phrase *common responses* in the very first paragraph? How does it affect how we understand the whole text about human reactions to trauma? ***Discuss these questions with your teacher.***

LIFE SKILLS
Story of Resilience
Read this story about a family whose life was changed by a terrible shock.

Develop your reading skills:
Read and re-read. Remember that you will understand more if you read a text more than once. Read this story *quickly* once. Or if you would like to practice your ***skimming***, skim the text once. Then go back and read more slowly, paying closer attention to the order of events.

Pay attention to how writers order events. Stories do not always tell events in the order that they happened. Essays that reflect on the effects of an event (like the one below) may put the events in a different order. Since stories are usually told in past tense, look for instances of the past perfect verb form (HAD + 3rd form of the verb). When you see that verb form, you will know the events happened earlier than the situation being described currently

Example: Look at these first three lines from the story below:
My daughter, younger son and I <u>had</u> just <u>arrived</u> in Karachi from London. My husband <u>was posted</u> on a diplomatic° assignment there. Some of us <u>were sitting</u> at the breakfast table at my brother's house. My 3-year-old nephew <u>blurted</u>° out, "Auntie, <u>do</u> you <u>know</u> that the robbers <u>have taken</u> Faisal and Junni-bhai?

The verb tenses here are a little difficult. The perfect forms (*had* or *have* + past participle) signal things that happened <u>before</u> the "past" that the writer is telling about. There are also present tense verbs in these lines, like "<u>do</u> you know." The writer is reporting the words of her nephew just as he spoke them, but these words were spoken in the past, as the verb "blurted" shows us.

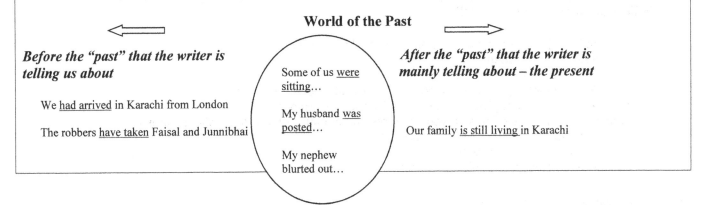

A Family Shocked and Shaken
by Ruxsana Arshad

In 1989 Ruxsana Arshad's son and nephew were kidnapped when they were on their way to their grandparents' home in Karachi, Pakistan. In this essay, Ruxsana reflects on how this incident affected her and the whole family.

My daughter, younger son and I had just arrived in Karachi from London. My husband was posted on a diplomatic° assignment there. Some of us were sitting at the breakfast table at my brother's house. My 3-year-old nephew blurted° out, "Auntie, do you know that the robbers have taken Faisal and Junni-bhai? We all broke into laughter. But then my sister began crying and told us that this was no joke. Just
5 then my brother and sister-in-law walked in, looking miserable. ° My brother told us all the details. I could scarcely believe what they were telling me.

Before we arrived, the family had sat together and planned how they would break the difficult news to us. First, my brother had called my husband in London. But he never told me. Instead, he put me and the children on the next flight to Karachi. It was at breakfast that first morning in Karachi that I learned that
10 my son and nephew had been kidnapped.

On their way to my parents' house, my son Faisal and his cousin Junni had stopped at a friend's place on the way to collect something. As they were waiting for Junni's friend to come down from a block of flats, a car came and picked up my nephew. At first, since there were already 4 people in the car, they said, "Leave the younger one." Then one of them said, "No take him also; otherwise he will give
15 information about us." So they pushed Faisal between their legs and drove off. Since both of the boys were pushed to the floor of the car, they couldn't see where they were going.

My entire family was badly shaken by this event. They were in a state of shock for the first few days. The effect on every family member was different. My mother had to wear a collar° because of severe neck pain. My father seemed to have aged at least forty years since I had last seen him just six weeks ago.

20   After waiting for eight days, we paid the ransom° demanded by the kidnappers. Even today I get goosebumps° thinking about the agonizing° wait. During that time, I had a minor angina° attack. Some of my family started talking against God. Some became silent. Others were crying and asking God for help. All our extended family and lots of friends were praying at all times.

25   On the tenth day the kidnappers released the boys. Our son's first reaction was, "I don't want to serve my country anymore." He had served as a cadet° in the Pakistan Air Force for the last two years. His father was a serving officer, and so his expectations from the Air Force were high. But the Air Force had made so little effort to get him released from the kidnappers. So we had to do the paper work to get him out of the Air Force.

30   Earlier on, when we had first left for England, my son didn't want to come. He had said that he would come during his summer break. Now after getting released, he said, "I need to leave the country." He is now a British citizen and doing well for himself. At least we feel he is safe.

           Our family is still living in Karachi and facing many bad experiences day to day. We don't have any other choice. When my son comes to visit us every winter, we are nervous, fearful, and extra careful. If he goes out at night to visit friends, I stay up till he comes back home. All I do is pray he will have a safe holiday and a safe return to the UK.

°diplomatic (adj.) – serving the government in a foreign country
°blurted (v.) – said suddenly
°miserable (adj.) – sad, deeply upset
°collar (n.) – something worn to support the neck and relieve neck pain
°ransom (n.) – payment given for release of kidnapped persons
°goosebumps (n.) – the hairs on your skin raise up because of fear or emotional stress
°agonizing (adj. from the v. *agonize*) - painful
°angina (n.) – a pain in the heart
°cadet (n.) – a student in a military school

Understand what you read

Here are some events from the story above. Put these events in the order that they happened. The first event is already marked for you.

___Faisal and Junni stopped at a friend's house.

___Faisal moved to the UK and became a citizen.

_1_ Faisal said, "I don't want to go to London with you."

___My brother called my husband in London.

___We went to London to join my husband on his diplomatic posting.

___Faisal and Junni were pulled into the car and pushed onto the floor.

___We returned to Karachi on the next flight from London.

___The boys left for their grandparents' house.

___We paid the ransom on the eighth day.

___I couldn't believe what my brother and sister-law told me.

___Faisal got released from the Air Force.

Discuss
1. What words and sentences in the story describe Ruxsana's and her family's response to this trauma?
2. Look again at the diagram of the victim cycle. Where do the reactions of Ruxsana and her family fit on that diagram? What would you say about the reactions of Faisal when he was released?
3. Do you think that Ruxsana is still suffering effects of this trauma that occurred so many years ago?

4. What is your opinion—is it possible to recover completely from such a trauma? Is it possible that an experience like this can make you a more resilient person?

EXTEND YOUR LEARNING
1. Journal
Write about one or both of the following topics:
(a) In your culture, what are common responses to trauma? If people in your culture suffer trauma, how are their thinking, behavior, emotions, spiritual life, and bodies affected?
(b) What would you say about the health of your thoughts, feelings, behavior, body, beliefs, and memories?

2. Movement
Living Sculptures
Form three or four teams in the class. One member of the team will be the sculptor. Her or his job will be to mold the rest of the team members into a sculpture. Sculptures, remember, do not talk or move. They are still. The people in living sculptures take a position and they keep that position.

Each group will receive an assignment from the teacher to make a sculpture that exhibits the responses to trauma in thought, emotions, behavior body, or spiritual life. Everyone in the sculpture will show one of the responses to trauma. With the advice of the teacher, each group will appoint a sculptor. Groups will privately discuss ideas for the sculpture and practice performing their sculpture.

Finally, one by one the groups will present their sculptures. The class will watch as the sculptor molds her/his group into the poses that show the kinds of responses in emotions or behavior, etc. that people exhibit. The rest of the class will guess what kinds of response are being shown.

3. Music: Listen to "All I Can Do is Keep Breathing" by Ingrid Michaelson
Ingrid Michaelson is an indie-pop singer and song writer who has produced six albums. Her music has been used on several popular television shows in the United States. Listen to Ingrid Michaelson singing "All I Can Do is Keep Breathing." The words to the song will appear on the video.
https://www.youtube.com/watch?v=qe2BeQWR3HI

Discuss
1. Why are the same words repeated again and again? What do you think about the amount of repetition in this song? How does the music of this song reflect the repeated words?
2. The first verses of the song seem to carry an important message. Why does the singer not seem sensitive to storms coming, people dying, and the need for changes in the world?
3. How does this song relate to what you have been studying about coping with trauma or responding to trauma?

SELF-ASSESSMENT
Think about your learning. Complete a self-assessment for this chapter by using the template at the end of the textbook (p. 194).

Learning Tip: Pay attention to your feelings. Strong, positive feelings about English and about yourself as a learner can help you make faster progress.

Chapter 7 First Aid for Trauma

Get to Know Each Other Better

1. Look at the activities shown in each of the pictures below. Which activity or pictures do you like the best? Why?
2. Now find out which pictures or activities the other members of the class like the best. Be sure to ask <u>why</u> they like this activity.
3. Get up from your seat so that you can walk around the class and find someone who can sign their name under <u>one</u> of the pictures.
4. A class member can only sign your page <u>one time</u>. This means you need to talk to as many as five people in the class.
5. When you have names for all five pictures, you can yell out "Bingo!" and return to your seat.

Jon Gehman

Connect to the topic

What do the favorite pictures reveal about the members of the class?

How do you think the class's favorite pictures relate to the topic of this chapter, "First Aid for Trauma"?

READ

Develop your reading skills:

Topics and main ideas: Remember that in textbook readings, the first sentence of each paragraph signals the discussion of the main idea. (see chapter 6, pp. 76-77) A new paragraph means a new idea. The paragraphs in the reading below have been numbered for you. **Look at the first sentence of each paragraph.** Identify the key words in those sentences--participants and processes. *Hint: Processes are very important in this text. Note the title "How do we help ourselves" The word "how" signals some kind of actions.*

Text organization: look for signal words to mark the change from one topic to the next. We call these signal words *transitions*. The transition words help to mark the main ideas of the text. Examples of transition words are *first, second, next, then, another thing, finally,* and so on. Writers sometimes use numbers (1, 2, 3), letters (a, b, c), **bold** or *italic* print and <u>lists</u> to show how their ideas are organized. These kinds of transition words are used more in texts that give explanation or instructions than they are in stories. When you are reading the text below (or any text), try underlining or circling the transition words that you see.

How do we help ourselves and others?

1 (1) Resilient people know how to pay attention to the signals their bodies give them. If you get a small cut on your finger, you will have a small amount of bleeding, and you will know how to stop the bleeding and take care of the wound. Your body also tells you that you are feeling stress, fear or anger. You should learn to identify your personal signs of stress and intense emotion. (See the drawing activity
5 below). If you feel these intense emotions, here are some things you can do.

(2) First, breathe deeply. This will calm your body and mind. You have already learned and practiced two different breathing exercises in this course.

(3) Second, **imagine** being in a safe place. Sit in a comfortable place with your feet on the ground. Feel the solid ground under your feet and your back against a tree, rock, or chair-back. Imagine that you
10 are being held by someone you trust in a place of peace and safety.

(4) Third, relax your muscles as you learned in chapter 5. Make your muscles tense and then release the tension. This exercise helps you release stress. You can also release stress by **engaging** in physical exercise like running, walking, dancing, drumming and sports.

(5) Next, express your feelings. Keeping your feelings bottled up inside may make matters worse.
15 Learn to use the EFT tapping exercise that is described at the end of this chapter. In this exercise, you **acknowledge** that you have a **disturbing** feeling of some kind. Breathe in deeply, taking into yourself a sense of **harmony**, strength and healing. Then breathe out slowly. Use a sentence like this: "Even though I feel sad today, I deeply and completely accept myself." In doing this, you name the intense emotions as you tap sensitive points on your hand, head, and upper body. Engaging in music and art are also excellent
20 ways of expressing feelings.

(6) Another important thing is to talk to a person you trust. Tell them the story of your traumatic event. Lucas Baba Sikwepere of South Africa is a **survivor** of trauma. He was shot and blinded by a member of the South African security forces. He said to a group of people, "I feel…what has brought my… eyesight back is to come here and tell the story." But we need to be careful. Telling the story can
25 be very painful because it reminds us of the trauma event. While telling the story, mention your thoughts and feelings before, at the time, and after the traumatic event. You can massage your fingers and hands as you speak to help you **process** these intense emotions.

(7) There are three more things you can do. (a) Recognize what may trigger your trauma responses. What reminds you of the traumatic event? This may be a sight, sound or smell. Try to **eliminate** these
30 triggers if you can. (b) Identify feelings that prevent you from healing (anger, **guilt**, shame or desire for revenge) and let go of them if possible. (c) Seek healing and support in your faith community and through meaningful personal spiritual practices.

(8) Resilient people not only know how to give first aid to themselves, but they can also give first aid to others who have suffered traumas. If you have a chance to provide **psychological** first aid to trauma
35 survivors, here is a **brief** summary of what to do or what to avoid.

(9)   **DO promote...**

    •Safety: food, shelter, medical attention

    •**Calmness**: Listen to the stories and feelings of the trauma affected; be friendly; offer **accurate** information.

40

    •**Connections**: Help them find families and friends.

    •Self-help: **Engage** people in meeting their own needs.

    •Hope: Direct people to available services.

(10)   **DO NOT...**

45

    •Force people to share their stories.

    •Give simple **reassurances** like "everything will be OK."

    •Tell people what they should be feeling, thinking or doing.

    •Make promises that may not be kept.

    •**Criticize** existing services or relief activities.

(11)   Remember the example of the small cut on your finger at the beginning of the story. Most people
50   know how to take care of small cuts. But what would happen if you had a large cut in your leg that was bleeding very much? To take care of that cut, you may need to go to the hospital or see a doctor. The same thing holds true if you are experiencing too much stress, fear or anger. You may need to get help from a doctor.

UNDERSTAND WHAT YOU READ

Did you notice that this text is divided into two main parts?

                1. how to help other people   2. how to help yourself

1a. The first part of the reading tells you _____.

1b. Which paragraphs give you advice on how to _____? Paragraph numbers:_____.

1c. Which sentence specifically introduces these paragraphs of advice?

_____

2a. The second part of the reading tells you _____.

2b. Which paragraphs give you advice on how to _____? Paragraph numbers:_____.

2c. Which sentence specifically introduces these paragraphs of advice?

_____

3. One sentence in the text has the important purpose of connecting the two main parts of the text. Which one is it?

_____

Now use the signal words to help you find all the main ideas in the first half of the text.

First, _____	a. know what causes trauma responses
Second, _____	b. tell someone else your feelings
Third, _____	c. loosen up your muscles (*see more items on the next page*)

Next, _____	d. be aware of negative feelings and try to let them go
Another thing, _____	e. breathe deeply
Three more things: _____	f. get help from your church, mosque, or temple
_____	g. get a picture in your mind of a safe place
_____	h. tell your story to someone you can depend on

Discuss
1. Which is the easier part of the text for you to understand? The first part (with the signal words) or the second part with the lists of *do's* and *don'ts*?
2. What do you think about the advice in the do's and don'ts lists? What do you or don't you understand about the advice?
3. What advice to help yourself could also be useful in helping other people?
4. Now that you have read the text, can you connect any of the pictures from the previous page with the advice in the text?

WORD STUDY
A. Define it yourself!

imagine (verb) _____
    Look at how this word is used in lines 8 and 9.

engage (verb) _____
    Look at how this word is used in lines 12 and 19.

first aid (noun) _____
    Look at this word as it is used in lines 33-34. Consider the separate meanings of the two words.
    Here are some more sentences with aid.
    Aid workers came to rescue people in the floods.
    After the floods, Pakistan received some aid from other countries.
    Many hungry families needed food aid.

B. Get to know verb meanings from context

Verbs: **acknowledge** (16) **criticize** (48) **disturb** (16) **eliminate** (29) **imagine** (8), **process** (27) **promote** (36) **engage** (12, 19)

The same verb goes in <u>both</u> *blanks for each of the sentences. Try to decide which verb makes the best sense in both blanks. The first one is done for you as an example.*

1. A woman is sad about the death of her son, but her friends never *acknowledge* her sadness. They never mention anything about her son. If someone has had a bad experience, then we should *acknowledge* that we are aware of their experience. We shouldn't hide our feelings or pretend we don't know about their sadness or anger.

2. Imagine that you and I are walking down the street together and we see a disturbing event. Talking about the event will not _____ our bad feelings, but it can help us to calm down. The truth is that no one can _____ all the evil things that happen in this world.

3. Sometimes we see things on the TV news that _____ us and make us feel sad or angry. When we see _____ [add –ing] things on the news, we should discuss them with other people.

4. Conversation is a healthy way to _____ difficult emotions. We can _____ our feelings if we can name them and if we acknowledge what caused them.

5. When we work with trauma-affected people, we need to _____ calmness and positive thinking. When we show people how to help themselves, then we also _____ hope.

6. When you feel tense, it is a good idea to _____ in physical exercise. _____ [add –ing] in music and art also helps to promote relaxation and calmness.

7. Our minds have the wonderful power to _____ things. We can calm ourselves down if we _____ things that are beautiful and peaceful.

8. During a disaster we should not _____ aid workers because their job is very difficult in a time of confusion. Instead of _____ [add –ing], we should work together in harmony to help needy people.

C. Get to know noun and adjective meanings from context:

Nouns: **calmness** (38) **connection** (40) **guilt** (30) **harmony** (17) **reassurance** (45) **survivor** (22)
Adjectives: **accurate** (39) **brief** (35) **psychological** (34)

Some items only have one blank. In those items, look for underlined words to give some clue about the meaning. In items with more than one blank, the same word goes in all the blanks.

1. Sometimes a natural disaster separates people from their families. Aid workers should help people make _____ (add –s) with family members and friends.

2. In a situation of pain and loss, words of comfort like "Everything will be okay" are not helpful. When someone has lost a loved one, this simple _____ is not honest. Everything will not be okay; life will never be the same again because a loved one is missing.

3. A good listener can help to bring peace and _____ to survivors of a traumatic event by speaking quietly and giving full attention to their story.

4. A person who lives through a difficult illness like cancer also needs to tell his or her story. We should listen carefully to the stories of these _____ (add –s) to help them heal in mind as well as body.

5. Survivors of a disaster or crime often have a sense of _____. They feel bad and wonder why they deserved to live and their friends or family died. They sometimes blame themselves for the bad thing that happened.

6. A peaceful society where people live in _____ with each other helps to build resilient persons. In this kind of society people learn how to get along with each other and solve problems together

7. The teacher wrote a _____ note in my journal.
    The teacher asked the class to write a _____ summary of the article.
    Chapter 6 gives a _____ description of how trauma affects people.

8. I think my journal entry gives an _____ picture of my experience.
    The description of trauma in chapter 6 is short, but it is _____.
    In a disaster situation, aid workers need _____ information so they can bring enough help to the right place.

9. A central topic in this book is _____ trauma.
    Many traumatized persons need _____ counseling.
    Violent TV programs have negative _____ effects on children.

D. More practice. *Play the game "Take Two" with your new vocabulary. Here are the rules.*
1. Divide the class into two or more teams.
2. Write all the 19 words on the board in two columns (10 in one column and 9 in the other)
3. Your teacher will put a number 1 beside two words (one from each column).
4. Teams must make one sentence that uses both of those words.
5. The team members may all work together in creating the sentence, and every person on your team must take a turn in saying a sentence. (One team member may not be the only spokesperson.)
6. If your team gets makes a good sentence, you may choose the next two words by putting a 2 beside them (and so on).
7. When all the words have been used up, you can erase the numbers and start again using new combinations of words.

Example: Suppose that the first two words are *disturb* and *survivor*. A sentence that combines these two words would be: The earthquake *survivors* were *disturbed* when they saw a TV program about the disaster.

Expressions:
bottle up – this idiom paints an interesting picture. Think of a bottle of soda when you shake it up. There are millions of little bubbles. If you open the bottle after shaking it, the bubbles will rush out of the bottle. If you leave the cap on, the bubbles are *bottled up*: they cannot get out. The reading above mentions "feelings that are bottled up."

pay attention to – you may think it is strange that we use the verb *pay* in English in expressions like *pay attention*. It does not cost us any money to *look at or listen carefully to* something. But when we *give our attention* to something we say that we *pay attention*.

bring back –this two-word verb literally means to *carry back,* as in the sentence She brought back *medicine from the doctor's office.* But that is not what it means in the text above (line 24): *what has brought my... eyesight back is to come here and tell the story.* Here the meaning is *restored.* Another meaning of *bring back* is to cause thoughts to occur in one's mind. *The pictures brought back memories of our trip.*

Use the expressions as you answer these questions:

1. Why isn't it healthy for our *feelings* to be *bottled up*? What else can be *bottled up*? [*Hint:* Think of specific feelings. Also think about things that we can keep in our mind.] Is it healthy to have anything bottled up inside of us?

2. Discuss the things that women *pay attention to* and the things that men *pay attention to*. What are some things that both women and men *pay attention to*?

3. What *brings back* memories for you? What kind of things *bring back* good feelings or bad feelings?

GRAMMAR STUDY

Consider the form of these sentences taken from the reading above.

Verbal group	Nominal group
Breathe deeply.	
Relax	your muscles.
Express	your feelings.
Do promote	calmness.
Don't criticize	relief activities.

Notice how the verb comes first. There is no subject expressed in these sentences. This way of writing or speaking makes you sound like a person who has power—like an expert. As an expert, you can tell people what to do. You can use this grammatical form, which is called the imperative. It is the same form that we use to give commands.

A parent can tell a child, "Sit up straight in your chair. Don't put your elbows on the table."

A teacher can tell students, "Take out a clean sheet of paper. Write your name at the top."

A boss can tell an employee, "Finish up your report and then meet me in the control room."

Any experts can use this kind of grammar in writing to people who seem ready to accept their advice.

This is the form also used in simple instructions on how to do something. Instructions for a product are not personal. They are addressed to everyone who needs to use that product. Look at the instructions for the various movement activities near the end of chapter 1 (pp. 25-26). Are those the same kind of sentences that you see in the table above?

But if you are not an expert, you might say these things in a different way. If you are a friend or equal and not a person in power, you will use a softer and more personal kind of grammar. You will use what we call modals.

Nominal group	Verbal group		Nominal group
	Modal	Verb	
You	can	express	your feelings.
You	could	breathe deeply.	
You	might	relax	your muscles.
You	should	promote	calmness.
You	should not	criticize	relief activities.

Even if you are an expert, you might choose to speak or write to people this way, as the writer of the reading sometimes did.

Examples:

a. You <u>could</u> imagine that you are being held by someone you trust in a place of peace and safety. (lines 9-10)

b. You <u>can</u> also release stress by engaging in physical exercise. (line 12)

c. There are three more things you <u>can</u> do. (line 28)

Look again at the chart above. Which of the forms are the softest and which are the strongest? Ask your teacher to give an opinion on which forms are the softest and strongest.

Practice:
Write each of the following instructions in three different ways

Imagine being in a safe place.

a. _____

b. _____

c. _____

Learn to use the EFT tapping that is described at the end of this chapter.

a. _____

b. _____

c. _____

Look for two other examples of instructions in the text. Copy them on your paper. Then rewrite them in three different ways

Now move around the class and use the **give one-get one** activity to collect more examples.

More practice: Class members can write short letters to Mr. or Ms. Advisor to ask for advice on any problem they might have. Redistribute the letters to other members of the class to answer. As you advise the writer about the problem, take care what modals you use. Do you want to sound like an expert? If you have a lot of personal knowledge and experience, then maybe you can write like an expert. If you don't know much, then you will want to use softer modals. When you answer, you can keep your real name a secret if you like!

Example:

Dear Ms. Advisor,
Gas prices are so expensive that I have a hard time keeping my car running. I need to save some money on gas and car care. Can you help me?
Thanks,
M.T. Pockets

Dear M.T.,
You should think carefully about when you need to drive somewhere and when you don't. You should plan to combine your trips whenever possible. For example, if your barber and the grocery store are near each other, you could plan to have your hair cut on the afternoon that you buy groceries. You should also think about using a bicycle for short trips. -Ms. Advisor

LIFE SKILLS
Story of Resilience
Read this story by an experienced giver of first aid to those who face difficulties in life.

Develop your reading skills:
Distinguish between background and actions. Texts that tell a story may first spend some time giving the background. Learn how to identify the background information. It often comes toward the beginning of a text. Verbs like BE (in its various forms), *feel, think, want,* and *have* are helpful signals. Verbs that signal actions that occurred repeatedly or continuously also point to background information. When a text gives the main actions of a story, then words that signal time or order will begin to appear. Verbs of doing or saying in the simple past tense express the main actions of the story.
Pay attention to words that signal time and order. Words like *first* and *then* commonly signal order in texts that explain ideas or events in a logical way. But prepositional phrases of time are important in stories that people tell: *in the morning, at the end of the week,* etc. Notice in the text below when these signal words begin to appear.

Lara Faces a Crisis
by Carolyn Yoder

Carolyn Yoder is a licensed therapist who specializes in working with individuals and groups living with trauma and challenging life situations: accidents, physical illness, war, torture, immigration, and betrayal. She has lived and worked in Asia, Africa, the Middle East and the Caucasus. Names and other identifying information have been changed to protect the woman who faced her crisis with courage.

5   Lara faced a crisis at the hospital where she worked. Her supervisor accused° her of spreading rumors° about a colleague° and wrote up the charge and put it into her personnel file. Lara found herself thinking constantly about the supervisor, about work, about the unfairness of it all. She was angry and could not sleep. She felt ashamed of what was happening. This problem came on top of all the other problems in her life—her difficult childhood in Colombia and her marriage in America to a man who criticized her because of her appearance.

10   Then she started having suicidal° thoughts. *I'm worthless. My daughter would be better off without me. I hate my body. I hate my life. I hate the supervisor.* She cried easily. She didn't want to get out of bed in the morning and go to work. She began to feel panic° when she was driving. Her heart would race, her mouth was dry, and she would feel hot and then cold. A part of her wanted to drive off the road and kill herself and a part of her was terrified that she would do so.

15   Lara told a friend about her troubles. The friend helped her meet with a counselor trained in EFT - Emotional Freedom Technique.° EFT involves tapping on acupoints° points while talking about the thoughts and feelings that are upsetting. This helps to calm the part of the brain that controls emotions and memory.

The counselor first asked Lara to identify where she felt the tension of anger, sadness, fear and panic in her body. Then she taught Lara how to tap on certain acupoints while tuning into the tightness in her chest,
20   the knot° in her stomach, the shortness of breath. Lara was surprised to find her body soon started to feel calmer. Then the counselor asked Lara to talk about what had happened at work while she continued to tap the acupoints. Whenever Lara started to feel very upset, the counselor told Lara to stop telling the story and focus on the emotion or disturbing thought while she tapped. In this way Lara learned to calm herself. At the end of the hour, Lara was amazed how much better she felt. For now, she did not want to kill herself.

25   The counselor told Lara the overwhelming feelings might come back. She showed her how to tap on acupoints on her fingers so she could tap whenever she felt upset even if she was in public. She helped Lara identify other people and community resources she could turn to in an emergency. She told her to pull off the road if she panicked and tap until she felt calmer and to call her or another resource person. She told her to take a walk every day and to tap whenever she could on her fingers or the other acupoints.

30   The bad feelings sometimes came back. But Lara knew what to do. She tapped and it made a difference. For a short time, Lara saw the counselor twice a week. After a few weeks, she was surprised to realize that she no longer felt suicidal. When she felt strong feelings like fear or shame, she tapped. She began to read about EFT and other helpful techniques and practiced them every day. Facing her crisis helped Lara build a healthier life and future.

94

°accused (v.) – blamed, said someone is guilty of doing wrong
°rumors (n.) – talk that comes from what other people say and not from witnessing directly
°colleague (n.) - coworker　　°suicidal – thoughts of killing oneself
ᵛacupoints (n.) – sensitive places in the body where acupuncture doctors insert needles
°technique (n.) – a method or way of doing something
°knot (n.) – a feeling of tightness or sickness (when used with *stomach*)

Understand what you read

Look at the sentences below, taken from the reading. Which ones provide background information and which ones are part of the series of actions? Write the sentence number in the appropriate box below the sentences.

1. I made Lara stop telling the story and focus on the emotion.
2. She was angry and could not sleep.
3. Her heart would race, her mouth was dry, and she would feel hot and then cold.
4. She was surprised to realize that she no longer felt suicidal.
5. She began to feel panic when she was driving.
6. She felt ashamed of what was happening.
7. Lara told a friend what was happening.
8. I taught her how to tap on certain acupoints.
9. She didn't want to get out of bed in the morning and go to work.
10. I first had Lara identify where she felt the tension of the anger, sadness, fear and panic in her body.

Background information	Sequence of actions

Teacher Story

Listen to your teacher tell a story about a time when she or he gave first aid to someone else or received first aid from someone else. As you listen to the story, make some notes about points in her story that are <u>similar to</u> and <u>different from</u> the ideas you got from readings in this chapter.

Discussion

1. What are some of the similarities and differences between your teacher's experience and Lara's experience?
2. How do people in your culture feel about going to talk with a counselor? What's your opinion?
3. What do you do when you feel tension in some part of your body? What do you think about the tapping that the counselor taught Lara to use? What could be some other ways of dealing with tensions like these?

EXTEND YOUR LEARNING

1. Movement: *EFT Tapping Practice*
Preparation

1. First **practice** finding and tapping on the points pictured in the drawing here. Use your pointer finger and middle finger to tap with. Tap lightly 3 to 5 times.
   a. Start with the karate chop point on your hand.
   b. Then move to the crown of your head. Next move to the point between your eye-brows.
   c. Now use two fingers of both hands and tap on the sides of both eyes.
   d. Tap under your nose. Then move to your chin.
   e. Use two fingers of both hands to tap on both sides of your collar bone and then under both arms.

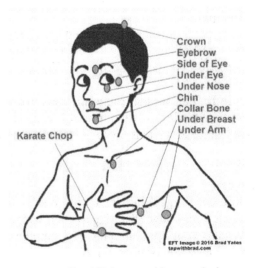

Brad Yates, used by permission

2. **Prepare the sentence** you will use in the tapping exercise. *"Even though I have _____ (or feel _____), I deeply and completely accept myself."*
In the blank space, name a specific problem that is bothering you; it can be a physical, mental, or emotional problem. ***Examples:*** Even though I <u>have a very sore knee and I can't walk easily</u>, I deeply and completely accept myself." or Even though I <u>feel very sad because my mother is angry with me</u>, I deeply and completely accept myself."

Now begin the EFT tapping exercise
3. Breathe in deeply and let your breath out slowly.
4. Begin tapping at the karate chop point on your hand. As you tap, say to yourself the sentence you have prepared.
5. Keep repeating your sentence and move on to the other tapping points. Move to the crown of the head, the point between your eyebrows, the side of your eyes, and so on. Repeat your sentence at every point where you tap. Tap lightly 3 to 5 times.
6. You can repeat the whole tapping as many times as you like.
7. Breathe in a sense of harmony, strength and healing.
8. Then, breathe out slowly, releasing bad feelings and problems.

When you feel upset or need to calm yourself, practice this tapping exercise. If you have a friend or family member who needs to find some relief from a problem, teach them to do this tapping exercise.

If you would like to see a demonstration of EFT tapping, there are many videos available. Try using the search terms "EFT tapping lesson" or "EFT tapping demonstration." Search on Google or directly on Youtube. Brad Yates, who has given permission to use his drawing (above), has his own Youtube channel with lots of videos about EFT tapping. Brad's channel is https://www.youtube.com/user/eftwizard

2. Drawing/Coloring
Draw your own human body outline. Make an outline of the human body from head to toe.
Color the places in your body where you hold stress.
Use different colors to show the intensity of the feelings (red, yellow, green, blue, black, etc.)
Are they hot/cold? tense/loose? aching/tingling?
After you do your drawing, share it with a partner. What are some similarities and differences that you see?

3. Role play
Work in pairs or teams of four to prepare a role play. Here are your roles:
Person A: You are feeling tense and stressed. You have aches and pains in your body. You have headaches. You are nervous. You don't sleep well. You go to a trusted and knowledgeable friend to explain your situation and ask for advice.
Person B: You are the friend and you have some knowledge about how to help yourself and other people who have stress. Use the information from this chapter and give advice to your friend. Remember to practice the grammar for giving suggestions to a friend as explained earlier in the lesson.

4. Journal
Choose one of the following topics to write about in your journal, or use the topic given by your teacher.
1. What things have you tried to calm yourself down and relax? What method works the best for you?
2. What is your opinion of the EFT tapping exercise? Does that way of coping with your emotions seem reasonable to you or not? Why?

SELF-ASSESSMENT

Think about your learning. Complete a self-assessment for this chapter by using the template at the end of the textbook (p. 194).

> *Learning Tip:* When you feel that your learning is being blocked, try using some of the advice for relaxation from the reading about first aid for trauma. When you use imagination, don't imagine yourself being held by someone you trust. Instead, imagine yourself speaking English fluently to an American friend or co-worker.

Chapter 8 Compassionate Listening

Get to Know Each Other Better

Divide into pairs. One of you will talk for 3 minutes and the other person will just listen. Then you will reverse roles. The other person will talk for 3 minutes and the partner will just listen. Share about <u>one good thing or one new thing in your life</u>.

Connect to the Topic

1. How did you feel when you were just listening to your partner? Was it difficult <u>not</u> to talk?
2. How did you feel when it was your turn to speak? How did you know that your partner was listening to you?
3. From what you learned in the last chapter about giving psychological first aid to trauma victims, what do you think is the importance of listening?

Look at the pictures

The first duty of love is to listen.
- Paul Tillich

Jon Gehman

1. What would happen if you said this in your classroom?
2. What other persons could stand in place of the teacher – as someone who does a lot of talking and needs to listen?
3. Do you agree or disagree with Paul Tillich's statement?

READ

Develop your reading skills:

Practice your skimming skills. Prepare to read this text more carefully by first skimming. Read only the first line of each paragraph, and when you get to the numbered points read only the first few words of each point. Now ask yourself, what did you learn about the text and from the text by skimming. Then go back and read more carefully.

Interact with the text. You can increase your understanding of a text if you *interact* with the writer. This text asks you (in paragraph 3) to interact with the text by putting a check in front of the rules that you usually practice when you listen well to others. In the last paragraph, the text tells you that you will practice following these rules as you listen to others. So doing what a text says is another way of interacting with it. Can you think of other ways that you can interact with texts?

Listening that Heals and Connects People

1.   Linda O'Brien's daughter went through a horrible experience. Her boyfriend was shot and killed in front of her during a robbery. Linda says she found it very difficult to share her daughter's story with others. After all, bad things like murder are not supposed to happen to white middle-class American families. Whenever Linda started to tell her story, other people would show **discomfort**. But then Linda

5 took a class in trauma awareness and resilience. Other participants in the class included women from the Middle East who were dealing with refugees and **mass** trauma, mass injuries and mass horror. They listened with **sympathy** and understanding. Suddenly, Linda felt it was easier to share her story. She said, "I could tell my story and not be a **freak**. The experience was very healing. I felt like I could be a whole person."

10   There are ways of listening to the stories of trauma victims that gently move them toward healing. Effective listening can also be a powerful tool for reducing tensions, **resolving** conflicts and building bridges between people. Hearing each other's stories allows for **mutual compassion** and understanding. Careful listening connects us to each other more closely. Listening in ways that heal is a skill that can be learned and is known as *compassionate listening* or ***reflective listening***.

Principles

15   Here are ten **principles** you can follow to be a **compassionate** listener to the sometimes difficult stories that people have to share. As you read these principles, think about which ones you usually practice when you listen to others. Put a check (√) in front of that principle.

1. Be present for the person who is sharing their story. As much as possible, leave your own concerns behind. Try not to act hurried, distracted or restless.

20
2. Listen with **empathy**. That means try to see the world through the eyes of the other person; and try to feel what the speaker is feeling.

3. Follow the ground rules of good listening. Don't ask too many questions or **interrupt** the speaker. Don't give advice unless the person asks for advice.

4. When listening to another, don't tell your own story or share personal problems except on **rare**
25   occasions.

5. Through words and **nonverbal** behaviors, **communicate** these things to the speaker: "I am interested in what you are saying," "I am trying to understand your emotions and feelings," "I am not judging you."

6. Be like a mirror: **reflect** back to the person what you think they are saying and feeling. After hearing
30   about the speaker's frightening experience, you might say something like this. "You must have been

very frightened. I am not surprised you were crying and shaking."

7. Be careful not to ask a lot of questions. If you do, ask **open-ended questions** (questions that can't be answered with a "yes" or "no") to clarify and encourage the person to share in greater depth.

"What has happened to you?"
35 *"Tell me more about..."*
"What was most frightening to you?"
"How has this affected you?"
"What signs of courage and kindness did you see?
"What other difficulties have you survived in the past and how did you do that?"
40 *"How can I help?"*

8. Listen for **indications** of strength, resilience, and ability to survive hardship. Identify and **affirm** these qualities for the person who has shared a story.

9. Be **alert** for stories that keep repeating a **sense of defeat**. In such stories the speaker sees herself (or himself) as a victim with no power. You can gently help this person to focus on possibilities for
45 healing and growth.

10. Encourage people to identify their own sense of inner strength and direction. Affirm them when they show courage to move forward in their lives.

The only good way to learn these principles is to practice them. Later in this chapter you will spend time practicing these ways of listening that heal and connect people.

UNDERSTAND WHAT YOU READ

How well did you understand the ten principles of compassionate listening? Which of the following sentences are true and which are false? How would you change the false sentences to make them correct?

1. ____ Share your own personal problems when they are similar to the problems of the speaker.

2. ____ Try to listen for positive things that the speaker says about him- or herself.

3. ____ If the speaker keeps telling stories of personal defeat, just ignore them.

4. ____ Ask questions that will help the speaker to share more about his or her experience.

5. ____ Be sure to give good advice if the speaker shares a problem.

6. ____ You can show the speaker you are interested by your words, your body, and the look on your face.

7. ____ A compassionate listener tries to understand what the speaker is feeling as well as saying.

8. ____ You can look at your watch and look out the window while the speaker is telling his or her story.

9. ____ Compliment the speaker for the strength and courage that he or she shows.

10. ____ You do not need to repeat anything that the speaker said to you.

Discuss
1. Why is it important to use listening as a way to connect people with each other?
2. What made it easy or difficult for Linda O'Brien to share her story? What about you—what helps you or hinders you from sharing your stories?
3. Which principles do you usually practice? Compare your answers with a partner.
4. Are there any principles of compassionate listening mentioned in the reading that would be strange in your culture? Why? Are there any other principles of compassionate listening that should be mentioned?

WORD STUDY
A. You Define It!

principles _____
> *Notice what words come just before "principles" and the material that appears between the two uses of the word (lines 15 & 48).*

empathy _____
> *Hint: remember to look for definitions of a word in the surrounding sentences (line 20).*

reflect _____
> *Hint: Sometimes you don't see a definition in the surrounding sentence, but you get examples (line 29).*

reflective listening _____
> *You should be able to use the item above to help you define this one (line 14).*

open-ended questions _____
> *Hint: Look for definitions of a word in the surrounding sentences (line 32).*

B. Word meanings
Choose the answers that mean the same thing as the boldfaced word for each sentence. Cross out the word or words that do not mean the same thing. Every item has <u>two</u> correct answers and <u>one</u> wrong answer. Cross out the wrong answer.

1. Whenever Linda started to tell her story, other people would show **discomfort.**
     feeling of worry   anger   emotional pain

2. In the class were women from the Middle East who knew personally about **mass** trauma, **mass** injuries and **mass** horror.
     harmful   widespread   a lot of

3. They listened with **sympathy** and understanding.
     shared feeling   kindness   intelligence

4. Linda said, "I could tell my story and not be a **freak**."
     a normal person   a strange person   an odd person

5. Effective listening can be a powerful tool for reducing tensions and **resolving** conflicts.
     questioning   settling   finding a solution for

6. Hearing each other's stories allows for **mutual** understanding.
     common   shared   accurate

7. We can all admire someone who listens with **compassion**.
     calmness   kindness   sympathy

8. A **compassionate** listener tries to understand what the speaker is feeling as well as saying.
     understanding   excited   kind

9. Don't **interrupt** the speaker.
     stop   eliminate   cut off

10. On **rare** occasions, you can share your own experiences.
     regular   few   unusual

11. You can show your interest in the speaker by your **nonverbal** behavior.
    without words   psychological   body language

12. You should **communicate** by words and body language that you are interested in the speaker's story.
    give an idea   tell   concentrate

13. Listen for **indications** of strength, resilience, and ability to survive hardship.
    fantasies   signs   expressions

14. **Affirm** the positive qualities of the persons who are sharing their stories.
    acknowledge   avoid   give approval to

15. A good listener is **alert** to repeated stories that show the speaker as a victim with no power.
    paying careful attention   ready to hear   numb

16. You can help the speaker move away from a **sense of defeat** to a feeling of hope.
    feeling of guilt   feeling of loss   feeling of failure

C. Classify the words. Think about the 16 words in the sentences of part B plus the words *principle, sympathy,* and *respect* from part A above. These words are all connected with some actions, feelings, or values. Which words can you connect with positive actions, feelings or values? Which do you connect with negative actions, feelings or values? And which words are difficult to connect with either positive or negative?
    1. Use the table below to work on your classification.
    2. Compare your answers with a partner or with the whole class.
    3. Discuss why you agreed or disagreed about classifying specific words.

Positive	*Negative*	*Not clearly positive or negative*

Word family
In chapter 6 you learned the verb *sympathize*. In this chapter you met the noun *sympathy*. Look at the examples in the left-hand column. Write your own sentences in the right-hand column.

sympathize (verb) – this form of the word refers to the act of showing agreement with some else's feelings of sadness or with their ideas

When I am sad, I feel better when someone *sympathizes* with me.

sympathy (noun) – this form means "agreement with someone's feelings or ideas;" when we *sympathize* with others, we *show sympathy*.
    (example sentences are on the next page)

The other students did not have any *sympathy* for my ideas.

They didn't show *sympathy* when we were suffering.

Expressions:
build bridges – A person who *builds bridges* across rivers is an engineer. But we can all be people who connect other people with each other and with ourselves by *building bridges*. This is the kind of bridge building referred to in our reading (line 11-12). Ordinary people can build stronger relationships among people: they can be *bridge builders*.

be present for – The phrase *be present* usually mean *to attend* or *to be some place*, as in "She was present at the party." We can also say, "He was present for his friend's wedding." But *to be present for someone* also has a special meaning. In the reading (line 18), it means to give special attention to someone, to think carefully about what someone is saying or doing in the present moment.

ground rules – This compound word is especially an American expression. It comes from ***American baseball***. These are the special rules that apply in certain stadiums (or grounds) where baseball games are played. In general English it means the basic rules that apply to some behavior or process, in the case of our reading (line 22), the *basic rules of good listening*.

spend time - In the last chapter you practiced the idiom *pay attention*. This is another idiom that uses a word related to *money—spend* (line 49). To *spend time* means to *use time* for some purpose or to *pass the time* in a certain way. If *time* is like money, then speakers of English believe that time is valuable.

Use the expressions to answer these questions:
1. Share your opinions about solving conflicts in different parts of the world. Which countries or leaders need to work harder at *building bridges* with certain other countries or leaders?
2. What hinders you from *being present for* other people?
3. What are the *ground rules* for discussion in your class? What other settings have *ground rules*?
4. What do you like to *spend time* doing?

GRAMMAR STUDY
A good listener needs to have the grammatical tools for getting others to share their ideas and feelings. One essential tool is making questions. As the reading states, we need to ask open-ended questions and not yes/no questions. Here are some examples to help you understand this advice.

Yes/No questions begin with a form of the verb *to be*, an auxiliary (like *do, did, have* or *had*) or a modal.
a. Was this the most frightening thing?   Yes. This was the most frightening thing.
b. Did you see any signs of courage and kindness?   No. I did not see any signs of courage and kindness.
c. Has this affected you?   Yes. This has affected me.
d. Can I help?   Yes. You can help.

Open-ended questions begin with a *wh-* question word. Those words are *who, which, what, when, where, why* and *how*. Not all of these *wh-* words make open-ended questions. The best ones for open-ended questions are *what, why,* and *how*. Here are examples from the reading:

e. What has happened to you?
f. What was most frightening to you?
g. What signs of courage and kindness did you see?
h. What other difficulties have you survived in the past?
i. How has this affected you?
j. How can I help?

Watch out for common errors in making questions:
1. Don't forget to move the auxiliary verb in front of the subject of the sentence.
Wrong: What hardships <u>you have</u> experienced?
Right: What hardships <u>have you</u> experienced?

2. Don't forget that the wh- word moves to the front of the sentence and needs nothing to mark its place (like a pronoun).
Wrong: How have you <u>felt it</u> since you had that experience?
Right: How have you <u>felt</u> since you had that experience?

Other ways of getting information: polite requests
k. You can use a simple imperative form: <u>Tell</u> me more about that experience.
l. You can use polite questions with modals *can* or *could*: <u>Can</u> you tell me about your feelings at that time? <u>Could</u> you explain what made you feel sad?
m. You can use a statement with the modal *would:* I <u>would</u> like to hear more about the day this event happened.

Practice:
Change these yes/no questions into open-ended questions. Try writing more than one version of some questions. Try to use all three *wh-* word: *what, why* and *how.*

1. Did that news disturb you?

_____

2. Were you angry about that?

_____

3. Have you felt sad since you had that experience?

_____

4. Can I do anything?

_____

5. Now, change any two of the open-ended questions to make them polite requests.

_____

_____

More practice
Try again the activity that you did at the beginning of this chapter. Try to practice what you learned in the reading about principles of compassionate listening. Also practice the grammar that you have just reviewed.

Divide into pairs. One of you will talk for 3 minutes and the other person will listen and ask open-ended questions as needed. Then you will reverse roles. The other person will talk for 3 minutes and the partner will listen and ask open-ended questions as needed. Share about <u>one thing that has recently surprised you or made you angry or made you laugh.</u>

Discuss: How was your experience of being a speaker or listener this time different from your experience the first time you did this exercise?

LIFE SKILLS
Story of Resilience
Read this story by a person who really knows how to listen.

> **Develop your reading skills:**
> **Practice distinguishing background information and main actions.** Remember that background information often comes in the beginning of a text. Notice the kind of information presented in the first two paragraphs, and especially present tense verbs in the second paragraph. What is the purpose of the first two paragraphs? Where does the main sequence of actions begin? How do the verb tenses change in paragraphs 3 to 6 to signal the main actions? Finally, what is the purpose of the last paragraph?
> **Think about what you already know.** Before you read any essay, be sure to think about what you already know about the topic of sharing in circles. You can make some notes about what you know before you read. Earlier in this course you had some experiences using a circle for sharing your ideas and experiences (during chapters 2 & 3). What do you remember about your experience using a circle? Earlier in this chapter, you read about good principles of listening. How many principles can you name? Now you are ready to read—as you keep in mind what you know about circles and principles of listening.

The Healing Work of Circles
by Charito Calvachi-Mateyko

Charito Calvachi-Mateyko was a human rights lawyer in her native Ecuador. Now she lives in the state of Delaware in the USA and teaches classes on restorative justice (see chapter 13) and circle processes.° She also serves on the Governor's Advisory Council on Hispanic Affairs in Delaware as the Chair of the Historic and Cultural Committee. In 2010 she was invited to lead a workshop on circles for Hispanic women at a meeting in Pennsylvania.

I was invited in September 2010 to present a workshop on circles at a Latina women's meeting in Reading, Pennsylvania. I called this workshop Circle of Women's Power. The circle was a perfect symbol° for the stories we were going to hear. The endless flow of life experiences is like the circle without beginning or end.

5   During a circle workshop, people sit in a circle. Sometimes objects that have special meaning for the people are placed in the middle of the circle. They remind participants of the values they share as a group. One member of the group holds a special object, called a *talking piece*. Whoever holds the talking piece is allowed to speak. All other participants must give their complete attention to this person and listen carefully. They may talk when the talking piece is passed to them. As Kay Pranis writes in *The Little Book*
10   *of Circle Processes*, "Circles aim to create space in which participants are safe to be their most authentic° self." This means they may share their ideas and stories freely and without fear.

     The women who came to the Circle of Women's Power workshop shared great stories. These stories came from their own lack of power at a certain moment of their lives. There were 12 of us in the workshop, all Latinas. Bouquets° of flowers were in that room for the awards at the end of the day. We
15   collected them in the center of our circle to remind us that life is beautiful and fragile. Each participant wrote a value to guide us during the conversation. We placed these papers at the center, too.

     Now we felt safe enough to start the sharing. I asked members of the circle to answer this question: "What was the event in your life that made you the leader you are today?" The first woman who spoke said it all came from her visit to a therapist.° The therapist asked her to think of five personal qualities that she
20   possessed. To her surprise, she could not come up with even one quality. That was the moment, she said, when she understood the extent to which domestic° violence had affected her life. The abuse she had suffered from her husband eliminated all positive thoughts about herself.

     As I sat there listening, I recalled how powerful this woman had seemed to me during all the years of knowing her. She organized events for her community. She created ways to promote Latino culture and
25   help elderly° people. And I never knew what drove her life until she told her story. The day at the therapist's office changed her life. She had to divorce her husband because of the unending abuse. She became an independent woman who chooses to serve her community and promote the gathering of other Latina women

to gain strength.

My surprises didn't end with that story. The next woman told us that her leadership started the day her mother was shot and killed in front of her. She was seven years old. And here she was, a wonderful woman who supports other women in every way possible. She has even trained herself in massage° and other forms of healing as a side business besides her regular job. I have heard David Anderson Hooker say: "Hurt people hurt people; hurt people heal people. We can heal together." This 27- year-old woman embodies° the word *healing*. She helps to heal in others the wound that she also works so hard to heal in herself.

These stories moved the participants and opened a sacred° space where all the others wanted to pour out their own soul journeys. And they did. We lost track of° time. Suddenly, a knock on the door announced that the next workshop was coming. We all knew this circle could not just break up; we all got to the center and hugged in a circle and looked up at each other saying: "We are powerful! We are the wise Latinas!"

°processes (n.) – a series of actions or steps
°symbol (n.) – something visible that stands for something else (e.g. a flag is a symbol of a country)
°authentic (adj.) – real
°bouquets (n.) – bunches
°therapist (n.) – counselor who listens to people's psychological and social problems in order to help them
°domestic (adj.) – in the home, involving family members
°elderly (adj.) – old
°massage (n.) – rubbing parts of the body to relax the muscles
°embodies (v.) – is an example of, shows the meaning of by her life
°sacred (adj.) – holy, divine, related to God or religion
°lost track of (v. - idiom) - forgot about or didn't think about

Understand what you read

First, find the right ending for each of the sentences below. Write the letter of the ending in the blank spaces. These sentences form a summary of the essay. In the boxes to the left, use the numbers 1 to 8 to show the correct order of the sentences. One example has been done for you.

	Then the women discussed the question	___
	She explains how a circle discussion allows	___
	All the participants shared great stories	___
1	In her essay Charito shares her experience	*f*
	This woman became a community leader because of the hardship	___
	The second woman, who witnessed her mother's murder,	___
	The first woman explained how she became a leader	___
	First, she arranged the circle and got the women	___

Sentence endings

a. after she realized her life was being destroyed by domestic violence.
b. and felt stronger because of the circle sharing.
c. that she suffered in her marriage and divorce.
d. "What event in your life made you the leader you are today?"
e. people to share their ideas freely and without fear.
f. leading a workshop for Latino women in Pennsylvania.
g. became a supporter and healer of other women.
h. to decide the values that would guide the conversation.

Discuss

1. What do you learn about methods of listening from reading what Charito has written? How do her ideas and experiences compare with what you read in the chapter's first reading?
2. What do you learn about the effects of compassionate listening from reading Charito's essay?

3. What do you think about your experiences with circle processes? How does Charito's essay help you to evaluate circles that you have participated in? How does your experience with circles help you to evaluate Charito's opinions about this method of sharing and listening?

EXTEND YOUR LEARNING

1. Circle process
Work as a class or in small groups to plan a circle for sharing your answers to questions that you as a class want to discuss. Decide what symbols you will place in the middle of your circle and what you will use for a talking piece. When you hold your circle, remember that only one person at a time can share, only the person who is holding the talking piece. You can hold your circle at the beginning of class as part of the "Get to Know Each Other Better" section of the lesson. You can also hold circles at the end of class to discuss your responses to important issues raised in the lesson.

Here is a suggestion for your first student-led circle. You can answer the question, "What values do you want to promote in our circle sharing?" Ask your teacher to take notes on what you say and prepare a list of values agreed on by the class. Feel free to use a different question.

2. Music: Listen to "Chiquitita" by ABBA
Listen to the song "Chiquitita" written and performed by the pop group ABBA. ABBA was a group from Sweden that became popular all across Europe, North America, Australia, and other parts of the world. In 2010 ABBA were voted into the Rock & Roll Hall of Fame. The group consisted of four musicians, two female singers and two men, who sang and played the piano and guitar. The song "Chiquitita" was one of ABBA's biggest hits. They performed it for a United Nations Children's Fund (UNICEF) fund-raising event in 1979. ABBA donated half of all the money they made from this song to support the work of UNICEF. ABBA recorded songs in both English and Spanish. "Chiquitita" also has a Spanish version, as well as this English version with just one Spanish word— "chiquitita," which means "little girl." This version of the song has the words on the video:
https://www.youtube.com/watch?v=S68Sc_SoelY

First listen to the song without watching the video. Your teacher should prepare a version of the lyrics, leaving blanks for some of the rhyming words. Listen to the song again and see if can fill in the missing words. Now watch the video while you listen and check your answers.

Use this help only if you need it. Here are the words (out of order) that your teacher erased from the song: *before, go, grieving, handle, quiet, rely on, sky, together, tomorrow*

Discuss
1. How does the singer invite the little girl (chiquitita) to tell her story?   Point out the words used.
2. What parts of the song give us some idea about how chiquitita feels and what is disturbing her?
3. How do the song's words or music offer comfort or hope to listeners?
4. What are some stresses that girls and women face that boys and men do not have?

Optional follow-up activity:
Go to this website: http://pressplaytogive.com/ When you play the song "Chiquitita," the website owner will make a small donation to UNICEF to support education for girls. At the bottom of the page there is a short video message from the writer of this song, Björn Ulvaeus.

3. Movement
Self-massage
Charito Calvachi-Mateyko mentioned that one of the women in her circle learned about massage as a way to help women under stress. It's great to get a massage from a person who has special training. But we can't always afford to do that.   But you can very cheaply learn some self-massage techniques. You might be able to use these

techniques on friends who need to relax. Review the instructions for self-massage in chapter 1, page 26. Give yourself a massage.

Suggested class project: Do some research on the website eHow.com and learn how to do relaxing self-massage for specific areas of the body. Watch the videos there, and then give short presentations to the whole class. Demonstrate for the class and ask them to do the massage on themselves.

4. Journal

Choose one of the following topics:

1. Write about something that you would like to discuss with other people because you want them to listen to what you say.
2. Write about any of your own experiences as a listener. What makes it hard or easy for you to listen to what others have to say?

SELF-ASSESSMENT

Think about your learning. Complete a self-assessment for this chapter by using the template at the end of the textbook (p. 194).

> *Learning Tip: Listening can be a secret to success in language learning. Listen again and again to the songs that you have encountered in this course. Use all resources available to you to practice listening to English.*

Chapter 9 What If We Ignore Trauma?

Get to Know Each Other Better

Do a student-led circle (as suggested at the end of chapter 8). If you cannot think of a topic, your circle could be a general check to get the mood of the class. How are people feeling at the beginning of the class period? You can rate their feelings on a scale of 1 to 5 (with 5 feeling the best and 1 the worst). If class members want to, they can explain why they rated themselves as 1, 2, 3, 4 or 5.

Look at the pictures

1. Divide yourselves into four groups.
2. The teacher will give each group a number 1 to 4, corresponding to one of the pictures below. Don't tell the other groups what your picture is. Keep it a secret.
3. Your group will create a little dialog between two or three people and then act out your dialog. The rest of the class will guess which picture you are acting out.

Example: Andre: Hey, what's up? **Max:** I'm feeling really good today, man. **Andre:** You look like you're high on something. **Max:** Yea, I've been taking these (*shows something from his pocket; holds it in the palm of his hand; then he puts his hand to his mouth and swallows.* These help to take away all your worries.
Can you guess which picture Andre & Max are acting out?

1

2

3

4

Jon Gehman

109

Connect to the Topic

Most of the pictures above show different kinds of behaviors. In the case of picture #4, you can decide how to understand those pills: are they for a sick person or a drug addict?.

1. What differences did various class members have in understanding the meaning of each picture? Remember that it is all right to have differences. Being able to see more than one meaning in a picture is a strength.

2. How could you relate any of these pictures to trauma?

READ

> **Develop your reading skills:**
> **Make connections among texts.** Review what you learned in chapter 5 about trauma energy during the freeze response. As you read the text below, how do the ideas from chapter 5 help you understand this reading better?
> **Know what kind of text you are reading.** By now, you know that the first reading in a chapter of this textbook is not a personal story. It usually explains something about resilience or awareness of trauma. In chapters 3 and 4, you read texts that were based on *classification*, texts about different kinds of violence and trauma. In chapters 5 and 6, you read about *causes and effects*: What reactions do threats cause? How does trauma affect people? Knowing what kind of text you are reading can help improve your understanding. ***Look at the title of this text.*** According to the title, will the text be based on *classification* or *cause and effect*?

The Results of Ignoring Trauma

If we don't use the energy **accumulated** during the freeze response for something productive, we may use it against ourselves or others. The main reading in chapter 5 ***put it*** this way. Trauma energy "wreaks havoc on the bodies and spirits of the people who experience it. It wreaks havoc on communities and societies as well." When we ***turn*** trauma energy ***against*** ourselves, we call it ***"acting-in."*** When we

5 turn trauma energy against others, we call it ***"acting-out."***

We act in when we turn unhealed trauma energy on ourselves. We can hurt ourselves in many ways. Some people may try to **cope with** the trauma by using alcohol or drugs. These **dull** the pain of trauma. But they can also cause addiction and health problems. Other persons ***use up*** the traumatic energy by **overworking**. Overworking helps them forget about their pain. Sometimes trauma victims have eating

10 **disorders.** Some people seek comfort in food, so they eat too much and gain lots of weight. Other times, people starve themselves or eat a lot and then make themselves vomit. Children who have suffered sexual abuse are more likely, when they grow up, to engage in **risky** sexual behaviors with others. This behavior **exposes** them to HIV infection and other sexually transmitted diseases. Persons who have suffered trauma are more likely to be **compulsive** shoppers or gamblers. This behavior can **ruin** them **financially** and hurt

15 anyone who depends on their **financial** support.

As you have already learned, there are also physical and emotional responses to trauma. If trauma remains unhealed, the physical and emotional responses continue. Months or years after the event, victims who have not healed may have pain in their back or joints, headaches, changes in **appetite**, weakness, high blood pressure, or stomach problems. Emotionally, they may suffer from **depression**. Sad and hopeless,

20 they withdraw from contact with others. They may feel numb, **anxious**, ashamed and guilty because they suffer all these trauma responses. You can imagine how their **moods**, behaviors, and chronic physical problems affect their family members. Not only are they acting-in and hurting themselves. They are affecting others around them.

Unfortunately, persons with unhealed trauma can hurt others more directly. By acting-out they turn

25 their trauma energy onto others. As Catholic priest, Father Richard Rohr says, "Pain that is not **transformed** is **transferred**." Persons with unhealed trauma may be **irritable** and **aggressive**, blaming others for their problems. They are sometimes unable to be flexible or **tolerant** or show empathy toward others. As a result, they may ***get into* repeated** conflicts with others. In the home, they may act-out in domestic violence. In society, they may become guilty of sexual abuse, **criminal** behavior or violent acts. As victims

30 of trauma themselves, they might always be on the look-out for enemies in order to keep themselves safe and **preserve** their identity.

Acting-in and acting-out behaviors lead to cycles of violence--violence against self or others. Many destructive acting-in behaviors are attempts to quiet the raging trauma energy and calm oneself. Trauma healing involves helping people find healthy ways to comfort and calm themselves. You need to remember this important message about trauma. Don't just ignore it and hope it goes away. It won't! **Generations** now and in the future will be affected by these acting-in and acting-out behaviors.

Have a second look

Look for the most important idea. The most important idea for a whole text can often be found by reading the first and last paragraphs. The first paragraph introduces the main idea. The last paragraph often emphasizes the main idea.

Look for main ideas in the body paragraphs. Remember that you can usually find the main idea for each *body paragraph* among the first sentences of the paragraph. The *body paragraphs* develop the most important idea stated in the introduction. Remember to look for *participants* and *processes* to find the main ideas.

UNDERSTAND WHAT YOU READ

Choose the best answers from the choices given.

1. This reading discusses the trauma energy that comes from the
       a. flight response   b. fight response   c. freeze response

2. Which of the following sentences expresses the most important idea of the whole reading?
       a. unhealed trauma harms both the victim and others
       b. acting in affects a person's body, behavior, and emotions
       c. we should help people find healing from trauma

3. Which of these sentences express the main ideas of paragraphs 2, 3, and 4? (choose <u>three</u> answers)
       a. acting in affects a person's behavior in harmful ways
       b. by acting in, persons with unhealed trauma try to calm themselves
       c. acting in harms a person's physical and emotional condition
       d. by acting out, persons with unhealed trauma harm others

4. Which paragraph ends by showing how *acting-in* behaviors affect other people? Paragraph
       a. 1   b. 2   c. 3   d. 4

5. Persons with unhealed trauma may have problems with food because they
       a. eat too much   b. don't eat anything
       c. make themselves vomit after eating a lot   d. all of these

6. Some of the emotional problems related to unhealed trauma are
       a. smoking, back pain, and anger
       b. shame, guilt and sadness
       c. depression, drug use, and headaches

7. Persons with unhealed trauma directly harm others through behavior problems like
       a. conflicts and domestic violence   b. shopping too much   c. drinking too much alcohol

8. The last paragraph suggests that we can help trauma victims
       a. to forget about their pain
       b. to affect future generations for good
       c. to find calmness and strength

Discuss
1. How could a person's family (spouse and children or extended family) be affected by changes in his or her behavior, emotions, and physical condition caused by unhealed trauma?
2. If a person ignores the effects of his or her trauma, what can other people or social organizations do to help?
3. Some of the behaviors discussed in the reading can be considered crimes. How do you think society should deal with persons who break the law as a result of their unhealed trauma?

WORD STUDY

A. Define it yourself!

dull (7) _____

overworking (9) _____

repeated (28) _____

generation (35) _____

B. Word meanings. *Match the words from the text (first column) with the words that mean the same thing (last column). First, find the words in their original sentences using the line numbers. To make your work easier the words have been divided into two sets.*

SET 1

New words	Line #	Words with similar meanings
1. ___ ignore	title	a. destroy, make poor
2. ___ accumulate	1	b. handle, deal with
3. ___ cope with	7	c. make open to danger, put in danger
4. ___ disorder	10	d. related to money
5. ___ risky	12	e. desire for food or drink
6. ___ expose	13	f. pay no attention to
7. ___ compulsive	14	g. dangerous, daring
8. ___ ruin	14	h. become more, build up, gather
9. ___ financial, financially	14-15	i. having a strong psychological drive or desire
10. ___ appetite	18	j. illness, disease

SET 2

11. ___ depression	19	k. worried, nervous
12. ___ anxious	20	l. low spirits, sad feelings
13. ___ mood	21	m. threatening, warlike, unfriendly
14. ___ transform	25	n. easily angered or bothered
15. ___ transfer	26	o. accepting different beliefs or behavior, open-minded, patient
16. ___ irritable	26	p. move, pass on from one to another
17. ___ aggressive	26	q. breaking the law, bad
18. ___ tolerant	27	r. keep safe or guard from harm or change
19. ___ criminal	29	s. change completely
20. ___ preserve	31	t. state of mind or emotions

C. Fill in the blanks. Your new words have been introduced in relation to the subject of trauma. But these words can be used in other situations, too. Read the paragraph on *banking* below and use the words in the box to fill in the blanks.

> *repeated, accumulate, criminal, transform, financial, preserve, risky, ruin, transfer,*

If you save some money in the bank every month, you will be surprised by the amount that you

_____ by the end of the year. Month by month, _____ saving will quickly build up

112

your _____ resources. It is _____ to keep your cash at home under the mattress. There may be _____ activity in your neighborhood and your money will get stolen. If you lose your job, you won't he _____ (add –ed). At most banks you can get a checking and savings account. You can easily _____ money from one account to the other. Having a savings account won't _____ your life. But it can help you _____ a good standard of living.

D. Answer these questions using your new words in complete sentences. Then do the **give one/get one activity** with your classmates. Ask as many class members as you can to share two or more sentences with you.

1. What makes you feel <u>irritable</u> or <u>anxious</u>?
I feel irritable when I don't get enough sleep _____

2. What is a good way to <u>cope with</u> people who are <u>irritable</u> or <u>aggressive</u>?

3. How can a person always remain in a good <u>mood</u>? What advice would you give?

4. If you know anyone who has suffered from <u>depression</u>, how did that person behave?

5. Are you a <u>tolerant</u> person? Is there anything you cannot <u>tolerate</u> (accept)?

6. When you have a healthy <u>appetite</u>, what do you like to eat?

7. Do you know anyone who is a <u>compulsive</u> drinker of _____? (you fill in the name of a drink)

8. If you hurt yourself, what do you do to <u>dull</u> the pain?

9. What advice would you give to a person who <u>overworks</u>?

10. What are the dangers of <u>ignoring</u> your friends' problems?

11. What hopes do you have for the next <u>generation</u>?

Expressions:
act in and **act out** are key words for this chapter. First, notice that they can be used as two-word verbs:
    a. *Teenagers <u>act in</u> by trying drugs or alcohol.*
    b. *Children <u>act out</u> when they feel stressed by a difficult home life.*
When we add *–ing*, we can use these terms as nouns as in sentence c. When these nouns modify other nouns, we spell them with a hypen (-) as in sentence d.
    c. *<u>Acting in</u> and <u>acting out</u> are common ways of coping with stress.*
    d. *But many <u>acting-in</u> and <u>acting-out</u> behaviors are not healthy.*

Look at the pictures on the first page of this chapter. Which pictures could you use to talk about *acting in* and *acting out*?

The verbs below (*put, turn, use,* and *get*) occur in <u>many</u> different expressions. You will need to use your learner's dictionary to help you discover the meanings of these verbs with different prepositions and in different contexts. The reading above uses the verbs with prepositions as described here.

to put it: to express or communicate something in a certain way. The pronoun **it** seems to refer to the idea that someone wants to express. So the verb gives the idea that we "put our thoughts into words." *When King wanted to inspire people to work for racial equality, he put it in terms of a dream.* Or *No matter how I put it, I can't tell you how thankful I am.* Who or what expresses an idea in a certain way in the reading? (see line 2)

turn X against someone: to point or aim something against someone as a kind of weapon. Example: *She became angry and turned the knife against him.* What is turned against someone in the reading above? (see line 4)

113

use up something – The preposition *up* gives the meaning to *use all of something*. Example: *We used up the milk last night, so we don't have any for breakfast.* What gets used up in the reading? (see line 8)

get into something – This phrase can actually mean three quite different things. (a) to enter – *They got into the car and drove off.* (b) to put oneself or someone else into a situation, usually a bad situation – *My cousins always got into trouble when they visited my house.* (c) to become used to something or to like something – *I couldn't get into that movie; I fell asleep after the first 30 minutes. He has really gotten into bird watching; he goes out every weekend.* Which way is this phrase used in line 28 of the reading?

Picture these expressions:
1. Work by yourselves, in pairs, or in groups to make pictures to illustrate the idioms above. Write one sentence with the idiom to go with each picture.
2. Trade your pictures—but not your sentences—with another group.
3. Now make sentences to go with pictures you received from the other group.
4. Show the pictures to the class and share your sentences.
5. Compare your sentences with the ones written by the group who made the pictures.

GRAMMAR STUDY
Open conditionals
Open conditional sentences help you to express a relationship between a certain condition or cause and the effect that is possible, likely, or even certain to occur under that condition.

Condition clause	Result clause
a) If trauma <u>remains</u> unhealed,	the physical and emotional responses <u>continue</u>.
If + simple present tense	*simple present tense*
b) If trauma <u>remains</u> unhealed,	the physical and emotional responses <u>will continue</u>.
If + simple present tense	*future with will*

In the first part of the sentence, we state the condition in the simple present tense. A common mistake of learners is to use the future with *will* in the condition clause [**Wrong:** If trauma <u>will remain</u> unhealed…]

One of the conditional sentences (a) or (b) comes from the text. Which one was in the text? Version ___ appears in line ____. In both sentences (a) and (b), the writer is very certain about the result. Under the condition of unhealed trauma, physical and emotional response will <u>certainly</u> continue. There are many conditional statements that we can make about which we are very certain. For example, *If you are thirsty, you will feel better when you drink some water.* Can you make some other simple conditional statements about which you are very certain?

In the field of psychology and trauma studies, there are many things we are not certain about. We can also use open conditionals to express these uncertain ideas. But in the result clause, we need to use a modal other than *will*. Can you find in the reading above conditional sentence (c) below? It is in line _____.

Condition clause	Result clause
c) If we <u>don't use</u> the energy accumulated during the freeze response for something productive,	we <u>may use</u> it against ourselves or others.
If + simple present tense	*modal + verb (expressing possibility)*
d) If trauma <u>remains</u> unhealed,	the victim <u>could become</u> addicted to drugs.
e) If we <u>don't use</u> the energy accumulated during the freeze response for something productive,	we <u>might use</u> it against ourselves or others.

The result clauses in sentences (d) and (e) use modals other than *may* or *will*. Do sentences (c) and (e) mean the same thing? According to the reading, is sentence (d) true or not?

114

Sentence practice:

A. *Here are some more sentences related to the reading above. Use your understanding of the reading to complete these sentences by supplying either the result clause or condition clause.*

1. If they are unable to be flexible or tolerant or show empathy toward others, _____

    _____ (*hint: see line 27-28*)

2. _____, generations now and in the future will be affected.

    (*see lines 35-36*)

3. If they use alcohol and drugs to dull the pain of trauma, _____

    _____ (*see lines 7-8*)

4. _____, you may have chronic stomach aches or headaches. (*see lines 17-19*)

5. _____, your family members might be negatively affected.

    (*see lines 21-23*)

Round-robin conditionals: Think of personal states or behavior that you want to explain. Here are some example topics. Use these examples to help you write conditional sentences that explain the behavior or state.

sleeping well or restlessly	eating a lot or a little	feeling anxious or calm
feeling stressed or relaxed	working hard or not at all	feeling confident or shy
able or not able to sympathize with others	having strong or weak motivation	having good relationships or conflicts with others

1. On a blank sheet of paper write one part of a conditional sentence, either the condition clause or the result clause (like the sentences you completed above).
2. Draw a line to show the blank space that needs to be completed.
3. Write two more like this.
4. Pass your papers to the person on the right to complete the first sentence.
5. Pass your papers again for the next person to complete the second sentence.
6. Pass your papers one more time to complete the third sentence.
7. Now return the papers to the original writer and share the results with the whole class.

LIFE SKILLS
Story of Resilience

Develop your reading skills:

Pay attention to how a writer develops characters. Sometimes writers want us to pay more attention to the people in their story than to the sequence of actions. This story has three main characters. You find their names in the first two lines. As you read the story, look for two things. First, how does the writer describe the character? In sentences where writers describe a character, the main verbs are often *was* or *became* or *seemed*. Second, what actions does the writer tell us about? Writers who want us to learn more about the people in their story choose to tell us about certain kinds of actions. The actions show what kind of person this is. As you read this story, make some notes about each of the three characters.

Pay attention to how writers order events. Review what you learned toward the end of chapter 6 about how writers refer to events that happened *before* the world of the past. They use the *past perfect* verb form, e.g. in line 1 below: *Karina had coped with a difficult childhood.* There are two places in this story where the writer needs to tell about events that happened *before* the past events that she is focusing on. She uses *past perfect* in the first paragraph, where she needs to give us some background information before the story starts. Where else does she use the *past perfect* verb form? Why does she need to use it there?

The Effects of Untold Trauma
by Carolyn Yoder

Carolyn Yoder is a licensed therapist who specializes in working with individuals and groups living with trauma and challenging life situations: accidents, physical illness, war, torture, immigration, and betrayal. She has lived and worked in Asia, Africa, the Middle East and the Caucasus.

Karina* had coped with a difficult childhood. But she never talked about it with her children, Alexander and Yulia. They knew she had come to the United States before they were born. From a few comments and letters that came occasionally from Russia, they knew she had lived with relatives as a child. Karina was vague° and even seemed angry when they asked about their relatives or grandparents or her
5   childhood. So they learned early on not to ask their mother questions about the past.

Karina and her husband divorced when her children were small. The children didn't see their father or his family after that. Karina worked hard as a maid in a hotel to support the family. Although money was scarce, Karina always made sure there was plenty to eat. She was very self-disciplined° and followed a strict schedule in her own life. She pushed her children to study hard and do well in school. Alexander and
10 Yulia knew she was proud of them. But it was never enough. Their mother always pushed them to study even harder.

The children felt secure physically. But emotionally, Karina was tense and hard. She got angry quickly. She rarely laughed and never seemed relaxed. She could not tolerate displays° of feeling from her children. If they cried, she scolded° them and told them to stop being weak. If they were noisy, she shouted
15 and told them to quiet down. If they got excited about something, she warned them not to get their hopes up. Once in awhile, Karina bought vodka. ° She shut the door to her bedroom and often did not come out until late the next day, quiet, gloomy° and disheveled. ° Alexander and Yulia talked about their mother's strange behavior.

Both Alexander and Yulia went to university. Alexander studied engineering and Yulia studied
20 psychology. Karina was not pleased with Yulia's choice and urged her to study medicine. But Yulia wanted to understand more about human behavior. Although she felt guilty, she went against her mother's wishes. Studying psychology helped Yulia understand emotions and how she had hidden her true feelings as a child.

One day she made an appointment to talk to a counselor at the university. The counselor helped
25 Yulia talk about her feelings of sadness and anxiety. She asked Yulia about her family and the kind of relationships they had with each other. Yulia realized how cut off she was from family and how little she knew. She felt relieved and less sad as she talked with the counselor.

With the counselor's encouragement, Yulia began to ask her mother about her life. At first Karina became angry and refused to talk. But gradually Karina told her daughter the basic facts. Her parents had
30 been arrested° for political reasons. They never returned from the labor camps° where they were sent. Karina had lived with various relatives and in an "orphanage" ° for children of political prisoners.

As Karina got older, she drank more and more and was unhappy and critical.° Yulia tried to get her to talk more about her past or to go to a counselor, but she angrily refused. Alexander was a successful engineer but had a short temper and had difficulty showing affection to his wife and children.
35 Yulia continued to do research and learn all she could about the family. She contacted relatives in Russia. She searched for her father. She continued with counseling and learned to understand and express her feelings. She worked hard to build a happy marriage. She delighted° in her children and was able to show affection° to them. Although she felt sadness that her own relationship with her mother was not close or warm, she was at peace. She was able to treat her mother with respect and love even when it was difficult.
40 Yulia took great satisfaction in knowing that although she was not perfect, she would not pass past trauma on to her children in the same way it had been passed on to her. She was breaking a cycle of trauma.

*names and some circumstances in this story have been changed to protect the identity of the family

°vague (adj.) – not specific, not clear
°self-disciplined (adj.) – showing strong control of one's behavior

°displays (n.) – showing or acting
°scolded (v.) – told them in an angry way they were doing something wrong
°vodka (n.) – an alcoholic drink that comes from Russia
°gloomy (adj.) – sad, depressed
°disheveled (adj.) – having messy hair and clothing
°arrested (v.) – taken by the police for breaking a law
°labor camps (n.) – *labor* means work; a place of punishment for people accused of crimes
°orphanage (n.) – a place where children without parents can be cared for
°critical (adj.) – pointing out wrong things, even very small things
°delighted (adj.) – to enjoy, to be happy with
°affection (n.) – kind and loving feelings

Understand what you read

1. There are sixteen facts and characteristics in the box below. Put these items in the table below with the person that they describe. Some items can describe more than one person.

was divorced	was born in Russia
got angry quickly	had problems showing love to family members
became an engineer	was unhappy and critical
learned about the family's past	studied psychology
lived in an orphanage	talked with a counselor
felt sad and anxious	was born in the USA
her parents were sent away	had a happy marriage
passed trauma on to the next generation	did not pass trauma on to the next generation

Karina	Yulia	Alexander

2. Look at your notes or review the story. What other actions or qualities can you add for Karina and Yulia?

Discuss

1. Which of the characters ignored or tried to ignore the trauma that happened to them? What was the trauma?
2. What were some of the results of ignoring the trauma in that person's life? How were their behavior and emotions affected?
3. Which of the characters dealt with trauma in a positive way? How did that affect their emotions and behavior?

Teacher Story

Listen to your teacher tell a story about a student who realized that some trouble from the past or problems outside of school were having bad effects on his or her work as a student. Listen for the teacher's explanation of how like Karina this student took steps to address those problems. What resources did the student use to deal with these problems?

EXTEND YOUR LEARNING

1. Journal

Write about <u>one</u> of these topics

1. Compare yourself or some member of your family with one of the three persons in the "The Effects of Untold Trauma." How are you the same or different?
2. You learned in chapter 4 that trauma can be collective. This means that whole groups or nations can suffer trauma and ignore trauma. How do you see untold trauma on the national level affecting the behavior of a particular country?

2. Music: Listen to "One-X" by Three Days Grace

Listen to the song "One-X" by the Canadian alternative metal and hard rock band Three Days Grace. This song was written by band member Adam Gontier when he was in rehabilitation for addiction to a painkilling drug called OxyContin. Gontier became addicted when he was facing a lot of stress in his career as a band member. While addicted to this drug, Gontier experienced anger, depression, and many other emotions. This version of the song has the lyrics on the video: https://www.youtube.com/watch?v=F3lRg1yR100

Listen to the song without watching the video. Your teacher can write on the board the four questions in the first verse, leaving the first word of each question blank. Can you supply the words that go in the blanks to make correct questions? Now as you listen again, watch the video and check your answers.

Discuss

1. Who are the people referred to by the pronouns "you," "I," and "we"?
2. What does it mean to "get knocked down"? And then what does it mean to "stand above the crowd"?
3. Why are some parts of the song sung softly and others very loudly, with the singers almost shouting?
4. What does Gontier show us about intense stress in our daily life compared with the effects of trauma?

   Explore on your own: If you like this kind of music, you could explore other songs that Adam Gontier wrote when he was in rehabilitation for his addiction. These include "Pain," "Over and Over," and "Animal I Have Become." How do these songs express Gontier's struggle with his addiction? Do they express more or less hope than the song "One-X"?

3. Circle

Do a student-led circle (as suggested at the end of chapter 8). Students should choose any topic related to the class.

4. Make a collage

A collage is a collection of photos, pictures and pieces of pictures that are glued on a flat surface to make a work of visual art. Gather some old magazines. Cut out pictures that symbolize the ideas in this chapter. Look for pictures that symbolize *effects of trauma that have been ignored*. Look also for pictures that symbolize *hope in overcoming the effects of trauma*. Paste your pictures on a blank sheet of paper. Make short presentations about your collage to the rest of the class. As your teacher directs, work in small groups or individually to make and present your collage. To see examples of collages, do a Google image search.

SELF-ASSESSMENT

Think about your learning. Complete a self-assessment for this chapter by using the template at the end of the textbook (p. 194).

> *Learning Tip: When you read, make notes on your reading as you go. Underline important words or phrases. Write little notes in the margin of the book or on a separate piece of paper. This kind of active reading will help you understand more.*

Chapter 10 – The Cycle of Violence

Get to Know Each Other Better

Have a **student-led circle** related to any question that students would like to pose to each other about the countries that they come from. *Or* do the Common Ground activity described below.

Common Ground

This activity will help you see what you have in common with the other class members.
1. The teacher will read some sentences. These sentences will help you find out interesting similarities and differences among the places from which your class members come.
2. When the teacher says a sentence that is true for your country, you should stand up. If the sentence is not true for you, then do not stand up.
3. If anyone wants to question someone or say something about any of the topics, they are free to do so.
4. Look around and see who else is standing for each sentence.

Example sentences: If it never snows in your country, stand up.

                                  If your country touches one of the great oceans, stand up.

                                  If your country has good relations with an English-speaking country stand up.

                                  If your country has tensions with a neighboring country, stand up.

                                  Stand up if your country was involved in a war in the last 25 years.

                                  Stand up if there are free elections in your country.

                                  Stand up if there is sometimes political violence in your country.

Discuss this activity:
1. What did you notice as you and other students were standing up?
2. What surprised you?
3. What was comfortable or uncomfortable for you?
4. What is the value of sharing similarities and differences about each others' countries?
5. What did you learn about your classmates or the countries from which they come?

Connect to the Topic

So far most of our readings have focused on individual trauma. Remember that chapter 4 also introduced you to collective trauma. Collective trauma occurs "when large numbers of people in a society share a traumatic experience" (p.54). Natural disasters in many countries cause collective trauma. But the worst kinds of trauma on any level are caused by other humans. Human-on-human violence in the form of crime, political assassinations, riots, civil war, or war between nations causes the most serious trauma.

Look at the pictures

Look at the pictures and diagram on the next page. What do you learn about trauma caused by human violence?

The Aggressor Cycle

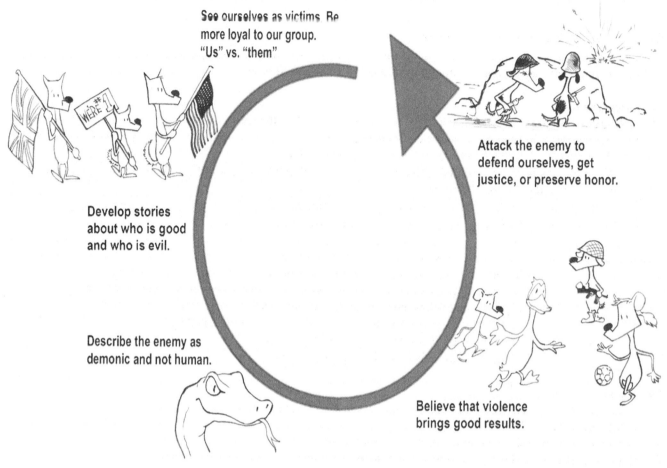

See ourselves as victims. Be more loyal to our group. "Us" vs. "them"

Develop stories about who is good and who is evil.

Describe the enemy as demonic and not human.

Attack the enemy to defend ourselves, get justice, or preserve honor.

Believe that violence brings good results.

Jon Gehman

READ

Develop your reading skills:
Connect what you are about to read with what you have already read.
As you saw clearly in chapter 9, those who ignore the effects of trauma in their lives act in to harm themselves and they act out to harm others. Review the victim cycle in chapter 6. What is the last stage in the victim cycle?
Use visuals provided with the text and graphic organizers to ease your understanding. As you read this text, refer to the diagram of the cycle of violence above. Write on the diagram the paragraph numbers that relate to the topics mentioned there.
Rely on examples to help you understand the concepts. One example has been given in the textbox below to help you understand a concept. What concept is it? Where else in the text do you find examples? Can you provide your own examples for any ideas?

The Cycle of Aggression

(1)   Cycles of violence occur when a person or group chooses to respond to violence with more violence. Those who get trapped in the victim cycle are in danger of moving into the **aggressor** cycle. In that cycle they will act violently against others. Victims of violence feel many negative emotions. Shame, **humiliation**, anger, and a desire for justice are emotions that can lead a victim in the direction of **aggression**. When these emotions build up without release, they can lead to a hunger for revenge. The cycle of aggression describes what may happen when a person or group chooses the way of violence.

(2)   The aggressor cycle often begins when emotional healing has not occurred. Groups or individuals see themselves as victims who have been wronged. Perhaps a recent **crisis** has occurred which threatened their pride, identity, or security. Take the traumatic experience of losing a job, for example. A person who loses his job because of an economic **recession** might become angry at immigrants because he **perceives** them as taking away jobs. They seem to be a threat to his **identity** as a hardworking Briton or American. Bad economic conditions sometimes lead to increased violence against immigrants.

(3)   Sometimes leaders will point to an historical event that threatened the **security** of the nation or community. This event becomes what historian and psychologist Vamik Volkan calls a **chosen trauma**. Usually, the more a group's security is threatened, the more the members hold on to their group identity. They develop a strong sense of "us **versus** them." **Patriotic** or cultural symbols such as flags, songs, dress, food and other customs become more **visible**. (See the box below for an example of "chosen trauma.")

An example of chosen trauma to justify violence: Professor Thomas Scheff tells about a conversation he had in 2004. He attended a memorial to American soldiers killed in Iraq. The father of a soldier who died in Iraq was showing him pictures of his son in uniform, a handsome young teenager. "After viewing photos from his childhood to just before his death, I began to cry," says Scheff.

Father: (surprised): What's the matter?
Me: I was wondering if the war in Iraq is worth the death of your son.
Father: (again surprised). But we had to do something.
Me: Why is that?
Father: 9/11.
Me: But Iraq had nothing to do with 9/11.
Father: Well, they're all Moslems."

http://www.soc.ucsb.edu/faculty/scheff/main.php?id=38.html

(4)   In a hypervigilant atmosphere following a threat, individuals and groups tell the story of what happened in terms of good versus **evil**. "We" are the good, and "they" are the evil ones. In these stories, the "good" side **projects** evil onto the "enemy" and takes away all their human goodness. These stories also shift attention away from our own **shortcomings**. We don't talk about how we might have contributed to the conflict that led to an attack on our country because that would seem **unpatriotic**.

(5)   When a group or nation buys into a story of good versus evil, it is easy to **demonize** and **dehumanize** the "other." The group labels the enemy as *terrorists*, *communists*, **axis** *of evil*, **savages**, or *animals*. A belief that the "other" is not human **justifies** getting rid of them, even killing them.

(6)   Another common theme of victims' stories is that violence is **redemptive**. Violence is believed to have the power to give us security and keep us free. It can restore a sense of pride and honor. Violence will save the nation. Violence will even put an end to violence. It's not true, but that's what people believe.

(7)   When victims see themselves as good and their enemies as evil and inhuman, and when they think that they can only save themselves by violence, then they will turn to violence. They will justify an attack on "the enemy" in the name of self-defense, justice, security, honor, or freedom. But one thing we know for certain about violence is this: it creates more victims. These victims, then, become trapped in their victim cycles. From the victim position, they will **eventually** move into the aggressor cycle. In this way, the cycle of violence goes on and on.

(8)   It is important to note that the cycle of aggression does not necessarily happen in a linear way as presented in the diagram. An individual or group may not experience all the steps described. They may experience several of the steps at the same time. They may find themselves or their nation at times in both cycles—as victims and aggressors.

UNDERSTAND WHAT YOU READ

There are eight paragraphs in the reading above. Look at the reading again and match each topic with the number of the paragraph in which it is discussed. The first one has been done for you.

Topic	Paragraph number
Attack "the enemy" to defend ourselves, get justice or preserve our honor	___
See ourselves as victims	___
The aggressor cycle is not linear, one step after another	___
Develop stories about who is good and who is evil	___
Be loyal to my group: "us versus them"	___
The aggressor cycle explains how victims can become violent	1
Believe that violence brings good results	___
Describe the enemy as inhuman or as demons	___

Pay attention to the details of the reading. Solve these riddles by matching the words on the right with the sentences.

1. ___ These feelings can push victims toward aggression
2. ___ These are names we give to the enemy
3. ___ These are symbols of our group's identity
4. ___ These things could make us feel like victims
5. ___ Some victims think violence can provide these things

a. bad economic conditions, losing a job, terrorist attacks
b. flags, songs, dress, food, national customs
c. security, justice, honor, freedom
d. terrorists, communists, axis of evil, savages, animals
e. shame, humiliation, anger, desire for justice

Pay attention to important ideas in the reading. Match the correct ending with each sentence.

1. ___ Victims' negative emotions
2. ___ People become more loyal to their group
3. ___ Our stories of good and evil focus on
4. ___ Our stories of good and evil leave out
5. ___ Leaders sometimes use historical events
6. ___ Violence cannot eliminate violence,

a. the bad things we have done.
b. but it does create more victims.
c. to unite their people against threatening enemies.
d. increase their hunger for revenge.
e. when they feel their safety is threatened by others.
f. the evil done by the enemy.

B. Discuss

1. Can you think of "chosen traumas" that people in your country point to? What other examples of "chosen traumas" can you think of?
2. What are some "good versus evil" narratives that you have heard?
3. What's your opinion: Can violence be redemptive? Is violence an acceptable way to solve some problems?

WORD STUDY

A. You define it!

aggression (noun) _____

aggressor (noun) _____

versus (preposition) _____

evil (noun & adjective) _____

chosen trauma (noun phrase) _____

B. Find the word meanings. Which of the words below can replace the underlined words in the following sentences? (line numbers give you a clue to help you choose the right word.) Write the correct vocabulary item above the underlined words. The vocabulary has been divided into two sets to ease your work.

SET 1 (for items 1-6)

aggression (noun)	project (verb)
crisis (noun)	recession (noun)
humiliation (noun)	security (noun)
identity (noun)	shortcoming (noun)
patriotic/unpatriotic (adjective)	visible (adjective)
perceive (verb)	evil (adjective & noun)

1. Victims of <u>violent attacks</u> (5) don't talk to others about their experience because they want to avoid <u>painful loss of self-respect</u> . (4)

2. When bad economic conditions cause a <u>time of emotional upset or a dangerous situation</u> (8) in the community, immigrants may feel a lack of <u>safety</u> (13) because people blame them for the hard times.

3. During a(n) <u>economic slow down,</u> (10) many people lose their jobs.

4. While some people welcome immigrants, others <u>think of</u> (10) them as threats to their national and cultural <u>sense of who they are as a people</u> (11).

5. When the United States was attacked in 2001, <u>faithful</u> (16) Americans flew the country's flag. Those who questioned whether US policies might have caused the attack were considered <u>unfaithful</u>. (26) The shock of all Americans was <u>seen</u> (17) in the church services and special meeting that they held to honor the dead.

6. Psychologists observe that people often <u>transfer</u> (21) their own <u>bad or hateful</u> (20) qualities onto others. They are very uncomfortable accepting their own <u>weaknesses.</u> (24)

SET 2 (for items 7 to 10).

aggressor (noun)	evil (adjective and noun)
axis (noun)	justify (verb)
dehumanize (verb)	redemptive (adjective)
demonize (verb)	savage (noun + adjective)
eventually (adverb)	versus (preposition)

7. Sadly, in a time of intense conflict, people create stories that <u>make</u> their enemies <u>into devils</u> (28). The enemy becomes a <u>wild human being without culture or civilization</u> (30) or even an animal. They see enemy countries as the <u>center</u> of <u>all that is bad and hateful.</u> (30)

8. <u>Making</u> people <u>into less than human beings</u> (28) is one way to <u>make</u> an attack on them <u>seem right</u> (31).

9. When we are victims, we see ourselves as a good, peace-loving nation <u>against</u> (16)our enemies who are cruel and violent.

10. Many people support high spending on the military because they believe that violence will free and save the nation from the power of enemies. This belief in the <u>saving and freeing</u> (34) power of violence will <u>after some time</u> (43) result in war between nations.

11. Violence creates more victims. And in creating victims, it also creates more people who can become <u>doers of violence.</u> (2)

C. Practice your new words. Review the pictures of the victim and aggressor cycles in the beginning of chapter 6 and the beginning of this chapter. The victim cycle begins with a traumatic event. It ends with a desire for revenge. This desire leads directly to the aggressor cycle. That cycle ends with an attack on the enemy. This attack creates more victims. Where would you put the new words from this chapter on these circles? Which words relate to the victims and which ones to the aggressors? Can some words belong to both cycles? **_Write the words where you think they belong._** Discuss your choices with the class.

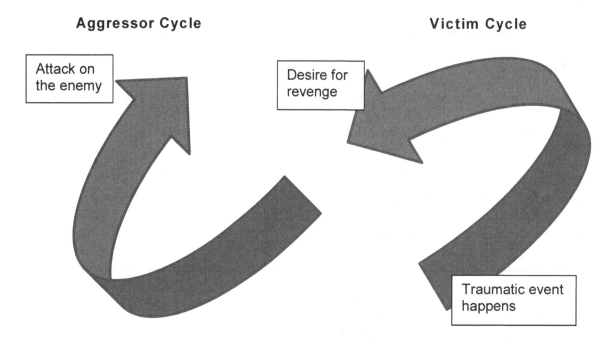

Aggressor Cycle   **Victim Cycle**

Attack on the enemy

Desire for revenge

Traumatic event happens

Word family: In chapters 9 and 10 you have studied three words that belong to the same family. Here is a summary of those words to remind you how they are used. You write your own sentences in the right hand column.

An **aggressor** (noun) is a person or a group.

In countries where there is a lot of conflict, it is hard to know who the victim is and who the **aggressor** is.

Aggression (noun) is a behavior that a person or group exhibits

Teachers need to watch carefully bigger children who show physical **aggression** toward others.

124

Aggressive (adjective) can describe people, but more often it describes a kind of behavior that is threatening, violent or unfriendly.

*The government took **aggressive** action against people who disagreed with its policies.*

Expressions:
buy into – In the text above (line 27) this two-word verb does <u>not</u> have anything to do with spending money. It means *to believe in something—usually with enthusiasm, without thinking carefully about it.*

put an end to – This multi-word verb means *to stop something* or *to cause something to stop.*

in the name of – This phrase is not really about names. It is about doing something *as an excuse or reason for the thing that is named.* It also gives the meaning of doing something *for the benefit of the thing that is named.*

Use the expressions as you answer these questions:
1. According to paragraph 5, what do people *buy into*? What are some ideas or programs that people you know *buy into*?
2. In line 37 what do some people believe will *stop* violence? Do you agree that this will *put an end to* violence? What will *put an end to* violence? What will *put an end to* _____? (you name the problem)
3. According to paragraph 7, what *reasons* do people give for attacking their enemies? In *what or whose name* do they attack? If you do good things, *in what (or whose) name* do you do them?

Extra activity: Do a Youtube search for songs containing the words "in the name of love." Or go to elyrics.net and type the search term; choose to search "within the text" of songs.

GRAMMAR STUDY
Learn to use correctly both the verbs or adjectives and their related noun forms. In everyday English, both forms are used. But you will find the noun forms used more in technical academic writing.

1. respond – verb / **response** – noun (1)
a. Often people <u>respond</u> to violence with more violence.
b. Often a violent <u>response</u> will trigger more violence.

Sometimes writers will use the noun form because it provides a shorter way of communicating an idea. Notice how the sentences with the verb forms (a above and c^1 & d^2 below) mention some kind of human actor (in bold print). The sentences with the noun forms [b above and c^2 & d^1 below) do <u>not</u> mention the human actors. This is another reason why writers sometimes use noun forms of the verb or adjective: they want to focus not on human actors, but on a process or an idea. For example, in chapter 9 you saw the terms *trauma response* and *freeze response*. Look at how the sentences below focus on the process or the people.

(c^1) Sometimes, **people** <u>respond</u> to threats by freezing. (c^2) This is called the *freeze <u>response</u>* for short.
(d^1) Trauma *<u>response</u>* is a short way of talking about the ways (d^2) that **people** <u>respond</u> to traumatic events.

Compare the use of *violent* (the adjective) and *violence* (the noun) in sentences 1a and 1b above. There are many other adjectives in English with related noun forms. In fact, since a *verb+ing* can be used as a noun or adjective, English has many, many verbs, adjectives, and nouns that are related. Technically, the *–ing* form of the verb is called a *participle* and it has several different uses. Look carefully at the adjective-noun examples in 2a & 2b and verb-noun-adjective examples in 3a, 3b, & 3c.

2. **secure** – adjective / **security** – noun (9, 13)
a. Even a <u>secure</u> nation fears foreign aggression.
b. Leaders fear foreign aggression because it threatens the <u>security</u> of the nation

3. **heal / healing** (7)
a. If a wound does not <u>heal</u> properly, it may become seriously infected.
b. A bone may break again when <u>healing</u> has not occurred.
c. Compassionate listening is a <u>healing</u> response to a traumatized person.

One of the common English noun endings for words that have related verbs is *–tion* or *–ation*. We use these nouns, like the ones mentioned above, to express abstract ideas or processes. *Humiliation* is one of the abstract nouns in the reading; the verb from which it comes is *humiliate.*

4. **humiliate** – verb / **humiliation** – noun (4)
a. When we <u>humiliate</u> people for crimes they have committed, we feed their aggressive urges.
b. The <u>humiliation</u> of criminals can create anger and feed aggressive urges.

The main reading for this lesson has several other verbs that have commonly known noun forms ending in *–ation or -tion.* Here are the verbs, followed by their noun forms and the line number where they appear in the reading.
5. direct/direction (4)
6. contribute/ contribution/ (25)
7. justify/justification (31)
8. demonize/ demonization (28)
9. dehumanize / dehumanization (28)

Which form of the word goes in the blank? In deciding your answer, remember to think about these two questions: (a) Is there an actor <u>doing</u> something? – Use the *verb* form in that sentence. (b) Is the focus on a process? --Use the *noun* form in that sentence to talk about the <u>action</u> as a <u>thing</u>. (*Use the past tense ending on the verb when needed.*)

justify/justification
1. The rebels_____the destruction of the bridge by explaining that it kept the army from attacking the
village.

2. Their _____ for destroying the bridge was not accepted by village leaders.

demonize/ demonization
3. Through the _____of the rebels, the government hopes to earn the sympathy and support of
people all over the country.

4. Newspapers_____the rebels, describing them as the most evil criminals that ever lived.

dehumanize /dehumanization
5. The strategy of _____used by both sides in the conflict affected many people in all parts of
the society.

6. During the civil war, the army and the rebels_____the people by destroying their homes,
burning their crops, forcing them to flee to the jungle.

Share the best pairs
Work with each other in pairs and write a sentence for each word. One person in the pair will take the verbs of
number 1, 2, & 3 (above) and the nouns of 4, 5, & 6. The other person will take the nouns of 1, 2, & 3 and the verbs

of 4, 5, & 6. When you have finished your sentences, share them with each other for correction and improvement. Then each pair in the class will share their best pair of sentences.

LIFE SKILLS
Story of Resilience
Read about two generations who had to cope with wars.

Develop your reading skills:

Think about the title. The title suggests that you are going to read not just one story but two stories. How do you know that? As many languages do, English has ways of leaving out words that do not need to be repeated. (We call this ellipsis.) The meaning of the title is this: "In Grandma's Story I Find My Own Story" or "When I listen to Grandma's story, I find my own story as well." So when you read this text, you will discover two stories: Vesna's story and her grandmother's story. Can you identify which paragraphs tell whose story?

Identify and track the participants. When you read a story, you need to be clear about who the participants are. The title of this story suggests that there will be at least two main participants: *grandma* and *I* (the author Vesna). Since Vesna is telling the story, she will appear in the story as *I*. Her grandmother, though, will be referred to as *she*. Many times, a participant in a story can have more than one name. In this story *grandma* is referred to by three different names (*grandmother, Baka Naka,* and *Grandma Naka*). There are other important participants, especially *Croatian soldiers* (*they*) and *Serbs and Croats* (also *they*). If you have colored pencils or highlighter, you can mark the participants with different colors as you read the story.

In Grandma's Story I Find My Own
by Vesna Hart

Vesna Hart, currently a doctoral candidate in psychology, is an educator, practitioner of peacebuilding, mother of two, and wife, seeking to make a difference by listening and sharing stories with others. She has written a set of materials for training youth in trauma awareness and resilience.

My grandmother lived in nine countries, but she never moved from her little village. She was born in 1912 and lived through many wars. When she died, her village was ruled by what is now the country of Croatia. Sometimes the Serbs and Croats would fight together against one of two great empires. For they were trapped° between the Ottoman and the Austro-Hungarian Empires. But sometimes they would also
5   fight against each other. The conflicts between Serbs and Croats came to a climax° in the 1990s when Croatia became independent of the Federal Republic of Yugoslavia. I am a survivor of the war of 1991.

In 1983, when I was 12 years old, my grandmother became sick. There was no medical care in her area. So she left her small village and came to stay at our house in the city for about six months. My twin brother and I asked Baka Naka (Grandma Naka) to tell us stories. At first, she told us folk stories° that had
10   been passed down from our ancestors° for centuries. Then she ran out of those stories and began telling us stories of her own life. One of those stories was about her experience during World War II.

One day Baka Naka learned that the Croatian army, allied° with Nazi Germany, had come to a village across the mountain. This was the village where her sister and her mother were living. She heard that the situation in the village was very bad. So she took her one-month old son and she walked across the
15   mountain. On her way there, she was stopped by Croatian soldiers. They were not kind to her, but she managed to continue her journey.

As Baka Naka approached° the village, she could see that it was burning. When she reached her family's house, it was on fire. Her mother and brother-in-law were inside that house. She found her dying sister outside the house with some of her children. Baka Naka told us in detail how she held her sister while
20   she died. She told us how the Croatian soldiers had chased her nephews° and nieces° in the village and cut their throats.

I could tell that Baka Naka felt a lot of pain as she remembered these events. It was difficult for her to tell the story to us. But she never said anything negative about Croats as people. She was angry at those soldiers. But she never taught us to hate Croatian people because of what those soldiers did.

25   Little did I know at the time, but nine years later I would be experiencing a war between Serbs and Croats. My brother and I fled our hometown in Croatia and went to Serbia. Our parents stayed in their house. We could not contact them, but we listened to the news every two hours to find out what was happening. Fighting was going on all the time. I listened to the news reports that blood was flowing in the streets of my hometown. I became very angry. Some of my Serbian relatives believed that the Yugoslav

30 Army should come and bomb my hometown to stop the war there. I was upset about that because I feared for the safety of my parents. I was angry whenever people talked about anything related to the war.

        I was especially angry with the political leaders. They were greedy° for power. I dreamed about the best solution to this conflict. Bring the presidents of the two countries to the city square in my hometown. Then let all the bombs fall on them. I thought that would stop the war. I wanted revenge for the three months

35 of constant° violence in my city. I wanted revenge because they seemed not to care about causing so many ordinary people to suffer.

        Several years later, when the fighting had ended, I had a different idea. This time I still thought that we should bring the two presidents to the square of my hometown. But there they should listen to the stories of how people suffered because of their actions. Then, the community could grieve,° and we could start to

40 think about what we all need no matter what our ethnic° background is. I thought this kind of storytelling could help the people of my city to escape from the cycle of violence. I think Baka Naka would like this approach. She told us stories of suffering, but she did not promote revenge.

°trapped (v.) – caught between two or more things, not able to escape or get away
°climax (n.) – the high point, the most intense part
°folk stories (n.+ n.)– stories that are typical of a particular nation or people; traditional stories
°ancestors (n.) – the people in your family who came before your generation
°allied (v.) – joining with, supporting
°approached (v.) – came towards or came near
°nephews (n.) – sons of your brother or sister
°nieces (n.) – daughters of your brother or sister
°greedy (adj.) – wanting to have more food, money, or other things than is normal or fair for people to have
°constant (adj.) – something that happens all the time
°grieve (v.) – cry and feel sad about a loss or a death
°ethnic (adj.) – relating to a particular cultural or racial group

Understand what you read

A. Sort the sentences. Which of the following sentences re-state what happened in Vesna's story and which sentences belong to her grandmother's story? Write the number of the sentence in the boxes below.

1. She left her home and went to her sister's village.
2. She left her home and went to Serbia.
3. Her story happened during World War II.
4. She walked over the mountain carrying her baby son.
5. Her parents were in danger because of the fighting.
6. She listened to news about the war on radio or TV.
7. Her mother, sister, and other relatives were killed.
8. She could not talk with her parents.
9. She saw the village on fire.
10. Her story happened in 1991.

Vesna's story	Her grandmother's story

B. Give short answers to the following questions:

1. How did Vesna learn about her grandmother's story?
2. Who attacked the village where Baka Naka's sister lived?
3. What do you think was the saddest part of Baka Naka's story?
4. How did Baka Naka feel about the Croatian soldiers and about Croatian people?
5. Who was doing the fighting in Vesna's hometown?
6. How did Vesna feel about the war?
7. How did Vesna want to get revenge for the suffering caused by the war?
8. What did Vesna think might end the cycle of violence in her hometown?

Discuss
1. What are some similarities and differences between Vesna's story and her grandmother's story?
2. In the first reading of the chapter, you learned about "good vs. evil narratives." Is Vesna's narrative of this type? If it is not "good vs. evil narrative," what changes would make it into that kind of narrative?
3. At the end of the story, Vesna gives two possible solutions for ending the violence in her hometown. Which do you think is the better solution? Can you think of other ways to end the violence?
4. What hints do you find in this story about the roots of the violence that was experienced by Vesna and her grandmother? What do you think the situation might be for the present generation in Vesna's hometown of Vukovar, Croatia?

EXTEND YOUR LEARNING
1. Journal
Choose one of these topics to write about:
1. Write your opinions about one national trauma that you know about which might be the reason for that nation becoming an aggressor.
2. Do you know anyone who moved into the cycle of aggression after they experienced abuse of some kind or suffered humiliating punishment?
3. Write about anything related to the topic of this chapter.

2. Readers' Theater
Create your own drama to act out the ending of Vesna Hart's story. Your drama will need to have three or more characters: the leader of Croatia, the leader of Serbia, and one or more people affected by the war.
1. You will work in small groups.
2. In your groups prepare a script for your drama. When the leaders came together and listened to the people affected by the war, imagine what they would all say. What kinds of things would the people say? How would the leaders respond?
3. Each group will perform its drama for the rest of the class. You may read from the prepared script.

3. Movement
Calm those raging feelings of aggression
Sit with your legs extended forward,
Cross one leg over the other.
Extend both arms forward.
Turn your palms to face each other.
Cross one arm over the other.
Turn your palms to face each other.
Clasp your hands and lace your fingers.
Pull your clasped hands toward your chest.
Rest your clasped hands on your chest.
Stay in this position and breathe deeply three times.
Roll your arms back out and unclasp your hands.

Do feel calmer now? You might need more exercise to use up some of the energy that is building up inside you. Go for a walk, a run, a bike ride, or a swim!

4. Listen to "Where is the Love" by the Black Eyed Peas

Black Eyed Peas is an American hip-hop group from Los Angeles, California. Their song "Where is the love?" came out in 2003 and was a sensation around the world. The song was ranked #1 or #2 in at least 16 different countries. Pop star Justin Timberlake helped to write the refrain and sang it on the recording. The song came out just after the US invaded Iraq. What are some of the words in the song that people who liked it might have related to the invasion? You might not understand all the lyrics in the verses, which are sung in rap style. That's okay. Just enjoy the rapping. Pay closer attention to the refrain. You will probably understand it well. Think about what the refrain says in relation to the cycle of aggression. It's very hard to rap the verses, but you can try if you like. Everyone can sing the refrain! Before you listen to the song, go to the AZ Lyrics website and read the words, http://www.azlyrics.com/lyrics/blackeyedpeas/whereisthelove.html, because Hip-hop lyrics move fast and there are many words. Then watch this video and follow the lyrics as you listen: https://www.youtube.com/watch?v=kzXNvBBs8PY. See some notes below on the language.

Notes on language in "Where is the Love"

1. As in some informal spoken English, the –ing at the end of verbs is pronounced as –in (and spelled –in'). *Wanna* and *gotta* come from *want to* and *got to* (meaning *have to*)
2. The apostrophe (') is used to show missing sounds or letters. Notice in the refrain *'cause* for the word *because*.
3. CIA = US Central Intelligence Agency (spy agency)
4. Bloods and Crips = names of violent gangs
5. KKK = Ku Klux Klan, a violent US group that believes white people are superior to all other races
6. In the refrain, the word *Father* refers to God
7. Two of the lines include well known English sayings:
    a. "practice what you preach" = people should <u>do</u> the good things that they tell others to do
    b. "turn the other cheek" = from the Christian Bible, these are words of Jesus: "But I tell you not to try to get even with a person who has done something to you. When someone slaps your right cheek, turn and let that person slap your other cheek." (Matthew 5:39)

Discuss

1. What does the refrain of the song suggest about breaking the cycle of aggression?
2. Is the song optimistic or pessimistic about breaking the cycle of aggression? What's your opinion?
3. If you are a fan of hip-hop music, how would you compare this song to other hip-hop songs that are popular?

   Explore on your own: Do some research on the four members who make up this very diverse group Black Eyed Peas. Find out about their ethnic background, the difficulties some of them have faced in life, and their achievements.

5. Circle process

If there have been any tensions in the class discussions about the cycle of aggression, have a circle led by the teacher to conclude this unit.

SELF-ASSESSMENT

Think about your learning. Complete a self-assessment for this chapter by using the template at the end of the textbook (p. 194).

> *Learning Tip: Make extra time in your schedule to explore on your own beyond the lesson in this chapter. If the topic really interests you, then you will be motivated to read more. The more you read English, the easier reading will become to you.*

Chapter 11 – Breaking Free Through Truth

Get to Know Each Other Better

Facts and Opinions: Discern the Truth. Take two small strips of paper. On one strip write two facts about yourself that the members of your class are not likely to know about you. In addition, write <u>one</u> thing that is <u>not</u> true. On the other strip of paper write <u>two</u> opinions that you have about any issue that concerns you. Write <u>one</u> idea that is <u>not</u> your opinion. Turn by turn each class member will read his or her "three facts." The class will guess which "fact" is <u>not</u> true. After reading the facts, read your opinions. When you write and read the false facts and opinions, do your best to fool the rest of the class!

Example: **Fact:** I played on my high school volleyball team.
　　　　 Opinion: I think the United Nations is a corrupt organization.

Connect to the Topic

Life is full of facts and opinions. Do you want to know the *truth* about anything that happens in the world? You will have to sort through all the facts and opinions. You will have to decide whether facts are correct. Take the war in Iraq that began with the US invasion in 2003. The United States said Iraq had weapons of mass destruction. The US presented one set of facts and its opinions to the United Nations Security Council. Other countries presented different facts and opinions. What was the truth? It was certainly not simple at that time to distinguish the truth from lies or errors.

Jon Gehman

Look at the pictures

1. Describe what you see in each picture. Be careful just to give the facts of what is in each picture.
2. Now give your opinions about the meaning of each picture. How do the pictures relate to the chapter topic of breaking free from the cycles of violence through truth?
3. After you complete the first reading, discuss the pictures again. Have any of your opinions changed about the meaning of the pictures?

Note: Pictures that go with a text need to be interpreted. There may be room for different opinions about the relation of the images and the text. Don't be upset if your opinion differs from the opinions of your teachers and classmates. But also be willing to listen to their opinions and understand them.

READ

> **Develop your reading skills:**
> **Use the sub-headings.** Before you begin reading an article, look at the bold sub-headings. These headings help you to know about the topics and organization of the article. If you need more information, skim (read only the first sentence following each heading).
> **Make predictions.** Based on your survey of the main topics, what questions do you think the reading will answer? What answers do think the author will provide for those questions? As a way to train yourself to do this, write down your questions and predictions. Here are some examples for the <u>first section</u> of the article.
> > *Questions:* "What is the healing journey? How long is the journey? Where does it begin and end?"
> > *Predictions:* "Getting healed from trauma is like going on a journey; it must be a long process (like a journey); I don't know where it begins, but maybe it means getting away from danger; the journey ends with a healed person."
> Now you try this kind of questioning and predicting with the other sections of the article. Try not to read the paragraph; just look at the bold sub-headings. Then question and predict.

Truth: The First Stop on the Healing Journey

Beginning the Healing Journey

The cycles of violence can be repeated many times. But they can also be broken and transformed. First, people must become **aware** that they are **trapped** in a cycle.
5   They must acknowledge that they do not have to continue harming themselves or others. They can choose to *break free* and begin walking the healing path.

The most important condition for *breaking out* of the cycle of violence is safety. Both victims and aggressors need to feel physical, emotional, and spiritual safety.

There is another part of breaking free that is closely related to
10   safety. That is the **restoration** of supportive and trusting relationships with other people. We often feel safe if we can trust people around us. In the first part of the journey, trauma survivors will naturally find it nearly impossible to trust those who hurt them. But others, who were not involved in the hurt, also need to be trusted again. Because humans are social beings, we need others to help in
15   healing our inner pain. Only in a safe and trusting environment can survivors begin to seek and speak the truth.

Grieving

One path to breaking the cycles of violence is to remember
20   and acknowledge what happened. Victims need to remember the events in all their **complexity**. They need to **grieve** what they have lost. Silent or silenced voices of victims and **offenders** only deepen

> **Rituals** that have helped to create a good atmosphere for telling the truth about trauma
>
> **Mozambique:** bathing; breathing and drinking herbal medicine
>
> **Somali refugees in N. Kenya:** a peace prize ceremony
>
> **Rwandans at a workshop in Kenya:** spotting wildlife on a safari; singing together
>
> **Fijians & Indo-Fijians:** kava drinking ceremony & dancing
>
> **White and Black Americans in Richmond, VA:** a walk to historical sites related to slavery & civil war
>
> **Mennonite Christians in US:** foot-washing ceremony
>
> *From* <u>Ritual and Symbol in Peacebuilding</u> *by Lisa Schirch*

the wounds of trauma. **Rituals** that are part of the culture can help people to ***break the silence***. Rituals are practices that people follow. See the sidebar for examples of practices that have opened up space for people to acknowledge and remember harms that have been done. While they are remembering and grieving, it is
25 important for them to use body/mind exercises, like the EFT tapping exercise (chapter 7), deep breathing, and other relaxation techniques. These allow the body to unfreeze and provide a way to tell stories and release emotions without being overwhelmed. Being overwhelmed again is a common fear after trauma.

Accepting a Changed Life
30   Accepting what happened is **essential**. Life has changed. Now victims must be able to name and **confront** fears about the "new reality." Only then can healing begin. One way to do this is by telling their stories to others. Sometime it is difficult for victims and offenders to tell what happened. It is too painful or it is not politically or socially safe. Sometimes parts of the story are unknown. Sometimes there is pressure to tell only one version or one part of the story. So people tell the version that makes their side look good and the other side look bad.
35   Usually there are **multiple** sides of a story, all claiming to tell the truth. Creating safe spaces allows people from all sides to tell their story and their truth. This can be done through talking or using the arts. Normally, the truth about traumatic events is complex. Storytelling helps people in ways that move them beyond helplessness and hopelessness (See chapter 8 on listening).

40 ### Memorializing
    Memorializing is a way humans ensure that what happened and those who died are not forgotten. **Memorials** are places or objects that allow us to remember loved ones and past hurts and to grieve. Some memorials are healthy. They provide a place to store our memories so that we can move on.
    Other memorials keep us in the cycle of violence. They either symbolize our victory (often at the expense of others) or our humiliation in defeat. This may prevent us from healing the wounds of the past
45 and healing present relationships. In addition to building memorials, people remember and memorialize by marching in parades, writing poetry and stories, creating art, establishing scholarships, etc. Healthy memorials remind us of what happened in the past so that the painful past does not need to keep repeating itself.

50 ### The Journey Goes On
    Facing the truth can be painful. But it is necessary for healing to occur. We must allow ourselves time and space to express thoughts and feelings rather than **suppressing** sadness and tears. Realizing the complexity of the truth opens us to healing and change. But truth is only the first stop on the healing journey. Depending on the nature of the trauma, people may need to spend time in several stops during the healing journey. They will also have to stop and consider **mercy, justice**, and peace (chapters 12-14). By setting out on this journey, they search for answers and learn new skills. And in the process, they build personal and collective resilience.

UNDERSTAND WHAT YOU READ
How did your predictions turn out for each section?

Topics	How were your predictions?
Beginning the healing journey (done for you above)	*yes, safety from danger is important, but so is awareness of being trapped & awareness of choices; the end of the journey means healing for the individual person and for relationships with others*
Grieving	

Accepting a changed life	
Memorializing	
The journey goes on *If truth is the "first stop" on the healing journey, what are the other stops?*	

Compare your answers with your classmates' answers. Work in pairs or as a whole class together.

Now pay closer attention to the details and find the answers to these 8 riddles by matching the answers in the right column to the statements in the left column.

1. If you want to feel safe, you need this. ____
2. This is necessary for the truth to be freely shared. ____
3. Rituals like these are helpful for breaking the silence. ____
4. These are useful for calming emotions while telling stories ____
5. In order to bring out all sides of the truth, you can use these. ____
6. Creating memorials like these can help us remember our pains and losses in a positive way. ____
7. This can be a cause of pain. ____
8. This can slow down or block healing, ____

a. singing together, marching in an annual parade, having a special meal
b. not allowing tears and sadness to be shown
c. trusting relationships with other people
d. a creating scholarship fund , building a monument, naming a bridge for someone
e. facing the truth
f. a safe and trusting environment
g. storytelling and the arts
h. deep breathing and tapping

Discuss
1. How do people remember the hurt in your community? What are some of the rituals for grieving in your community?
2. How can telling the truth about events be difficult or even dangerous? What creates safety?
3. What is an example of a "healthy memorial" in your community? Are there any unhealthy memorials in your community?
4. Remember to talk about the pictures again, now that you understand the reading.

WORD STUDY
A. Define it yourself!

multiple _____
(see line 35 – be sure to look carefully at the following sentence, too)

memorial _____
(see line 42 - also look at the following sentences)

memorialize _____
      (see line 41, along with the definition you just completed)

ritual _____
      (see lines 23, also relate the information in the sidebar to the sentence that defines the word)

B. Word meanings

*Choose the answers that mean the same thing as the **boldfaced** word for each sentence. Cross out the words that do not mean the same thing. Every item has <u>two</u> correct answers and <u>one</u> wrong answer.*

1. First, people must come to know about the victim and aggressor cycles in which they are **trapped**.

      caught   stuck   freed

2. They must become **aware** that there are ways of getting free from these cycles.

      knowledgeable   anxious   mindful

3. It is important to promote the **restoration** of trusting relationships with other people.

      healing   removal   rebuilding

4. They need to **grieve** what they have lost.

      acknowledge   express sadness for   cry about

5. Victims need to remember the events in all their **complexity**.

      messy detail   complicated tangle   simplicity

6. Silent or silenced voices of victims and **offenders** only deepen the wounds of trauma.

      guilty persons   suffering persons   aggressors

7. Accepting what happened is **essential** for healing to begin.

      unimportant   necessary   required

8. Victims must be able to name and **confront** fears about the "new reality."

      face   avoid   meet

9. Usually there are **multiple** sides of a story.

      very few   many   several

10. It is normal that the "truth" about traumatic events is often **complex**.

      not simple   confusing   easy to understand

11. **Memorializing** is a way humans ensure that what happened and those who died are not forgotten.

      honoring the memory of something   eliminating the shame   remembering a trauma

12. **Rituals** that are part of the culture can help people to acknowledge their loss in healthy ways.

      natural responses   traditional actions   ceremonies

13. Some war **memorials** are healthy expressions of a society's grief for those who died in war.

      reminders   symbols of remembrance   emotions

14. We must allow ourselves space to express thoughts and feelings rather than **suppressing** sadness and tears.

      holding back   exhibiting   stopping

15. Victims face an important decision about whether to show **mercy** to their offenders.

     revenge   kindness   compassion

16. Ensuring **justice** for all is required for establishing peace.

     fairness   legal rights   prejudice

C. Practice your new words. Use what you have learned about the meaning of the new words. Decide which sentence is the best example for each word. The first one has been done for you (see the checked answer)

1. trapped
  a.   √ The leaders could not find a way to get out of the financial difficulties caused by the recession.
  b.   The leaders discussed how to create more jobs so that people could support their families.

2. complex and complexity
  a.   There was one simple cause for the shortage of electricity: the government didn't have enough money to pay for fuel to produce electricity.
  b.   There were many reasons why the government couldn't borrow money from international banks; it's very difficult to explain them all.

3. aware
  a.   The people knew that it would be difficult for their country to recover from the floods.
  b.   The people didn't understand how badly the whole country was damaged by the floods.

4. restoration
  a.   Workers cleared away all the bricks, wood, and trash from the buildings that were destroyed.
  b.   Workers fixed the damaged buildings so that the factory could begin producing shoes again.

5. grieve
  a.   Throughout the country people held a moment of silence to remember the hundreds who died in the flood.
  b.   When everyone woke up, they remembered the dark storm clouds and rain that frightened them yesterday.

6. suppress
  a.   The women were weeping and wailing loudly, showing all their emotions of grief.
  b.   Dressed in black suits, the men stood sadly and silently with their heads bowed.

7. memorializing and memorial
  a.   The community decided to build a park near the river in honor of those who died in the flood.
  b.   The community chose new leaders to help them solve the problems created by the flood.

8. ritual
  a.   The community holds a special program with prayers, songs, and speeches to open the park every spring.
  b.   Members of the community come to the park all the time to relax, play, and enjoy the beautiful scenery.

9. offender
  a.   Several store owners were satisfied that the police tried to protect their stores during the emergency.
  b.   Several people were arrested and jailed for stealing furniture, clothing, and food from stores during the emergency.

10. essential
  a.   Visitors to the jail may bring newspapers and magazines to share with the prisoners.
  b.   Anyone who visits the offenders in jail must first be carefully checked for weapons.

11. confront
   a. ___In court next week, the judge will listen to arguments by the lawyers of the men accused of stealing.
   b. ___In court next week, the men accused of stealing will have to face the shopkeepers whose shops were looted.

12. multiple
   a. ___In order to make a good decision, the judge must discover the truth of what happened.
   b. ___The judge will have to consider every side to the story from the police, the shopkeepers and the accused men.

13. mercy
   a. ___The shopkeepers asked that the men who stole from their shops be given a harsh punishment.
   b. ___The shopkeepers decided that they should forgive the men who stole from their shops.

14. justice
   a. ___The judge decided that the men who stole from the shops should pay money equal to the value of everything they stole.
   b. ___Even though the men stole goods worth hundreds of dollars, the judge warned them not to steal again and let them go free.

D. Word families. In this chapter you learned two pairs of words that belong to the same families. Write your own sentence for each word in the right hand column.

complex (adject) – a way to describe a thing or action that is difficult, complicated, and confusing.

The process of solving a complex social problem may take many years.
The issue of forgiveness is very complex.

complexity (noun) - we use this word to talk about confusion, difficulty, and complication as a kind of abstract thing

The complexity of our country's financial system makes it difficult for the government to take effective action to end the recession.

memorial (noun) - a thing or object that helps us remember
We want to build a memorial for this great leader because he achieved freedom for our country.

The family held a memorial service for their relatives who died in the past year.

memorialize (verb) – the act of creating an object or event to help us remember

It is healthy for people who suffer loss to memorialize those who have died.

Expressions

break free and **break out** – the word *break* (used as a verb) has 68 or more different meanings. The most common meanings relate to *damaging something* or *making it in small pieces.* But in these phrases, the meaning is *to get out of* or *to get away from.* In the first two paragraphs above, who is *breaking free*? What are they *breaking free* from?

break the silence – in this phrase we see the power of poetry at work in language. We see how word meanings can be stretched. Here we see the original meaning of *break* (*to damage* or *destroy*) being extended to something that is not an object—*the silence.* So here the word *break* means *put an end to* (see ch. 9, p.125). In paragraph 2 (above) who is breaking the silence? What are they breaking the silence about?

at the expense of – although we often use the word *expense* in relation to money, this phrase does not normally have anything to do with money. In the text above it means *to the harm of* others or *at the loss of* others. In lines 43-44, *at whose expense* does our victory come?

set out (on) – *Set* is one of those verbs in English that has many meanings and occurs in many different expressions (64 different meanings and 19 different expressions). Some common meanings are *to put* or *place something.* With the preposition *out*, the phrase *set out* can mean *put out*, but it also commonly means *to leave, depart,* or *begin a journey* or *start an activity.* In line 53, who *sets out* on a journey? What kind of journey is it?

GRAMMAR STUDY
The grammar of "I" messages

Because the truth in a violent situation is always complex, we need to acknowledge that we don't have the whole truth. We cannot speak for others involved in the situation. But we can speak honestly for ourselves. We can learn to speak the truth of our own experience without angrily accusing or blaming others.

a. You-messages: angry, blaming, accusing	b. I-messages: honest, fair, not blaming the listener
1a. "Can't you stop interrupting every time I try to say something?"	1b. "I feel that I never get a chance to say what I need to say without being interrupted."
2a. "You people only know how to make threats and engage in name-calling."	2b. "We don't understand what we have done to deserve these threats and bad names."
3a. "You're acting like animals. I have never seen such inhuman behavior before."	3b. "It's hard for me to understand why you have such a harsh attitude against immigrants."

Compare the pairs of messages above.
What makes the *you-messages* sound angry?
Where do sentences in column (a) focus the blame for bad things?
What makes the sentences in column (b) sound honest but more fair than the sentences in (a)?

Look at the grammar of I-messages more closely, so that you can learn to imitate them. Here are four different kinds of grammar structures you can practice with:

Structures	Example sentences
4a. *I think that* + complete sentence 4b. *I feel that* + complete sentence 4c *I don't like the feeling that* + complete sentence	4d. I think that we should be very careful about labeling anyone as evil. 4e. I feel that we don't deserve these threats and bad names. 4f. I don't like the feeling that we are responsible for what happened to your ancestors.

5a. *I feel like** + complete sentence * *feel like + sentence* is much more common in spoken English than *feel as if + sentence*, which is used more in written English	5b. I feel like we are often the victims of prejudice because of our religious beliefs
6a. *I don't understand what/why* + complete sentence	6b. I don't understand why they consider us unpatriotic. 6c. I don't understand what you will gain by denying our right to an education.
7a. *I want (_____) to* + complete verbal group 7b. *It's hard (important) for me to* + complete verbal group	7c. I want the offenders to acknowledge the harm that they did to my family. 7d. I want to speak without being interrupted. 7e. It's hard for me to hear immigrants being abused like this. 7f. It's important for me to see all people treated with respect.

Write your own sentences. Write four sentences—one for each of the types shown above. When you have finished your sentences, share them with a partner for correction and improvement. Then each pair in the class will share their two sentences. Or after writing your sentences, share them with other class members through the give-one/get-one activity.

If you need help to get started, try imagining…
*You are very angry with your friend (parent, brother/sister) because*_____. What will you say?

You disagree very strongly with your teacher (classmate, community leader) on the issue of _____. What will you say?

You have been hurt badly (or wronged) by another person. What will you say?

More practice later
You will have a chance to practice the grammar of I-messages with role plays following the second reading. See the activity called *Readers Theater*.

LIFE SKILLS
Story of Resilience
Read this story about what can happen when people speak the truth.

Develop your reading skills:
Skim to get an idea of the topics covered in the reading. Many articles do not use subheadings (like the first article in this chapter). You can use another method to find the topic of each paragraph: skimming. Read only the first sentence in each paragraph of the article. Many writers in English mention the main topic of each paragraph in the first sentence. You may be puzzled by the word "Bisho" in the title. See if skimming as directed here helps you to answer your question about "Bisho."
Make predictions.
Based on your skimming to find the main topics, what questions do you think the reading will answer? What answers do think the author will provide for those questions? As a way to train yourself to do this, write down your questions and predictions. Based on your skimming, will you be able to predict how this story ends?

Truth Comes Out in Bisho

Archbishop Desmond Tutu served as the chairperson of South Africa's Truth and Reconciliation° Commission.° In 1984 he received the Nobel Peace Prize. One of the stories in his book No Future Without Forgiveness *(1999, Doubleday, pp. 150-51) shares what happened when the truth was told in the town of Bisho.*

In 1995 the new president of South Africa Nelson Mandela established a Truth and Reconciliation Commission to find out the truth of the terrible violence that had occurred in the final years of the old apartheid° system. Mandela was elected in 1994 when South Africa held its first truly democratic elections. Both black and white South Africans voted in these elections. Before that time, the old political system
5   separated black from white South Africans. White South Africans had much more political and economic power than black South Africans.

Soon after the commission began its work, President Mandela spoke these words. "It is only natural that all of us should feel a collective sense of shame for the evils that as compatriots,° we have inflicted° upon one another. But even in the few days of these hearings° we can all attest° to the cleansing power of
10 the truth. It is to this that this Commission is committed. We are committed to the truth so that we can all be free. We are committed to the truth that we can all become reconciled° one to another. There is a very long road ahead. We are only just starting" (http://parishofmillend.blogspot.com/2013/06/truth-and-reconciliation.html).

In 1996 the Truth and Reconciliation Commission held meetings in the city of Bisho. The commission went to Bisho because members of the African National Party had held a protest march there in
15 September 1992. They wanted more political freedom in their country. When the protesters tried to enter a stadium, soldiers had fired at them and killed 30 people.

The meeting place was filled with people. Some of the people had taken part in the march. Some had even been injured in the incident or lost friends and family members. The feelings of tension in the room were very high. One of the first witnesses was the general who commanded the soldiers who shot the
20 marchers. The audience became very angry during his testimony° because he seemed very cold and hard. He seemed unsympathetic to the suffering caused by the shooting.

"The next witnesses were former officers of the defense forces, one white and the others black. The white officer, Colonel Schobesberger, was the speaker. He said that it was true that they had given orders for the soldiers to fire on the crowd. The anger of the audience rose even more. But then Colonel Schobesberger
25 turned toward the audience and said something surprising:

> I say we are sorry. I say the burden of the Bisho massacre° will be on our shoulders for the rest of our lives. We cannot wish it away. It happened. But please, I ask specifically the victims not to forget. I cannot ask you to forget, but I do ask you to forgive us. I ask you to get the soldiers back in the community, to accept them fully. Please try to understand also
30 > the pressure they were under then. This is all I can do. I'm sorry. This I can say, I'm sorry."

"That crowd, which had been close to attacking the witnesses, did something quite unexpected. It broke out into loud applause. Unbelievable! The change in their mood was surprising. The colonel's comrades° joined him in apologizing and when the applause died down." Archbishop Desmond Tutu said,

> "Can we just keep a moment's silence, please, because we are dealing with things that are
35 > very, very deep. It isn't easy, as we all know, to ask for forgiveness and it's also not easy to forgive. But we are people who know that when someone cannot be forgiven, there is no future. If a husband and wife quarrel and one doesn't say 'I'm sorry' and the other says 'I forgive,' the relationship is in danger. We have been given an example by our President, Nelson Mandela, and by many other people."

40 Afterwards, Tutu wrote, "No one could have predicted that day's events at the meeting. It was like someone had waved a magic wand.° The wand changed anger and tension into a display of communal° forgiveness and acceptance of the people who did the killing. We could only be humbled by it all. We were deeply thankful that ordinary people could be so generous° and gracious"°

°reconciliation (n.) – peace, friendship
°commission (n.) – a committee, a group working together to do special work
°compatriots (n.) – fellow citizens, people belonging to the same country
°inflicted (v.) - caused something bad
°hearing (n.) – meeting at which witnesses will be heard
°reconciled (v.) – became friends, became at peace
°testimony (n.) – words that represent official evidence in a trial or committee meeting
°massacre (n.) – killing of many innocent people at one time
°comrades (n.) – fellow soldiers
°wand (n.) – a special stick
°communal (n.) – of the community, collective, related to the group
°generous (adj.) – liberal, giving freely
°gracious (adj.) – full of grace or mercy

Understand what you read

How well did you understand the reading? Which of the following sentences are true and which are false? How would you change the false sentences to make them correct?

1. ___White and Black South Africans were treated equally before 1994.

2. ___Mandela said that telling the truth would bring about freedom for everyone in South Africa.

3. ___The African National Party was not satisfied with the political system and held a protest march in Bisho.

4. ___Soldiers stopped the Truth and Reconciliation Commission (TRC) when they tried to enter a stadium.

5. ___Some persons directly affected by the Bisho massacre attended the TRC hearings.

6. ___The commanding general was very sorry for the suffering his troops had caused.

7. ___Colonel Schobesberger told the victims that they should forgive and forget what happened.

8. ___The angry crowd began attacking these witnesses.

9. ___Archbishop Tutu was very surprised by the crowd's response to Col. Schobesberger's request.

10. ___One could have predicted that the TRC meeting that day would produce forgiveness, peace, & friendship .

Discuss

1. Nelson Mandela said that the truth is a cleansing power that can bring reconciliation. How does the story about the hearing in Bisho help you understand what he meant?
2. How do you understand this story in the light of the earlier reading in this chapter "Truth: The first stop on the healing journey"?
3. Look at the words of Colonel Schobesberger. What examples of I-messages do you see in his speech?

Teacher Story

Listen to your teacher tell a story about one time when telling the truth was very difficult or when hearing the truth was very important to her or him.

Discuss

Continue the discussion you had earlier on these questions: How can telling the truth about events be difficult or even dangerous? What creates safety? How can we influence truth-telling so that the result tends toward reconciliation?

EXTEND YOUR LEARNING

1. Journal
Choose one of the topics below to write about in your journal.
1 Write about a time when telling the truth was very difficult or hearing the truth was very important to you.
2. Write about a situation in your country or community's past or present where the truth is very complex.

2. Visual Arts
Think of a trauma or loss in your life or in the life of your community or nation. Make a memorial or draw a picture of a memorial. If you like photography, you can take photos. If you are good with computers, you can make a PowerPoint slide show or a web page. If you like to build things or make 3-dimensional images, you can do that, too. Prepare a short explanation of your memorial to share with the class.

Possible project: If there was recently a loss in the community where you live, what can your class do to help memorialize that loss?

3. Readers Theater
1) Work together to make the story "Truth Comes Out in South Africa" into a drama.
2) First, decide who the characters will be in this drama.
3) How many scenes will this drama have?
4) You can divide into groups to write dialogue for the different characters. When you write the lines for the general and for Colonel Schobesberger, remember to show the difference between I-messages and you-messages. Use the grammar you learned for making I-messages.
5) After you have written out the dialogue, practice reading it.
6) Then act out the drama. Do not use any special props or costumes. Just mime the actions.
7) Don't memorize your lines. Just read them.

Discuss: How did you feel when you were watching the drama? If you were playing one of the parts, how did you feel about your character?

4. Music
Listen to a song chosen by the class or to one of the following songs. What does the song suggest to about the complexity of the truth?
"Truth Hides" by the British electronica band Asian Dub Foundation which performs music that is a mixture of different cultural influences
    Lyrics: http://www.poemhunter.com/song/truth-hides/
    Performance: http://www.youtube.com/watch?v=KJtx3qZCZc0&playnext=1&list=PL4B74A09F7B87EBF7
"Truth?" by the British heavy metal band Def Leppard
    Lyrics: http://www.poemhunter.com/song/truth-original-version/
    Performance: http://www.youtube.com/watch?v=mrz4J1C1vnw
"What is truth?" by US country music icon Johnny Cash
    Performance with lyrics: http://www.youtube.com/watch?v=S0KQWTBljjg

5. Circle process
Hold a student-led circle to discuss any topic you choose. If there have been any disagreements because the truth about an issue was very complex, you can use the circle to process class members' feelings about that issue. Or you can use the circle to discuss the self-assessment (below).

SELF-ASSESSMENT
Think about your learning. Complete a self-assessment for this chapter by using the template at the end of the text.

> *Learning Tip: The meaning of texts is not always clear.*
> *There is not only one right way to understand a text.*

Chapter 12 – Daring to Forgive

Get to Know Each Other Better
How much of a risk will you take?
Work together as a class to make and play a simple ball toss game.
a. Get a large bucket or a waste basket and three small balls or bean bags. Even a tightly wadded newspaper could be used as a ball. Be creative in whatever materials you use for the game.
b. Draw three lines with chalk at the following distances from the bucket—one line 4 feet away; the next line 6 feet away; and the last line 8 feet away.
c. Every class member will get three chances to throw the ball in the bucket.
d. They must choose which line to throw from, and they have to throw all three times from the one line that they chose on their first throw.
e. Volunteers from the class will keep a record of students' choices and points. Write names, line choices and the score on the white board for all to see.
f. Scoring will be as follows: 10 points for each ball in the bucket from the first line; 15 points for each ball in the bucket from the second line; 20 points for each ball in the bucket from the third line.

At the end of the game discuss these questions:
1. Which class members took the least risk (choosing line 1)? Why did they take this level of risk?
2. Which class members took the highest risk (choosing line 3)? Why did they take this level of risk?
3. How did the class members do on their scoring compared with the amount of risk that they took? Who tended to have the highest scores—the high, the low or the medium risk-takers?
4. What did you learn about yourself or any of your classmates by doing this activity?

Connect to the Topic
In chapter 9 you learned that children who have suffered sexual abuse sometimes engage in risky sexual behaviors as they grow older. These behaviors put the child in danger of being harmed. These are not good risks to take. But not all risks in life are bad, even if they are dangerous. It's risky to drive in some cities because of the crowded highways and fast-moving cars. We take these kinds of risks all the time. The risks we want to consider in this chapter will feel very dangerous to those who have suffered trauma. It may be the risk of meeting and talking with the person(s) who hurt them. It may even be the risk of forgiving the aggressor. Are these risks worth taking? Think about this question as you work through this chapter.

Look at the pictures
1. Describe the two pictures below. What is similar and different about the two pictures?
2. What do you know about snails? How do snails behave?
3. The diagram on the right is called "the snail model" of the trauma healing journey. What parts of the snail model are already familiar to you from your study so far?

Are snails daring?
Do snails take risks?

Pearson Scott Foresman / Wikimedia Commons

Breaking Cycles of Violence • Building Resilience

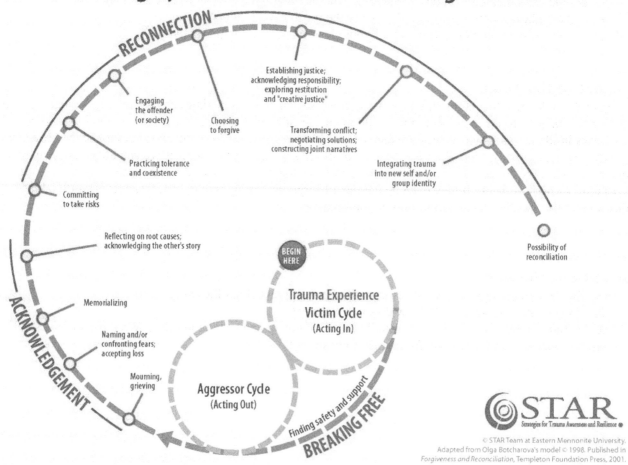

RECONNECTION

Engaging
the offender
(or society)

Choosing
to forgive

Establishing justice;
acknowledging responsibility;
exploring restitution
and "creative justice"

Transforming conflict;
negotiating solutions;
constructing joint narratives

Practicing tolerance
and coexistence

Committing
to take risks

Integrating trauma
into new self and/or
group identity

Reflecting on root causes;
acknowledging the other's story

Possibility of
reconciliation

BEGIN
HERE

Trauma Experience
Victim Cycle
(Acting In)

Memorializing

Naming and/or
confronting fears;
accepting loss

ACKNOWLEDGEMENT

Mourning,
grieving

Aggressor Cycle
(Acting Out)

Finding safety and support

BREAKING FREE

STAR
Strategies for Trauma Awareness and Resilience ®

© STAR Team at Eastern Mennonite University.
Adapted from Olga Botcharova's model © 1998. Published in
Forgiveness and Reconciliation, Templeton Foundation Press, 2001.

Eastern Mennonite University STAR Program

READ

The Complexity of Forgiveness

The apartheid[1] government of South Africa did not like Father Michael Lapsley. Lapsley was an Anglican[2] minister from New Zealand who came to South Africa. He served as a **chaplain** to black and white students. He **protested** government violence against schoolchildren. Eventually he became a member of Nelson Mandela's African National Party, which worked for **equality** between blacks and whites. Lapsley had to flee South Africa and lived for a while in the neighboring country of Zimbabwe. In 1990 he received some religious magazines in the mail. Hidden inside the magazines was a bomb. When it exploded, he lost both hands and the sight in one eye. It is almost certain that this bomb was sent to him by the South African **authorities**.

Reflecting on the Roots of Trauma

It is hard to remember that the people who hurt us are human beings. To protect ourselves, we may sometimes think of them as something less than human. Instead, we could ask, "Why did they do this to us?" Asking WHY questions is a sign of strength. It is a sign that we want to hear truth and **achieve** justice and peace.

We can take the WHY questions a step further. We can wonder, "Have the offenders been hurt, too?" Reflecting on the history of the offenders helps us understand and address root causes of the trauma. Fr. Michael Lapsley **identifies** some questions that individuals and groups need to ask to understand the roots of trauma.

What was done to me?	What was done to us?
What did I do to others?	What did we do to others?
What I did I fail to do?	What did we fail to do?

These are extremely difficult questions for a traumatized individual, group or nation to ask. Most victims of trauma will not be able to reflect on all of these questions until much time has passed.

Taking the risk

Asking these questions is risky. In answering the questions, we may understand why someone harmed us. And this understanding may lead us to realize that we ourselves can feel safe only if everyone around us feels safe. This realization may motivate us to **approach** those who harmed us. There are several ways of **approaching** them. We could work on a project together. We could learn together or participate in healing rituals. Through these activities we listen and start to understand their story. Honestly telling our own story and listening to their story or personal experience is a powerful way to create a space and a relationship where we may choose to forgive. But this is all a very risky business.

---

[1] See the second reading in chapter 10 to review what *apartheid* means and what the situation was in South Africa under the apartheid government.
[2] *Anglican* means "of the Church of England" – the main Protestant denomination in England and in English-speaking countries like Australia, New Zealand, and Canada.

Choosing to Forgive

Some people say, "Just forgive and forget." If we forget what happened, how can we make sure it will not be repeated again? If we do not forgive, will we be **tempted** to take revenge? We could say instead,
35 "Don't forgive and forget, but remember and change." Forgiveness is a choice we can make. To forgive is to gain peace by taking responsibility for our feelings of anger, fear, or humiliation because of the harm done. Forgiveness is a gift we give ourselves so that the harm done does not continue to control our lives and rob us of joy.

Forgiveness is complex
40 Father Michael Lapsley has never had a chance to forgive the person who sent him the letter bomb. No one has ever admitted responsibility for that act. Lapsley says that he is not full of **bitterness** or hatred. But even if someone came to his door and asked for forgiveness, he would have to ask some tough questions. He might speak to that person in words like these: "While of course I've forgiven you, you can't give me back my hands. They've gone forever and I will need to employ somebody to assist me for the rest of my life. Of
45 course, you will now help pay for that person."

The way out of trauma is a journey. And forgiveness is a complex part of that journey. Forgiveness, says Lapsley, "requires a **generosity** of spirit and ... **grace**." This is a journey that victims and offenders must **ultimately** walk together.

UNDERSTAND WHAT YOU READ
Choose the best answer to complete each sentence.

1. Michael Lapsley was attacked by
   a) terrorists   b) the government of South Africa   c) the African National Congress

2. Lapsley was attacked because he
   a) was against violence   b) was a Christian minister   c) promoted the equality of black people

3. Forgiveness is difficult because
   a) those who hurt us are inhuman   b) we need to protect ourselves from more harm   c) both a & b

4. People show they are getting ready to forgive when they begin asking a question like this:
   a)   Why did the offender do this to me?
   b)   What did the offender do to me?
   c)   How can I make the offender pay for this?

5. An important step in choosing to forgive is to
   a)   get to know the offenders by listening to their story
   b)   tell the story of our hurt to the offenders
   c)   both a & b

6. Those who forgive receive benefits such as
   a)   complete healing from their trauma
   b)   freedom from being controlled by harmful emotions
   c)   enjoying the humiliation of their offenders

7. The reading advises us not to forget the bad things that were done to us so that we can
   a)   remember and change   b) take revenge on offenders   c) protect ourselves from more harm

8. If we don't choose to forgive then we may…
   a) seek revenge   b) be filled with hatred   c) both a & b

9. According to the reading, forgiveness can mean that
   a)   the forgiver will decide a punishment for the offender
   b)   the offender would have to pay for the harm done
   c)   the forgiver must become the friend of the offender

10. The main idea of this reading can be summarized best in which sentence?
    a) Forgiveness is a long, complex, and difficult process.
    b) We should not forgive and forget but remember and change.
    c) Forgiveness is a journey that victims and offenders walk together.

Discuss
1. What is forgiveness? What is forgiveness not?
2. What makes forgiveness difficult?
3. According to the text, what are the benefits of forgiveness?
4. To what extent do you agree with this author about the importance of forgiveness?

WORD STUDY
A. Define it yourself!

identify (line 16) _____
                    (notice what follows this sentence)

approach (lines 26, 27) _____
                    (notice the examples that come after the second use of this word)

Word meanings
B. *First, match the vocabulary from the reading (in the left column) with the meanings in the right column.*

1. ___achieve	a)	a worker who meets the spiritual needs of others
2. ___authorities	b)	the people who have power, officials
3. ___bitterness	c)	finally, in the end
4. ___chaplain	d)	mercy, kindness
5. ___equality	e)	to reach, gain, get, win
6. ___generosity	f)	to attract, dare, test
7. ___grace	g)	being the same in importance or power
8. ___protest	h)	pain, distress, intense anger, hatred
9. ___tempt	i)	giving, readiness to give, freedom from being mean or nasty
10. ___ultimately	j)	to speak or act against something, to complain

C. *Now use these words in the sentences below. The words* identify *and* approach, *which you defined, will also be used in these sentences. You should think of this story as being similar to the one about the riot in Bisho at the end of chapter 12.*

1. Large crowds filled the street and _____ the government's unfair laws that were causing black people such great hardships.

2. They wanted _____ for blacks and whites, so that black people would have a fair chance for education and employment.

3. As the crowd _____ the security forces, they began firing.

4. When the people reflected on what happened, they realized that the security forces were not savages. Rather, they were _____ to shoot because they felt threatened by the angry crowd.

5. Even though the security forces fired on the crowds, there was some indication that the political _____ may have given them the order to shoot.

6. After a long investigation, the judges _____ the head of the security forces as responsible for this massacre.

7. As a _____ in a hospital, Maria visited all those who were wounded and prayed with them.

8. Some of the wounded were full of hatred and _____ toward the security forces.

9. Some of the soldiers expressed sympathy for the wounded. And some survivors of the attack affirmed these soldiers for their _____ and compassion.

10. The people showed great _____ by giving enough money to pay for all the hospital expenses.

11. The people engaged in actions like this until they _____ their goal.

12. _____, they transformed their country into a just and peaceful society for all people.

D. More practice. *Play the game "Take Two" with your new vocabulary. Here are the rules.*
1. Divide the class into two or more teams.
2. Write all the 14 words on the board in two columns (7 in one column and 7 in the other)
3. Your teacher will put a number 1 beside two words (one from each column).
4. Teams must make one sentence that uses both of those words.
5. The team members may all work together in creating the sentence, and every person on your team must take a turn in saying a sentence. (One team member may not be the only spokesperson.)
6. If your team makes a good sentence, you may choose the next two words by putting a 2 beside them (and so on).
7. When all the words have been used up, you can erase the numbers and start again using new combinations of words.

Example: Suppose that the first two words are *bitterness* and *tempt*. A sentence that combines these two words would be: In my *bitterness* I was *tempted* to shout at my boss because he ordered me to work on the weekend.

Word family: In this chapter you learned the word *identify*. This word belongs to the same family as the word *identity* that you studied in chapter 10. Study the information in the left column. Then make your own sentences to remember these words in the right column.

identity (noun) – your identity is who you are, it is made up of many things—your physical appearance, your relationships, your habits, your beliefs, etc.

*Chapter 4 kept the real **identity** of Carlos a secret because his family is in danger.*

*When people immigrate to a new country, often their **identity** changes.*

identify (verb) – to identify something is to say what it is; to identify someone is to say who they are; you recognize things and people by their characteristics

*After studying chapter 3, you were able to **identify** several kinds of violence.*

*Can you **identify** the parts of your body where you feel stress?*

Expressions

root – You may know that a *root* is the part of a plant that grows under the ground. But you also know that paragraphs 2 and 3 of the text above are not discussing plants! Here *root* means the beginning or source of something. The writer of this article is interested in finding the source of what?

take _____ a step further – To *take a step* normally has to do with walking. But you can see in line 15, that the writer is not talking about walking. In fact, he writes about *taking questions a step further*. The word *step* has many different meanings and is used in a dozen or more idioms. Here *a step* means a mental action. To *take WHY questions a step further* is to develop other questions, to move forward in asking more questions.

of course – This phrase is used sometimes as a way of saying "Yes." **Host:** *Would you like some more tea?* **Guest:** *Of course.* In lines 42 to 44 above, *of course* has the meaning of *yes*, but it also gives the idea of a certain assumption. *Yes, you may certainly assume that I have forgiven you.* And *yes, you may certainly assume* that you will help to pay for my assistant.

Practice with the expressions:
1. What are the problems and issues that you would like to find **the roots of**?
2. What skills or knowledge do you have that you would like to **take a step further**?
3. About what facts or truths do you have certain assumptions? (For example, if you have a good teacher, **of course,** you will have to do homework to prepare for the next class.)

GRAMMAR STUDY

A. **Statements of purpose.** There are two common ways in English of talking about the reasons for actions or the results that we expect actions to achieve. One way is shown in sentences 1 and 2 below. The second way is shown in sentences 3 and 4.

lines	Action (mental or physical)	Purpose, reason, or desired result
	Sentence	*to + verb + object or complement*
16	1. Individuals and groups need to ask questions like these	**to understand** the root causes of trauma.
43	2. I will need to employ somebody	**to assist** me for the rest of my life
	Sentence	*so that + sentence*
35	3. Forgiveness is a gift we give ourselves	**so that** the harm done does not continue to control our lives and rob us of joy.
	4. Political leaders demonize national enemies	**so that** they can justify a war.

You will also sometimes see the words *in order* placed in front of *to* as a way of signaling the purpose. For example:

5. Individuals and groups need to ask questions like these **in order** to understand the root causes of trauma.

You can see in lines 11-12 of the reading that sometimes it is possible, or even desirable, to give the reason or purpose *first* in the sentence:

6. **To protect** ourselves, we may sometimes think of them as something less than human.

Can you rewrite sentence #1 above so that it is like #6? Can you rewrite sentence #2 so that it uses the phrase *in order to* (like #5)? Which version of the sentences do you like the best? Talk about the sentences with your teacher.

Matching: Match these sentence parts to make statements that are true. Write the letter of the ending that makes the best sense for each sentence. Compare your answers with a partner. If you have different answers, discuss them. Are they equally good?

1 The South African authorities sent Father Michael Lapsley a bomb ___

a) **to find out** why they harmed us

2 We reflect on the history of the offenders ___

b) **in order to listen to and start understanding** <u>their</u> story.

3 We may approach those who harmed us ___

c) **so that** he would die in the explosion.

4 Victims could work on a project together with offenders ___

d) **so that** we can make sure it won't happen again.

5 We should honestly tell our own story and listen to their story ___

e) **so that** we may understand and address the root causes of trauma.

6 Even though we have forgiven the offender, we need to remember what happened ___

f) **to create** a space and a relationship where they may choose to forgive.

Practice: Now you answer these questions by using clauses of purpose like the ones above. Notice that the word **why** in these questions is not asking you to explain a cause but to explain the <u>purpose</u> for doing something.
Example: *Why might victims work together with offenders on a project?*
Victims might work together with offenders on a project <u>to create a space and relationship where they may choose to forgive</u>.

1. Why do victims use rituals?
2. Why do people create memorials?
3. Why do trauma victims need to tell their stories to others?
4. Why do we encourage a trauma victim to use body/mind exercises, like EFT tapping exercises, deep breathing and other relaxation techniques?
5. Why do some victims choose to forgive those who harmed them?

B. **Modals.**

One must be very careful in writing or speaking about the topic of forgiveness. It is a very difficult and complex topic. The last thing the writer of the article above wants to do is to tell hurting people that they <u>must</u> forgive those who have hurt them. The writer makes us <u>feel</u> the complexity of forgiveness by using lots of modals. Look, for example, at the fifth paragraph; the modals have been highlighted for you. Note that almost every sentence has a modal.

Understanding why someone harmed us **may** lead us to realize that we ourselves **can** feel safe only if <u>everyone</u> around us feels safe. This realization **may** motivate us to approach those who harmed us. There are several ways of approaching them. We **could** work on a project together. We **could** learn together or participate in healing rituals. Through these activities we listen and start to understand <u>their</u> story. Honestly telling our own story and listening to their story or personal experience is a powerful way to create a space and a relationship where we **may** choose to forgive.

Notice what the writer chooses **not** to say:
1. Understanding why someone harmed us **will** lead us to realize that we ourselves **will** feel safe only if <u>everyone</u> around us feels safe.

2. This realization **will** motivate us to approach those who harmed us.
     [*Comment:* Understanding why someone harmed us *might* lead us to hate that person more, and we *might* feel less safe than we did before. We *might* want to avoid this hated person more than ever.]

150

3. We **should** work on a project together. We **should** learn together or participate in healing rituals.
   [*Comment:* The writer of the text felt that she had no right to tell us what we *ought to do*. Instead, the writer offered suggestions or possibilities. We *could* do these things as a way to experience healing from our trauma.]

4. Honestly telling our own story and listening to their story or personal experience is a powerful way to create a space and a relationship where we **choose** to forgive.
   [*Comments:* The writer did *not* claim that this is a process that always leads to forgiveness. Forgiveness is possible, but it all depends on the choice made by the traumatized person. We cannot force anyone to forgive.]

Now you try it. Look at the next paragraph (the sixth paragraph). First, highlight all the modals. Then notice what the writer chose <u>not</u> to say. Why did the writer choose to use the modals that she did? Discuss your answers with the class.

LIFE SKILLS
Story of Resilience
Read this story of a man who took the risk of forgiving.

> **Develop your reading skills:**
> **Re-read.** Remember that you will not deeply understand a text in isolation on its first reading. You have already read and discussed a text about forgiveness in this chapter. When you read the second text, you will want to read it quickly once to get the main ideas in the story. Then read it again more slowly.
> **Make critical comparisons.** When you read the second time, compare the experience narrated in this story with the ideas about forgiveness in the first text. Before the second reading, you might want to review any notes that you made about the first text.

Escaping Anger through Forgiveness
by David Works

On December 9, 2007 a gunman attacked David Works and his family in a church parking lot in Colorado Springs, Colorado. Two daughters were killed and David was seriously wounded. This version of David's story is based on his telling it to an audience at Eastern Mennonite University in September 2009. As a descendant of Thomas Jefferson who has worked to "understand, acknowledge and heal the persistent wounds of slavery," David was a co-recipient of the Common Ground Award in 2010. You begin reading David's story when he is in the intensive care unit at the hospital the night after the attack.

It was some time after 11 or 12 at night. I was all alone, a little like Jacob having to wrestle with God.° "Where were You, God?" No answer. Dead quiet. A song came to my mind: "Lord to whom shall we go? You have the words of eternal° life?" That's all I had to hang on to.

⁵ The next morning the news came on. I watched just a little because that's all I could take. But I wanted to know what happened. I found out that a young man named Mathew Murray was behind the shooting. I'd never heard of him in my life. The news lasted a minute or two. I turned it off and went into a mini-rage.° "Listen, buddy, if ya gotta beef,° don't take it out on me and my innocent family." So I simmered° with that a little bit and I realized somehow that this was not going work for me. I had enough problems, and I didn't need to deal with <u>me</u>, too.

¹⁰ I was totally drugged out° because of all the pain. And I was trying to sort everything out. "How do I get out of this mess? I can't be wallowing° in anger the rest of my life." I didn't know what to do and all of a sudden a picture flashed into my mind: the snail diagram° that I learned about in trauma awareness training. The diagram shows how to break out of patterns of retribution° and revenge.

I thought, "No, I don't want to get into those cycles of violence because I know that once I get started ¹⁵ in there, I'll never get out." I said, "Okay, I'm not going to be mad at this guy." My wife came in and I told her about it. She remembered how excited I was, talking about the snail diagram when I came back from a seminar two years ago. So I told the whole family, "This is what we're going to do."

That's what we did. I was in the hospital for nine days, three days in intensive care, six days up on

20   the ward. The day after I got out, we did a memorial service for my daughters.

          I had seen on the news where the Murray family had already met with the families of the other victims of their son's killing spree.° My pastor called me and said, "I'm having the Murrays come because I think they have a need to see what their son did, where he did it, and also where he died."

          The Murrays came to the church and met us in the pastor's office. I can't tell you how surreal° that is

25   to meet the parents of the one who's killed your daughters. A tall man, Mr. Murray came in all slumped° over. He had been crying. He held out his hand. I said "No, we're not doing that." I grabbed my wife and we hugged them for 15-20 minutes, told them we forgave them, told them they didn't owe us anything because we didn't have any financial needs for the immediate future.° What more could they do? What more could the community do? This is practical Christianity. It's making something good out of something bad.

This story is a written and edited transcript of a spoken presentation made by David Works and used with his permission. You can read the complete story in the book by David and Marie Works, Gone in a Heartbeat: Our Daughters Died...Our Faith Endures. *ISBN: 978-1-58997-548-4. Tyndale House, 2008.*

°Jacob wrestling with God – reference to a story in the Hebrew Bible when Jacob, father of the 12 tribes of the Jewish nation, wrestled with an angel of God all night
°eternal (adj.) – lasting forever
°mini-rage (n.) – a small fit of anger
°ya gotta beef (idiom) – you have a complaint
°simmer (v.) – literally this means *to cook on a low heat*; here it means *to be in a low state of anger*
°drugged out (adj. from the verb *drug*) – under the effects of medicine and not thinking clearly
°wallowing (v.) – to lie or roll around in something comfortably
°snail diagram (n.+n.) – the healing path from trauma to resilience (see the diagram on p. 141)
°spree (n.) – a time of wild or careless activity
°surreal (adj.) – seeming to be real but not real; strange, like a dream
°slumped (adj. from the v. *slump*) – bent over, head and shoulders down
°immediate future (adj. + n.) – near future (as opposed to the far-away future)

Understand what you read

First find the correct ending for each sentence. Write the letter of the best sentence ending in the blank at the end of the sentence beginning. Then number the sentences in order so that they follow the order of events in the story. One has been done as an example for you.

___ He listened to the news for a little ___   a) he quickly thought about the benefits of forgiving the man who murdered his daughters.

___ The Murray family visited the church ___   b) to show their forgiveness to Matthew's parents.

___ He became angry with Matthew Murray, ___   c) the family held a memorial service for their daughters.

_1_ While he was alone at night in his hospital bed, _f_   d) to see what their son did, where he did it, and where he died.

___ After David got out of the hospital, ___   e) so that they wouldn't be stuck in the cycles of violence.

___ The Works family met with the Murrays ___   f) David wondered where God was in this time of trauma.

___ Because David remembered his training in trauma awareness, ___   g) who had attacked his innocent family in the church parking lot.

___ He told his family that they were going to forgive Matthew Murray ___   h) so that he could find out what happened.

Discuss
1. What do you learn from comparing David Work's experience with the chapter's main reading and what it teaches about forgiveness? How would you compare David Works to Michael Lapsley?
2. Because David Works studied trauma awareness, that affected how he responded to this trauma in his life. Now that you have been studying trauma and resilience, have you noticed any difference in the way that you respond to life's difficulties?
3. Do the readings for this chapter suggest that you need to be a religious person to believe in forgiveness? What do you think is the relationship between religious faith and forgiveness?

EXTEND YOUR LEARNING

1. Journal
Write about one or more of the following topics in your journal.
1. Why do you think the snail is a good model or not a good model for the trauma healing journey?
2. Can you identify any stages in the snail model that you have personally experienced?
3. Are there any religious practices that you draw on to get strength in difficult times?

2. Music
Listen to "Forgiving You Was Easy" by Willie Nelson
www.youtube.com/watch?v=u0kYf9KG9QA
At age 77 Country singer Willie Nelson is still going strong, performing regularly. He started taking music lessons when he was 6 years old; wrote his first song at age 7; and played in a small band when he was 9. His first album came out in 1962 and since that time he has recorded more than a hundred albums. He has also recorded music for more than 30 films. His 1984 song "Forgiving You Was Easy" was number one in the US and Canada. The lyrics of the song can be found on the AZ Lyrics website:
http://www.azlyrics.com/lyrics/willienelson/forgivingyouwaseasy.html

Discuss
1. What kind of difficulty or loss is the singer telling about? How would you compare his loss to other losses that we have read about in this chapter? Do you think his loss is any less overwhelming to him than the other losses?
2. Why was it easy for the singer to forgive the person who wronged him? Having paid careful attention to the phrase "forgive and forget" in the first reading, what do think about the singer's attitude toward forgiving and forgetting?
3. What was your opinion of the American country western music style of this song? Does this musical style work well with words like these?

   Explore on your own: Do a Youtube search for songs containing the words "forgive and forget." Or go to elyrics.net and type the search terms; choose to search "within the text" of songs.

3. Movement
Struggling with complex issues like truth, forgiveness, justice and peace can be stressful. The stress of reading and discussing in English will tire you out. Give yourself an energy message. You can use this energy massage anytime you are feeling a little tired in class or while you are studying at home.

Energy massage 1
Make a claw with one hand.
Relax your hand.
Make a claw with your hand.
Place your hand at your navel, thumb pointing up.

With the thumb and your finger of your other hand, find your collar bone
Slide your fingers down to your first rib.
Find a tender spot between the collar bone and rib.
Gently massage that point.
While you do this, put your tongue on the roof of your mouth.

[In the future, if the teacher says "Give yourself an energy massage," follow this procedure.]

Energy massage 2
Place your clawed hand at your navel, thumb pointing up.
Tap <u>above</u> your lips with your fingertips.
Tap <u>below</u> your lips with your fingertips.
Tap seven times above and seven times below your lips.
Keep your tongue on the roof of your mouth while you do this.

4. Circle process
Hold a student-led circle to discuss any topic you choose. If there have been any disagreements because you had different opinions about forgiveness, you can use the circle to process class members' feelings about that issue. Or you can use the circle to discuss the self-assessment (below).

SELF-ASSESSMENT
Think about your learning. Complete a self-assessment for this chapter by using the template at the end of the text (p. 194).

Learning Tip: Don't be afraid to ask your teacher about things that were <u>unclear</u> to you. If you ask a question in class, the answer will not only help you, but it will also help your classmates. And you will be a good example for other students to imitate.

Chapter 13 - Seeking Justice

Get to Know Each Other Better

Bean-bag-toss questions. Make a large chart divided into 10 boxes with the following questions in them. Lay the chart on the floor in front of the class. One student will come to the front. Standing 3 feet away from the chart, the student will gently toss a small bean bag (or coin) onto the chart. The teacher will read the question on which the bean bag lands and the student must answer it. This student will remain in the front while the next student comes forward and tosses the bean bag. The first student will read the question and the second student answers it. The first student sits down while the third student comes to the front of the class to take a turn with the bean bag. Each student may have as many turns to answer a question as the class likes.

1. How do you feel about people who blame others for problems?	2. How important is it for you to be understood by others?
3. How do you feel about people who do not follow the rules?	4. How important is it for you to fight for what is right?
5. How do you feel about people who do not do what they say they will do?	6. How do you feel when you see people being treated unfairly?
7. How do you feel about people who judge and criticize others?	8. How do you feel about watching violence on television and in movies?
9. How do you feel about people who are very honest and direct in stating their opinions?	10. How do you feel when you are around persons who have power?

Discuss the activity
1. What interesting things did you learn about your classmates by listening to their answers?
2. How many class members were able to toss the bean bag onto the question that they wanted to answer?
3. If the bean bag fell on a question that you did not want to answer, how did you feel about answering that question?

Connect to the Topic

The activity you have just done may reveal the way your class feels or thinks about justice. Maybe you felt it was unfair that you had to answer a question you did not want to answer. Maybe some of you feel uncomfortable about those who judge or have power over the lives of others. You may not like it when people blame others for problems, or you may think it is important to find out who should be blamed for problems. Maybe some of you have a strong sense of what is right. You don't like it when others break the rules. Perhaps you want to fight for what is right and help those who are being treated unfairly. You may feel ill-treated when others don't take time to understand you. As you can imagine, victims of trauma are very concerned about justice. But what is justice? Are there different kinds of justice?

155

Look at the pictures
Describe what you see in each picture.
Suppose that each one of these pictures says something about justice. What do you think each picture says about justice?

Jon Gehman

READ

Punishment or Restoration?

Defining justice

(1)   **Justice** is not easy to define. It is a complex concept with several **components**. Doing justice requires power. Those who have power can **ensure** that all people get the benefits that they have a right to receive. They can also use their power to demand **penalties** against those who harm others or take away their
5   rights in the community. Justice ensures fairness.

(2)   Justice is about making sure the right thing is done. It is about <u>fair laws</u> and <u>equal treatment</u> under those laws. Justice or **injustice** is present in families, schools, communities, societies and the world. Injustice often gives rise to violence. If we become targets of violence, it is probably because there are conditions of **inequality** in the world around us.

10   ### Different approaches to justice

(3)   People deal with injustice in different ways. Some people do nothing and are harmed over and over again. Others take "justice" into their own hands and get revenge for the violence they have suffered. In countries where the rule of law is well established, people allow the police to arrest offenders. Then the courts decide how to punish them according to the laws. In some communities there may be a council of
15   elders or leaders who approach justice in a very different way. These communities **pursue** justice as a healing process for the whole community. They bring together the offenders and victims. They decide how to make things right and help both the victim and offender to take their place in the community again.

The justice you get depends on the questions you ask

(4)   Below are two sets of questions that **illustrate** two contrasting approaches to justice. Imagine that
20   Tomas has stolen the jacket of his classmate Amadou. What would bring justice in this situation?
One set of questions focuses on the one who did the harm and the punishment he deserves.

        What happened? _____
        Who is to blame? _____
        What is the punishment? _____
25   The other set of questions focuses on meeting the needs of all affected by the violence. They ask you to consider the harm that was done to Amadou and find a solution that would make things right for all parties.

        What happened? _____
        Who has been affected and how? _____
        What do those affected need? _____
30   How can we make things right? _____
Take time to write the answers to the questions before you read on.

Retributive justice

(5)   The first set of questions above is typical of retributive justice. This kind of justice makes offenders pay some kind of penalty for their actions. The central African country of Rwanda provides an example. In
35   just 100 days in 1994 an **estimated** 800,000 people were killed because they belonged to a certain **ethnic** group. This kind of killing is called genocide. Once the situation **stabilized**, the government began trials for those accused of participating in the genocide. About 22 people were publically **executed** for leading in the **genocide**. By 2002 there were 120,000 people in Rwandan jails on charges of genocide. These are examples of retributive justice. The focus is almost solely on punishing the persons who did the crime by giving them
40   prison time or the death penalty.

Restorative justice

(6)   The second set of questions above is typical of restorative justice. The aim of restorative justice is to find some way to make things as right as possible for all people affected by the violence. This means rebuilding right relationships among people. The 120,000 Rwandans jailed for genocide were many more
45   than the country's prisons could safely hold. In addition, there were several hundred thousand more **suspected** of genocide crimes. The retributive approach could not deal with so many offenders. Thus, the

157

Can you find a picture or video on the Internet of a Rwandan *gacaca* (pronounced ga-CHA-cha) **court?**

50

government allowed local village courts called *gacaca* courts to **try** offenders. The accused who come before the *gacaca* court have a chance to confess their guilt. If they admit their guilt, then they are **sentenced** to a reduced time in prison with additional years of community service.

(7)   Former prisoners returning to their communities frequently find it difficult to settle again into community life. Their property has been taken away, their homes lie in ruins, and their **livestock** are long since lost. People in their home villages, especially those who survived the genocide, distrust the returnees. 55 In some villages, a program has begun that provides **structured**, safe spaces in which offenders and victims can meet each other to request and grant forgiveness. But the program takes justice a step further in arranging for victims and offenders to work on teams building houses for needy members of the community.*

(8)   Restorative justice allows victims to meet their offenders. With the support of the community, victims can question the offender and tell freely about the pain that the offender caused them. The offender has a chance to admit guilt, express sorrow for what he or she did, and ask for forgiveness. The community finds ways that the offender can make things right for the whole community and be restored to its life.

*Information on *gacaca* courts and the reintegration program comes from MCC Peace Office Newsletter 39.2 (April-June 2009).

UNDERSTAND WHAT YOU READ

1. Identify the <u>four</u> words or phrases that are part of what justice is. Cross out the words or phrases that are <u>not</u> part of what justice is.
   a) inequality
   b) fair laws
   c) power to make things right
   d) getting all the benefits
   e) penalties for harming others
   f) rights for all people

2. Choose the <u>one</u> statement below that correctly states the relationship between violence and injustice.
   a) If we are harmed, it is probably because we caused some injustice to other people.
   b) Injustice and violence exist together in families, schools and societies.
   c) If people are not treated fairly, they may engage in violence that affects us.
   d) Violence occurs when societies lose the power to punish people who do wrong.

3. Identify the <u>four</u> approaches to justice that are mentioned in paragraph 3. Cross out any approach that is not described there.
   a) The community takes revenge for the victims.
   b) The victims take revenge on the offenders.
   c) The community finds a way to bring healing to victims and offenders.
   d) The victims let the police and the court deal with the offenders.
   e) The community decides what punishment to give the offenders.
   f) The victims do not do anything although they are repeatedly harmed.

4. Identify <u>three</u> questions that you should ask if you want to <u>meet the needs of everyone</u> who was affected by a violent action. Cross out the <u>one</u> question that does not belong.
   a) Who was affected and how?
   b) Who is to blame?
   c) What do the affected persons need?
   d) How can we make things right?

5. Identify below the <u>four</u> ideas that represent ***retributive justice*** and the <u>six</u> ideas that represent ***restorative justice***.

Ideas
a) sometimes offenders and victims work together on projects
b) communities take or destroy the property of offenders
c) offenders do work to help the community
d) offenders are put to death as a punishment
e) victims and offenders face each other in a local court
f) victims can express their pain and question offenders
g) offenders are put in prison purely as a punishment
h) offenders can tell their story and ask forgiveness
i) both victims and offenders become part of the community again
j) offenders appear before a court in a distant city

Write the letters in the appropriate boxes

Retributive justice	Restorative justice

Discuss
1. Discuss your answers to the questions about Tomas stealing Amadou's jacket (in paragraph 4 of the reading). What variety of answers did the class members give?
2. Think of a time when someone hurt you or your group. What did you want to ask the ones who did harm? What could they have done to make it right for you or your group?
3. What are some other real examples of retributive and restorative justice?
4. Which kind of justice seems to be more commonly accepted in the world? Is it accepted across cultures that you are familiar with?

WORD STUDY
A. You define it

injustice (noun) _____

retributive justice (noun phrase) _____

restorative justice (noun phrase) _____

genocide (noun) _____

execute (verb) _____
(pay close attention to how the last sentence of the paragraph [39-40] summarizes the example)

Word meanings

B. *Which vocabulary item can replace the underlined words or phrase? Write that word above the word or phrase that best matches the meaning.*

component (noun)	structured (participle of the verb)
ensure (verb)	suspect (verb)
illustrate (verb)	sentence (verb)
penalty (noun)	try (verb)

One morning a shop owner found gang symbols spray-painted on the front of his shop. The shop owner told police he believed (46) that two teenagers from the neighborhood did the painting. The two boys were put on trial (47) for this crime. The judge ordered that a fine of $800 be collected for the damage that the teenagers did to the shop, even though he knew the boys could not pay because they did not have jobs. Because the boys did not appear sorry for the crime they committed, the judge gave an additional punishment (4, 34, 40). He ordered as a punishment for (49) them to spend 90 days in jail. But it was not enough just to take away their freedom for 90 days. The judge also wanted to make certain (3) that the damage would be paid for. So he added another part (2) to their punishment. They had to work in an organized (55) program in the community to earn money to pay the shopkeeper. The judge's decision shows (19) his concern for the victim.

C. *Which vocabulary item can replace the underlined words or phrase? Write that word above the word or phrase that best matches the meaning.*

ethnic (adjective)	livestock (noun)
estimated (verb)	pursue (verb)
inequality (noun)	stabilize (verb)

One time in the village of Bambao a bad situation of prejudice and lack of fair treatment (9) developed. People belonging to a minority cultural or tribal (35) group began to feel afraid that the majority would harm them. They ran away at night because they didn't want their enemies to follow (15) them. When the situation in the village returned to normal, (36) these people returned to their homes. They found that some people in the village had taken away everything they owned, including their animals. A village court decided that the community should help these people get resettled in the village. The court guessed (35) that their goats, cows and chickens (53) were worth hundreds of dollars. Some people from the majority group expressed sorrow that they had sold the animals. In agreement with the court's decision, the whole community helped them to settle back into village life again. Every family gave one of their animals to the returnees.

D. Picture conversation. Use the new vocabulary to have a conversation about the picture of the gacaca court that you found on the Internet. You should also include the pictures from the beginning of this chapter. Here are the steps to follow:

1. Divide up the words and have everyone in the class write some of the words on his/her cards—one word on each card. The class should make 19 cards with 19 different words. (Be sure to include the words that you defined.)

2. Collect the cards, shuffle them, and deal them out to everyone in the class. In a class of 10 people, you could divide into two teams. Every student except one would receive 2 cards; the teams would have 9 or 10 cards each. Team members will help each other make sentences to contribute to the conversation.

3. You can begin your discussion with a question like this: What do you see in the pictures that *illustrates* a kind of justice? In order to take part in the conversation, you need to <u>use the words on the cards</u> that you have. Use those words in a sentence to make your contribution to the conversation. Remember to use the pictures and the knowledge you got from the reading to help you.

4. After discussing the pictures in your team, then discuss them as a whole class so that everyone gets to hear all the words used.

Word families

In chapter 3 you learned the word *structural* in the phrase *structural violence*. Now in this chapter you have met the word *structured*, the participle of the verb *structure*. In chapter 11 you learned the noun *restoration*. Now you see its adjective form *restorative*. Study the examples in the left-hand column; write your own sentences to the right.

structural (adjective) – this word refers to the pattern or organization of something; most commonly it refers to a building (a *structure*).

The earthquake caused *structural* damage to many buildings in the area.

Structural changes in our economy are necessary if we want to reduce the gap between poor and rich.

structure (verb) – this verb refers to the act of organizing something or building it to a plan; its participle form *structured* refers to something organized or built in a certain way.

They *structured* the meeting so that everyone would have a chance to speak.

Teachers need to use *structured* activities to keep the children under control at all times.

Both of the following words come from the verb **restore** (to cause someone or something to be in the same condition it was in before).

The United Nations should *restore* peace to the region. (There was peace before; the goal is to have peace again.)

restoration (noun) – this word refers to the results of action to *restore* someone or something.

The goal of the United Nations should be the *restoration* of peace in the region.

restorative (adjective) – this word is used to show that the follow noun has the quality of restoring something.

Restorative approaches to justice take seriously the needs of victims and offenders.

Expressions

be to blame- English has other ways of saying that a person *deserves blame*, words like *blameworthy*, *blameful* or *blamable*. But the expression *be to blame* is <u>much </u>more common than these words. *They are to blame.*

give rise to – This expression is another way of saying *cause, start, create, or bring about something.* The verb *arise* might be used to say something like *Last year trouble arose in that village.* Then to ask about the cause of the trouble, someone might ask, *What gave rise to that trouble?*

lie in ruins – If a building or a city is *destroyed* or *falls down*, we can say it that *it lies in ruins.* But this expression has also come to apply to things that are not physical. *After the war, the economy of Japan lay in ruins.*

take something into one's own hands – This means to take control of something and do it for oneself, not depending on someone else to act. The most common variant of this phrase is *take the law into (your/his/her/their) own hands.* But in line 12 above, what is it that some people take into their own hands? We can *take other matters* into our own hands as well. *Even though my mother was very sick, she didn't want me to call the doctor. But I <u>took matters into my own hands</u> and called the doctor anyway.*

Practice with expressions
1. Who or what is *to blame* for the climate changes we are experiencing?   Who or what is *to blame* for rising food prices?
2. What *gives rise* to food shortages in some countries? How does injustice give *rise to* violence?
3. What did the city of Port-au-Prince look like after the earthquake? After the devastating 2010 floods in Pakistan and Australia, how did the countryside look? *(use "lie in ruins")*
4. What frustrates you? What problem would you like to fix by *taking matters into your own hands*?
5. There are many other different expressions using the verb *take*. You can use a website like freedictionary.com to explore these expressions. Look for idioms with *take*.

GRAMMAR STUDY
A. How to talk about processes as things
In chapter 10 you studied some nouns made from verbs that help users of English to talk about a process (or action) as a thing. Another important way that English uses to talk about processes or actions as things is to use the verb + *ing*. Since verbs can be followed by nouns, adjectives and various phrases, these all become part of a phrase naming the process.

Noun or nominal group	Verb + *ing* describing a process
as subject of a sentence 1. <u>Justice</u> is not easy to define. (line 2) 2. <u>Justice</u> ensures fairness. (line 5)	*as subject of a sentence* 3. **Doing justice** requires power. (line 2-3)
as a complement of the verb 4. Restorative justice means <u>a return to right relationships in the community</u>.	*as a complement of the verb* 5. Restorative justice means **rebuilding right relationships among people.** (lines 43-44)
as object of a preposition 6. Justice is *about* <u>fair laws and equal treatment</u> under those laws (line 6)	*as object of a preposition* 7. Justice is *about* **making sure the right thing is done.** (line 6)

Notice that verb + *ing* does <u>not</u> always refer to a process. In sentence 8 below, *contrasting* acts like the adjective *different* in sentence 9. See line 19 in the text "Punishment or Restoration."
   8. Below are two sets of questions that illustrate two **contrasting** approaches to justice.
   9. Below are two sets of questions that illustrate two <u>different</u> approaches to justice.

Practice 1:

1. Look at the text to find more examples of verb + *ing* for talking about processes. Paragraph 5 is an especially good paragraph to search for examples.

2. Write your own sentences using your choice of the following phrases. Use the sentences in the chart above as your models. After you have composed four sentences, then move around the class and do the give one/get one activity.

Example:

ensuring justice (or *fairness* or *protection for victims*)

    <u>Ensuring justice</u> has been the purpose of the courts.

    A just constitution requires <u>ensuring fairness for all citizens</u>.

    The government must work harder at <u>ensuring protection for victims</u>.

a) punishing criminals (or *children* or *people*)
b) rebuilding communities (or *trust among neighbors* or *relationships with others*)
c) forgiving others (or *criminals* or *thieves* or *murderers*)
d) admitting guilt (or *your weaknesses* or *you are wrong*)
e) organizing a program (or *groups* or *your time*)

B. Ways of more clearly identifying people, places or things:

We use relative clauses beginning with *who, which, that,* and a few other words to identify more clearly the preceding noun.

10. Those persons can ensure that all people get benefits.

    Which persons can ensure that all people get benefits? If the important quality of those persons is that *they have power*, then we can use that idea to identify these people more clearly.

11. Those **persons <u>who</u> have power** can ensure that all people get benefits.

    Note that <u>who</u> replaces the word *they (persons)* in the short sentence *they have power*. The word <u>who</u> stands right after the word to which it is referring (or pointing).

    Now what about the benefits? What kind of benefits is the writer talking about? The important quality of these benefits may be that *people have a right to receive them (the benefits)*.

12. Those persons who have power can ensure that all people get the **benefits <u>that</u> they have a right to receive**.
(line 3) Note that the word <u>that</u> replaces the word *them (benefits)* in the short sentence *people have a right to receive them*. The word <u>that</u> stands right after the word to which it is referring (or pointing).

There is a rule in English that allows us to delete the *who* or *that* if it is followed by a form of the verb BE and one of the verb participles (verb+*ing* or verb+*en* – the past participle of the verb). We can call the resulting modifiers ***reduced relative clauses.*** These examples will make this rule clearer to you.

13. The government began trials for **those <u>who were</u> accused of participating in the genocide**.

    First, notice how the writer identifies "those (persons)" in the sentence. For which persons did the government begin trials? You will notice by looking at line 36-7 of the text that the author did not write sentence #13. Instead, he left out the words *who were* and used only the past participle of the verb (*accused*).

14. The government began trials for **those accused of participating in the genocide**.

    The phrase *accused of participating in the genocide* identifies who those people were.

15. **Former prisoners <u>who are</u> returning to their communities** frequently find it difficult to settle again into community life.

    How does the writer identify the *former prisoners*? You will notice by looking at line 51 of the text that the author did not write sentence #15. Instead, he left out the words *who are* and used only the present participle of the verb (*returning*).

16. **Former prisoners returning to their communities** frequently find it difficult to settle again into community life.

    The phrase *returning to their communities* identify who the former prisoners are.

163

Practice 2:
Do a running dictation activity. Find other examples in the text of relative clauses with *who* and *that* (like sentences 11, 12, 13 and 15). Also find more sentences in the text that use reduced relative clauses like sentences 14 and 16. Work on this as teams. If your teacher directs, you may divide the text into halves or thirds and let each team work on just part of the text. Send one team member to the board to write the examples that you find in the text. Those who do the writing must listen carefully to what the team tells them to write. No shouting is allowed. The writers must come back to their team to hear what should be written next. All team members should take a turn at running and writing. At the end of the time limit given by the teacher, the whole class can look at the sentences. Which team has found the most correct examples? Which team has written their examples with the fewest errors in grammar and spelling?

LIFE SKILLS
Story of Resilience

Read this story about prisoners caught in the cycles of violence who find hope and beauty in their lives.

> **Develop your reading skills:**
> **Use concepts learned from other texts.** What are the most important concepts you have learned in the first reading in this chapter? If you said something like *retributive justice and restorative justice*, you have the right answer. What if you think about important concepts you have read about in previous chapters? The number of possible answers grows wider. You might say *types of violence, acting out or acting in as a result of trauma,* or *the cycles of violence through which victims can become aggressors.* Which of these concepts can help you understand this new reading? If you actively use the information you know about *victims, aggressors, violence, ignored trauma,* and *restorative justice,* you will have a better understanding of this reading.

Victims on Both Sides of the Bars
by Brian Gumm

Brian Gumm is a licensed minister in the Church of the Brethren who has studied theology and peacebuilding at Eastern Mennonite University. Prior to graduate school, he was a volunteer with a state Department of Corrections as an advocate for ex-offenders. Brian is interested in creative expression as a way to help the process of healing and transformation. The names and some circumstances of the story have been changed to protect the women who have bravely sought justice and healing.

A victim's perspective°

Karen and I are at the Women's Residential° Correctional Facility° in Wichita, Kansas. We are leading a creative writing workshop.° Our students are criminals. Karen is an active volunteer for the Kansas Department of Correctional Services. She represents what they call the "victim perspective."

5 Before our class, she reads her own essay to me. She will read it again later to the whole group. Karen's stories bring focus to her listeners. When she reads them, people listen, attentively, sometimes tearfully. The women at the prison quickly pick up° that Karen can empathize with them deeply. They know that her life has not been very different from theirs even though Karen has never served° a prison sentence.

10 When she was twelve years old, over thirty years ago Karen survived a horrific murder-suicide in her family. Her abusive, alcoholic father charged into their house one night with a gun. He killed her mother as Karen watched. Then he turned the gun on himself, and in an instant he was dead.

Karen had been sexually abused throughout her childhood by her own father and one of his friends. For years she buried her unspeakable° pain in alcohol and work. In her mid-twenties Karen began to seek help. She talked about these horrible experiences with counselors. She formed a relationship with God. And 15 she began volunteering in prisons. Now in her 40s, Karen continues the healing process by helping others heal.

Writing as therapy°

The women in the writers' workshop file in and collapse° in the chairs. "All right, it's time to get rolling. Take out your notebooks and let's have 20 minutes of free writing," I say. Taking up my guitar, I 20 gently finger-pick a few soothing pieces. The room calms down, the quiet interrupted only by coughs, sniffs, and whispers.

I glance° at the clock. It's time to move on to group writing. Tonight's topic is "Your Body." Our writing topics were developed by a female professor for writers' workshops in female prisons. Now I'm the only man in the building. I know sexual abuse is a reality for some of the women in the class. Some may have
25 trust issues° with men. Despite reassurances from my superiors, I feel insecure.

But the women surprise me with light° and sometimes very funny pieces about fading youth, having kids, advancing years, and unfortunate physical changes brought about by all that. Our sides aching and faces sore from laughing, my fears were decidedly° put to rest.

On another night a promising young writer wrote an emotionally stirring piece. It recounted° the
30 violent neighborhood of her youth and how she and her sister coped.

Playing in the parking lot in front of their apartment complex, the girls heard gunshots close by. Running inside, the girls hid in a closet, low to the ground, holding each other tight. They began to tell each other stories of faraway lands where they were princesses, where there was no gunfire, and no death. Building these worlds in their collective imaginations, the girls hid until their mother told them it was okay to come out.
35 *The violence had passed.*

While reading this piece, the young woman wept openly. Others joined her, hot tears streaming down faces. Unfortunately for this woman, therapeutic° writing workshops couldn't cure all her problems. Soon she was gone from the group. The remaining women whispered rumors° of parole violations° and trips to the hospital.

40 **Celebration and satisfaction**

On the last night of the writers' workshop, we celebrated at a downtown coffee shop. Some of the women dressed up for the night out. When they saw the coffee shop had a stage and microphone, they wanted to do their readings from the stage.

Judy, bold and outspoken in the group, went to the stage first and read her piece, "Loss." Many tables were empty. But there happened to be a small crowd at the counter, placing orders. Judy's strong voice came
45 out of the speakers, filling the entire shop. When she finished reading, some of the applause came from the crowd at the counter. There were proud cheers and clapping from our tables. The reaction to Judy's reading encouraged a few others to read their works on the stage.

My co-facilitator, Karen, even took to the mike to read one of her stirring° pieces. When our cups ran empty and the stories had been told, a deep, warm sense of fulfillment° and satisfaction settled on the group. I
50 could see it clearly in the faces of all the women.

°perspective (n.) – a way of seeing things, a point of view, an opinion
°residential (adj.) – related to houses or places where people live
°correctional facility (adj.+ n.) – a prison or jail
°creative writing workshop (adj.+ n. + v.) – a class where people learn to write stories, poems, or essays by writing
°pick up (v.) – sense, recognize
°serve a sentence (idiom) – to go through a time of punishment in jail
°unspeakable (adj.) – cannot be spoken about, too bad or too good to be put into words
°therapy (n.) – treatment to bring about healing usually of a mental or social illness
°collapse (v.) – to come down or sit down suddenly
°glance (v.) – look at quickly
°have issues (idiom) – to have complaints, personal problems, emotional disorders
°light (adj.) – not serious
°decidedly (adv.) – very surely or certainly
°recounted (v.) – tell in detail, usually in a story
°therapeutic (adj.) – relating to healing treatment of mind or body
°rumors (n.) – reports or information that may or may not be true, gossip
°parole violation (n.+ n.) – breaking of the rules related to early release from jail
°stirring (adj. from the v. *stir*) – emotional, inspiring
°fulfillment (n.) – a feeling of success, of achievement, of reaching one's dreams

Understand what you read
Write short answers to these questions. You should easily be able to find the information from the text.
1. Why do the women prisoners like listening to Karen's stories?
2. What signs of ignoring trauma did Karen show before she began meeting with a counselor?
3. What does Brian do at these writing workshops?
4. What are examples of serious and funny topics that the women write about?
5. At the coffee shop, what encouraged some of the other women to read their pieces after Judy read hers?

Discuss
1. What surprised you the most about this story?
2. What kind of justice is being served to the women? Does the creative writing program represent a different kind of justice?
3. Why do you think the prison (correctional facility) allows a creative writing program like this?
4. If you could create a different type of program for these women, what would it look like?

Teacher Story
Listen to your teacher talk about the benefits that she or he has experienced through writing about an injustice that may have bothered her or him.

EXTEND YOUR LEARNING
1. Journal
Write about an injustice that bothers you. It can be an injustice that you personally have suffered or any other injustice that bothers you. What could be done to "make things right" for all the people affected by this injustice?

2. Debate
Our thinking about an issue can be sharpened by debating with others. In this debate, you will consider which kind of justice is the best.
(a) Count off and form two groups in your class (more groups for a bigger class). One group will think of reasons why retributive justice is the best approach; the other group will think of reasons why restorative justice is the best approach. Spend about 10 minutes discussing the issue with your group.
(b) Each group will present its reasons why their form of justice is better and the other form of justice is weak or deficient. Allow one side to speak, then allow the other side to speak. Then allow each group one more chance to make a response.
(c) End your session with a discussion of these two questions: (i) How should the situation affect the approach to justice that is used? (ii) What did you learn about taking "either/or" positions on an issue like this?

3. Role Play
a. Divide the class into at least three groups. Prepare a role play to act out for the whole class. One of the groups will choose a situation below and show how retributive justice would work in that situation. The other two (or more) groups will choose two (or more) different situations and show how restorative justice would work in that situation.
b. In your groups, work out the role play keeping in mind the following questions:
  - How many people will be involved in arriving at a just solution? Who are those people?
  - What will the different persons involved in the situation say?
  - What kind of penalty will you demand against those who have harmed others or taken away their rights?
c. Choose from these possible situations:
1) a student has shown disrespect to a teacher in front of the whole class
2) an employee at a restaurant has been caught stealing fresh meat from the refrigerator
3) the police arrest two neighbors who have gotten into a fist-fight on the street near their apartments
4) a taxi driver ran over and killed a school girl standing on the side of the road; some community members became angry and burned the nearby shops owned by people from the same ethnic group as the taxi driver

4. Music
Listen to "If I Had a Hammer" by Pete Seeger and Lee Hays

Listen to and then try singing this contemporary American folk song. This song was written in 1949 by famous American folk singers and songwriters Pete Seeger and Lee Hays. It only became popular in 1962 when it was recorded by the trio Peter, Paul, and Mary. You can view the Peter, Paul and Mary classic version here https://www.youtube.com/watch?v=XxWTDcP9Y5E .

Discuss:
Read over the verses of the song http://www.azlyrics.com/lyrics/peterpaulandmary/ifihadahammer.html

1. Think about this question: Why was this song popular during the movement to get racial equality and justice for African Americans in the 1960s?
2. What makes this song, as a folk song, different from most of the other music you have listened to during this course?

   Extra activity: Since 1962 the song has been performed in many different languages and styles. Listen to "I Have a Hammer" in some other versions. What do you think of the way the song changes?

   Trini Lopez (Latin sound with English words)
   http://www.youtube.com/watch?v=hZk2uMrQBSQ

   Wanda Jackson (US country western)
   http://www.youtube.com/watch?v=YCAxKFp3EXo&playnext=1&list=PL4B7C31698154E2AD

   Les Surfs - Si j'avais un marteau (in French from Madagascar)
   http://www.youtube.com/watch?v=A2AiOeilcyw

   Victor Jara - El martillo (in Spanish from Chile)
   http://www.youtube.com/watch?v=GKZwaN0JOU8

   Waldemar Matuška – Kladivo (in Czech from the Czech Republic)
   http://www.youtube.com/watch?v=H0TPFz9WXRg

   Choral arrangement for women's choir (USA)
   http://www.youtube.com/watch?v=Q-VVgF2c6eg

   Choreographed arrangement for mixed choir (USA)
   http://www.youtube.com/watch?v=9vZ25brTZSU

SELF-ASSESSMENT

Think about your learning. Complete a self-assessment for this chapter by using the template at the end of the text (p. 194).

> *Learning Tip: To make your learning more solid, review the readings and your notes within 24 hours after the class in which you discuss them. Set aside 10-15 minutes each night to review the main ideas from previous chapters.*

Chapter 14 – Building Peace

Get to Know Each Other Better
Trade Circles (a team problem-solving game)
1. Divide into two groups of about the same size.
2. Form two concentric circles (one circle inside the other). Hold hands with each other in your circle.
3. The inner circle must trade places with the outer circle without breaking either circle. If the circle breaks (because anyone lets go of a hand) the teacher will make you start from the beginning again.
4. You may talk as much as you want to decide on a solution to the problem.
5. Now the two circles must trade again, but they must solve the problem in a <u>different</u> way!
6. Your teacher will observe carefully how the teams work at solving this problem in two different ways. Then she or he will lead you in a discussion about problem-solving, creativity, cooperation, and communication.

Discuss
1. Which was the best solution? How was that solution created?
2. Which of the class members wa more active than others in suggesting solutions or giving directions?
3. If any disagreements arose, how did the groups settle them?.
4. If you did not say much to help solve the problem, how did it feel to cooperate in the solutions given by others?

Connect to the Topic
If you look again at the healing path out of trauma (ch. 11), you will see that making peace between victims and aggressors is almost at the end of the path. By the time persons affected by trauma have reached this point in the journey, they have recovered much of their strength. They are now more resilient than they were before they suffered violence. Remember David Works (also ch. 11) who had learned about the role of forgiveness in healing trauma. When he became a victim, he was ready to put that knowledge into practice. Actively improving your peacebuilding skills now, before you suffer trauma, will make you a more resilient person. You can improve these skills by practicing creative problem-solving and good communication.

Look at the pictures
Before you read the text, discuss the pictures on the next page. What do you think the pictures suggest about different ways of responding to violence? When you read the text following the pictures, compare your ideas with the explanation of the pictures given there.

Four Ways of Responding to Conflict

Avoiding

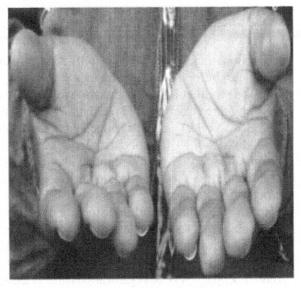

Accommodating

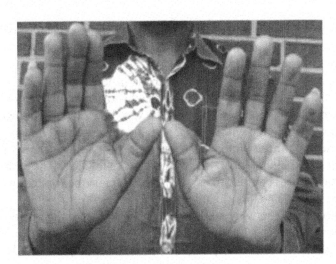

Using violence

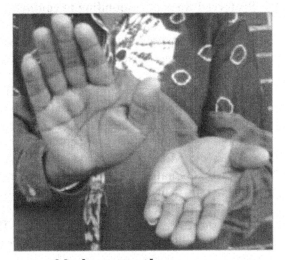

Using active
nonviolence

Eastern Mennonite University STAR Program

READ

Develop your reading skills:

Keep reading. Some parts of a text may be more difficult than others. Perhaps the vocabulary, the grammar or the ideas in some parts of the text are more difficult than in other parts. Don't let the difficult parts stop you. Keep reading and see if the next part of the text is easier to read and understand. You can come back and work on the more difficult part later. It may be that understanding the easier part of the text can help you unlock the harder part. Some readers of the following text might find the second paragraph more difficult than the rest of the reading. What do you think?

Responding to Conflict without Violence

Conflict and violence are not the same

Many people avoid conflict because they think it may turn violent. Conflict can be violent, but it does not have to be so. Conflict is bad only when it is settled with violence, which leads to broken relationships, destruction, trauma, and death. Conflict usually exists where there is injustice, where the situation needs to be made right for all those involved.

When conflict is approached **nonviolently**, many positive and creative solutions are possible, as in the following three examples. (1) In the first half of the twentieth century India struggled to **liberate** itself from British rule. Gandhi organized groups of people to **resist** unjust British laws in simple but creative ways. In March 1930 he organized a 250-mile march to the sea. This was to protest the British tax on Indian salt. Only 79 people set out with Gandhi. But thousands joined the march along the way. Upon reaching the sea, they scooped up handfuls of natural salt, **defying** the government's tax. (2) In 1960 African-American college students in North Carolina (USA) began **sit-ins** at lunch **counters**. They were protesting laws that **prohibited** stores and restaurants from serving blacks and whites together. Police would come and remove one group of students seated at the lunch counter. Another group was waiting in line to take their place. (3) In 1980 and again in 1983 thousands of **urban** South African students **boycotted** schools. They were protesting the white minority government's unjust **policies** toward black and colored people. Several organizations also organized effective black boycotts of white-owned businesses. These businesses eventually began pressuring the government to make changes. In every case, creative **nonviolent** actions led to positive changes.

Preferred ways of responding to conflict

Most people have a **preferred** way of responding to conflict or violence in their personal and social lives. There are three very common responses to conflict. The first is avoiding conflict. Conflict of any kind makes some people very nervous. They try to avoid conflict or violence *at any price*. They close their eyes to injustices in society. They flee or try to isolate themselves from the conflict. The second common response is **accommodating** conflict. This means living with the conflict and accepting whatever happens, no matter how unjust. Those who accommodate violence may not like war, but if their nation gets into a disagreement with another nation that leads to war, they will *sit back* and allow the war to happen without protesting it. The third common response is **counter-violence**. This means responding actively to conflict with violence. Some people feel the injustice being done to them is a kind of violence. They may not have **adequate** employment; they may not have **access** to resources; their freedom may be limited or **nonexistent**. They feel justified in using violence to change this situation.

There is a fourth way of responding to conflict. This way is illustrated by Gandhi and the others whose stories have been mentioned above. This response is active **nonviolence**. Active nonviolence peacefully and **persistently** resists oppression. Active nonviolence puts pressure on those in power to do justice.

Two-hands-of-nonviolence exercise

As you read the following description of the two-hands-of- nonviolence exercise, follow the instructions. Perform each of the actions with your hands. Use the pictures above to help you position your hands correctly. Hold each **pose** for 15-20 seconds. Pay attention to the sensations in your body and your emotions.

1. **Avoiding conflict**: Cover your eyes with your hands. This pose should give you a sense of retreating from the situation and not being involved.
2. **Accommodating conflict**: Extend your arms in front of you with your palms facing up. This pose symbolizes the experience of **passively** accepting whatever is happening.
3. **Counter-violence - meeting conflict with violence**: Extend your arms straight out in front of you, **parallel** to the ground, palms facing away from you, pushing outward. In this pose you aggressively push away the one who comes to do harm.
4. **Active nonviolence**: Combine the two previous poses. One arm is outstretched at a 45-degree angle with the palm facing up and the other arm is straight out in front, parallel to the ground.

50   While maintaining this position, pull your two hands closer to your body in a relaxed but steady way. This pose illustrates that active nonviolence is a process that holds two **realities** in **tension**. The hand in front of you is saying "I will not **cooperate** with your violence or injustice; I will resist it with all my strength." The open hand **indicates**, "I am open to you as a human being."

(Slattery, Butigan, Pelicaric, and Preston-Pile. *Engage: Exploring Non-violent Living*, Pace e Bene Nonviolence Service, 2005)

UNDERSTAND WHAT YOU READ

Answer these true and false questions. How would you change the false statements to make them true?
First, check how well you understood the main ideas:
1. Most conflicts have to be settled with violence.
2. Conflicts arise when people feel that they are being treated unfairly.
3. Nonviolent solutions to conflicts do not show much intelligence or imagination.
4. Individuals have ways resolving conflicts that they usually use because they like them better.
5. The most common way that people settle conflicts is through active nonviolence.
6. The four main ways of resolving conflicts can be symbolized by the position of your body.

If you need to, read the text again before you answer the following true/false questions about details.
Then check how well you understood the supporting facts and examples:
1. Indians were upset because the laws made by their British rulers did not seem fair to them.
2. South African children went to school and damaged the school property as a way of protesting injustice.
3. African-American college students ate their lunch at restaurants for white people.
4. Those who avoid conflict live with the conflict and accept unfair treatment.
5. Those who accommodate conflict try to run away and hide from the conflict.
6. Those who take the counter-violence approach, fight violence with violence.
7. Putting two arms straight out in front of you shows that you want to avoid violence.
8. Covering your eyes shows that you are accepting and agreeing with the violence.
9. Putting your hands with palms up in front of you shows you accept whatever is happening.
10. The hand positions for active nonviolence show that you are actively against aggression but ready to accept and talk with an aggressor.

Discuss
1. In your own life, which approach to conflict do you use the most? If you feel comfortable, give some examples.
2. Which approach do you use the least? Why don't you use that approach?
3. The reading suggests that fewer people tend to use creative nonviolent action although the examples in paragraph 2 show that the results of this approach are positive. Why don't more people use this approach?
4. In your opinion is it always possible to respond to conflict without using violence?
5. Which approaches to conflict allow the victim and aggressor cycles (and, thus, trauma) to continue and which work to end these cycles?

WORD STUDY

A. You define it
nonviolent (adjective), nonviolence (noun), nonviolently (adverb) _____
          (use your knowledge of word parts – what do you suppose *non-* means?)

_____

counter-violence (noun) _____
          (remember to look at the sentences nearby in lines 28-29)

accommodate (verb) _____
          (use the nearby sentence in lines 25-26 and the following example to help you)

indicate (verb) _____
          (review what you learned about *indication* in chapter 8)

Word meanings

B. *Most of the sentences below are taken from the text. They follow the order of the text. There are* two *correct answers that match the meaning of the underlined word. Cross out the wrong answer.*

1. India struggled to liberate itself from British rule.
   a. free   b. release   c. preserve

2. Gandhi organized groups of people to resist unjust British laws.
   a. oppose   b. neglect   c. fight against

3. The marchers defied the law and scooped up the natural salt.
   a. justified   b. openly broke   c. confronted

4. The students conducted a sit-in at stores that served lunch.
   a. protest   b. strike   c. ritual

5. When they sat at the counters, no one would serve them.
   a. memorials   b. long tables   c. eating places

6. The police prohibited them from staying in the store.
   a. rescued   b. stopped   c. did not allow

7. The most serious protests occurred in the urban schools, not the village schools.
   a. city   b. country   c. town

8. The students boycotted their classes.
   a. avoided   b. did not attend   c. threatened

9. It was the government's policy to arrest the protestors.
   a. rule   b. principle   c. threat

10. Some people prefer to avoid conflict.
    a. persist   b. like   c. choose

11. Those who accommodate injustice may not like it, but they allow it to continue.
    a. adjust to   b. sympathize with   c. live with

12. Victims of injustice may not have adequate employment.
    a. enough   b. acceptable amount   c. essential

13. They may not have access to resources.
    a. an appetite for   b. a method of getting   c. a way of approaching

14. Their freedom may be limited or nonexistent.
    a. absent   b. chronic   c. missing

15. Persistently struggling against injustice requires emotional and spiritual energy.
    a. firmly   b. physically   c. steadily

16. The four hand poses illustrate four different ways of responding to conflict.
    a. positions   b. ways of standing   c. moods

17. Persons who accommodate conflict passively accept whatever is happening.
    a. calmly & quietly   b. aggressively   c. without acting

18. Extend your arms straight out in front of you, parallel to the ground.
    a. motionless   b. in line with   c. in the same direction as

19. A person who is actively nonviolent can identify two realities: the aggressor is a human being and the aggressor is doing something unjust or evil.
    a. commitments   b. truths   c. facts

172

20. A person who is actively nonviolent feels a <u>tension</u> between actively opposing injustice and respecting the aggressor as a human being.
    a. tight pull   b. relaxation   c. stress

21. I will not <u>cooperate</u> with your violence or injustice.
    a. work along with   b. help   c. communicate

22. The open hand <u>indicates</u>, "I am open to you as a human being."
    a. exposes   b. exhibits   c. illustrates

C. Word practice – Get the context right! The underlined words in the sentences below are your new words for this chapter. But there is something wrong with the sentences. Part of the sentence does not go along meaningfully with the underlined word or words. You need to change the sentence to make its meaning agree with the meaning of the underlined word(s). The first one has been done for you.

1. When I go to a small restaurant, I <u>prefer</u> to eat at the <u>counter</u> because I like to sit by myself where it is quiet and I won't be disturbed by other people.
   When I go to a small restaurant, I prefer <u>not</u> to eat at the counter <u>because the counter is usually noisy and crowded.</u> I want to sit where it is quiet and I won't be disturbed by other people.

2. The people of India <u>resisted</u> British rulers by <u>cooperating</u> with the government's programs in all parts of the county.
   _____

3. The people <u>accommodated</u> the government's military <u>policies</u> by refusing to pay their taxes.
   _____

4. The laws were very fair because they <u>prohibited</u> the common people from having <u>access</u> to clean water.
   _____

5. The poor health of people in the community <u>indicates</u> that they have <u>adequate</u> supplies of food and water.
   _____

6. The students <u>passively</u> <u>defied</u> the school officials by calling off their <u>sit-in</u> at the principal's office and returning to class.
   _____

7. Because the students <u>persistently</u> <u>boycotted</u> their classes, they were able to graduate on time with excellent grades.
   _____

8. One of the <u>realities</u> of modern <u>urban</u> life is that there is very little to do at night; the streets are very quiet, and crime is almost <u>nonexistent</u>.
   _____

9. The newspaper reported that the government forces <u>liberated</u> the city from rebel control. In a <u>parallel</u> report, the TV news broadcast described how the rebels were celebrating in the streets as the government troops retreated.
   _____

10. In the aggressive <u>pose</u> of an angry person, we see a complete release of <u>tension</u> in his body as he confronts his enemy with violence.

Word Families. In this chapter you learned three new members of the word family *violence.* Write your own sentences to show that you know how to use the adjective, noun & adverb forms of these words. In addition, you met *indicate,* which is related to the word *indication* that you studied in chapter 8; and you met *persistently,* which is related to the word *persist* from chapter 4. Study the examples in the left-hand column and then write your own sentences in the right-hand column.

nonviolence (noun) *Gandhi and King both believed that **nonviolence** was the best way to approach conflict.* **nonviolent** (adjective) *They were able to think of creative, **nonviolent** method of confronting problems.* **nonviolently** (adverb) *They trained their followers to behave **nonviolently**.*	
indicate (verb) – to indicate is to show or point to something *A good appetite **indicates** that a person is healthy.*	
indication (noun) – an indication is a sign of something *Having a lot of energy is one **indication** of good health.*	
persist (noun) - to persist means that some action keeps happening; or someone keeps doing something *You must **persist** in practicing these new words, if you wish to learn them well.*	
persistent (adjective) - this word describes the quality of a person or things that keeps on doing something ***Persistent** language learners review and practice their new words every day.*	
persistently (adverb) – this word describes the quality of an action *If you **persistently** practice your new words, you will know them well.*	

Expressions

at any price (prepositional phrase) Here (in line 23) is another one of those English expressions that refers to money (*price*), but it does not literally have to do with money. If you are a runner and want to win your race *at any price*, you might work very hard in your training or you might even find some way to cheat.

close one's eyes to (verb phrase) The literal meaning here is to shut one's eyes physically. The meaning in line 23-24, however, *is to ignore.* You can *close your eyes to* (or ignore) problems all around you even though you keep your physical eyes open all the time.

sit back (verb) Literally, this verb means to sit down in a relaxing position. But in line 27 it also means to *do nothing.* If there is a fight in the classroom and you just *sit back*, someone will probably get hurt.

Practice your new expressions
1. When people *set out* on the healing journey from trauma, what are some things they need to do? When you *set out* to learn something about trauma, what were you expecting to learn? [*set out* was introduced in chapter 11]
2. What do you want to achieve in life that you are willing to *pay (almost) any price for*?
3. Sometimes you see problems that other people (leaders in government or other organizations) *close their eyes to*. What are some of these issues or problems that others *close their eyes to*?
4. When good people, who have knowledge and power to do something, just *sit back*, then what kinds of problems happen?

GRAMMAR STUDY
Notice the changes in tense and mood.
One way to increase your understanding of a text, is to pay attention to the verb tenses and moods that are used in different sections of the text. These small clues will alert you to the purpose of each part of the text. You can also produce your own texts more effectively if you know how to control these aspects of the verb.

Examples of tense:
Present: Many people <u>avoid</u> conflict because they <u>think</u> it <u>may turn</u> violent.
Past: They <u>avoided</u> the protest because they <u>feared</u> it <u>would turn</u> violent.

1. In which paragraph are almost all the verb tenses in the past? Why has the past tense been used so much in that paragraph? How does the tense help to signal the purpose of the paragraph?

Examples of mood:
Statement: Some people <u>respond</u> actively to conflict with violence. (the verb comes after the subject *some people* + *respond*)
Question: <u>How do</u> some people <u>respond</u> to conflict? <u>Do</u> they <u>use</u> violence? (the verb is split—and the subject comes in between: *[question word-how] + helping verb [do] + subject [some people* or *they] + main verb [respond* or *use])*
Command: <u>Use</u> violence to settle a conflict. <u>Don't respond</u> to conflict with violence. (the verb comes first and there is <u>no</u> subject mentioned)

2. In which paragraph do many of the sentences have verbs in the *command* form? Why has the *command* form been used there? How does this verb form help to signal the purpose of the paragraph?

3. What is the mood of all the other paragraphs in the text? Why?

Review how English uses verb + *ing* to talk about processes or actions <u>as things</u>. (See the grammar section of chapter 13). The first text for this chapter uses a lot of <u>verb + *ing*</u> from paragraph 3 to the end. Find some examples. When you have collected some examples, take out the verb + *ing* phrase and put it into your own original sentence.

Example: Most people have a preferred way of <u>responding to conflict</u>. (line 21)
  <u>Responding to conflict</u> is something that I don't do well.

1. Text sentence : _____

   Your sentence: _____

2. Text sentence : _____

   Your sentence: _____

3. Text sentence : _____

   Your sentence: _____

Speaking & thinking on the spot:
After you have done a few sentences, try doing a round robin speaking and thinking practice with the rest of the class. Seat yourselves in a circle. The first person picks out from the text one sentence that identifies a process as a thing using <u>verb</u> + *ing.* The student to right will then say an original sentence using the <u>verb</u> + *ing* phrase from the text. Then she/he will pick out another sentence from the text to give to the next person in the circle.

LIFE SKILLS
Story of Resilience
Read this story about neighbors in a serious conflict with each other.

> **Develop your reading skills**
> **Make predictions.** Under the guidance of your teacher, read one paragraph or section at a time from this text. Do **not** read the text before class. In class, your teacher will tell you exactly how far to read. Do **not** read farther ahead. Be patient and think about each section. After you read a section, ask yourself, "What conflict is going on here? What might happen next? Will the conflict become more serious? Will it be settled? How?"

Can Troubled Neighbors Make Peace?
by Charito Calvachi-Mateyko

Charito Calvachi-Mateyko was born and raised in Ecuador. She received her doctorate in law from the Pontifical Catholic University in Quito and her master in Conflict Transformation from the Eastern Mennonite University in Virginia, USA. She works as a restorative justice practitioner in Lancaster, Pennsylvania and Lewes, Delaware, where she makes her home.

I tell stories about restorative justice for a weekly radio program in Spanish. Some time ago, one of the program's listeners, a Cuban man, contacted me to tell me his frustrations° about an injustice that he experienced. Armando* was bitter and resentful. His dignity and his possibility to become an American were taken away because a false accusation° sent him to jail for six months.

5   After getting out of jail, he moved to a new neighborhood. After few months, he began feeling distrust toward his neighbors. The neighbor on one side and then on the other side of his house became his enemies. Someone tampered° with his air conditioning. His car got scratched. The barking of one neighbor's dogs became unbearable.° The music of the other neighbor really disturbed him and his wife and daughter.

Armando and his family didn't like to mingle° with anyone. They kept to themselves. Rumors went
10   up and down the street that Armando did this to "him" and that to "them." Someone spread garbage at his front door, even urine.° His daughter and wife felt unsafe.

One day, one of the neighbors became fed up.° His car had been scratched. Assuming that "the Cuban guy" did it, he went outside with a bat in his hand. Armando just happened to be outside with a machete in its sheath.° The two men exchanged nasty words and headed to the park to settle the dispute°.
15   Another neighbor saw the two from his window. He jumped outside to stop this madness.° Since he is a war veteran and a boxer, he used all his strength to grab Armando. Armando managed to hit his attacker in the shoulder with the machete just a moment before the boxer pinned° him to the wall. Meanwhile, the neighbor with the bat, taking advantage of Armando's vulnerability,° hit him in the legs.

The police came and charged° Armando and his attacker but did not put them in jail. Armando and
20   then the local police called me to assist with a meeting among these troubled neighbors. After two months of conversations and preparations, we finally came together in a restorative justice circle. Two city councilmen attended the circle as well as a police officer. In total there were 14 people

The time that I had spent visiting Armando's family really helped me to develop trust with his 8-year-old daughter. She was important in the environment created at the circle. She was brave enough to sing

25 a song at the opening ceremony, and she participated° fully in the group. Her gracious manner said so much about the effect that violence has on our children.

     I had asked the families to provide me with some photos of their children. I bought a nice frame to put them in. The frame had the word *DREAM* on it. And that was our talking piece. Every time one of the participants° spoke, they would hold that frame with the nice photos of the children. Seeing the children
30 made more important the gracious presence of Armando's daughter. People participated with respect and effort.

     Before we began discussing the conflict, I had asked the participants to write down the values they bring to this conversation. They placed their written values in the center of our circle. Then at the end, they gave those papers to the beautiful little girl as she sat in a special chair. They presented their papers one by
35 one, saying some inspirational° words pointing to the future.

     "So you can know that I care."

     "So you can sleep all night."

     "So you can grow up to be a peacebuilder."

     "So you know that you inspire° respect," etc.

40   Five long hours passed in the circle, and we felt we did a good job. We were inspired because this little girl represented our responsibility to do our best for her and the other children in the neighborhood. It takes relationship building and persistence to change people's hearts. When change occurred, I knew that our efforts were all worth it.

*The name has been changed to protect the person involved in this story.

°frustrations (n.) – feelings of disappointment or sadness or anger about something

°accusation (n.) – a statement of blame about someone for doing wrong

°tampered (v.) – did something to cause a change or even cause damage

°unbearable (adj.) – very bad, too much

°mingle (v.) – meet with, talk with

°urine (n.) – liquid waste from the body

°fed up (v.) – very bothered or annoyed by something

°machete (n.) – a large sharp knife for cutting plants

° sheath (n.) – a covering for a knife or sword

°dispute (n.) – disagreement, argument, or fight

°madness (n.) – something stupid or foolish (related to the meaning "serious mental disorder")

°pinned (v.) – held against

°vulnerability (n.) – condition of being weak or without help

°charged (v.) – officially blamed by the police for doing something

°participated (v.) – took part in the event

°participants (v.) – people who take part in an event

°inspirational (adj.) – something that makes a person work hard or be creative

°inspire (v.) – to cause someone to work hard or be creative

Develop your reading skills:
Make your own graphic organizers. When you read a story, remember that most stories have several important components: characters, settings (place & time), conflict (who or what is the conflict about) and plot (or series of events that happen). Take your own piece of paper and label it like this. Then **re-read the story** and fill in the information.

Characters	Plot
Setting(s)	
Conflict	

Understand what you read

1. Who are the characters in this story? If you had to choose the most important characters, who would they be?

2. Where does this story take place? (hint: there are two places)

3. What is the conflict about and who is involved in the conflict?

4. Read the sentences below and put them in order as they occur in the story. Use your graphic organizer to help you remember the order.

___Participants in the circle wrote down their values.
___Charito felt satisfied with the results of the circle process.
___Whoever held the picture frame with the children's pictures was allowed to speak.
___Armando's family moved into a new neighborhood.
___Charito visited Armando's family and became friendly with his daughter.
___Armando and his neighbor got into a violent fight.
___Armando went to jail.
___Armando didn't trust his neighbors, and his neighbors didn't trust him.
___Participants in the circle gave their papers to Armando's daughter.
___Armando's daughter sang a song.
___Charito received a call from Armando and the police.
___The police came and officially charged Armando & his neighbor for fighting

Discuss

1. In your opinion, did Armando experience any kind of violence before he got into a fight with his neighbor?
2. What are the different approaches to conflict that you can see in this story?
3. One fact that was left out of the story is this: One of Armando's neighbors who was invited to the meeting refused to come. He told Charito, "Things can be the way they are." What approach to conflict does this neighbor represent?
4. What are some important skills related to peacebuilding that you learn from this story?
5. What qualities should a peacebuilder have? Share your opinions.

EXTEND YOUR LEARNING

1. Journal

Write about the questions in the movement exercise below **or** write a story about a conflict that you have witnessed or been personally involved in. How would you analyze the approaches to conflict used by different people in your story?

2. Problem-solving

1. Brainstorm a list of possible conflicts that you could discuss. Have any conflicts arisen in your class during this course, conflicts that have not been completely settled? Are there conflicts in your community that you know about? Try to think about a conflict that touches your life or the lives of your classmates.
2. Work in small groups taking one or more of the conflicts that are on your brainstormed list. What are some creative nonviolent actions that your group could take to settle this conflict?
3. Each group will prepare a short presentation on how they would try to settle the conflict they chose to discuss.

3. Movement

Perform again all four of the different responses to conflict slowly. Hold each pose for 15-30 seconds. Notice any feelings or sensations you have.
Return to the approach you use most in responding to conflict or violence.
Now return to the approach you use least.

Discuss or write in your journal
What did you notice about yourself in doing the poses? What did you feel in your body?
How did that pose feel which represents the approach you use the most?
How did that pose feel which represents the approach you use the least?

4. Music: Listen to "We Can Work It Out" by the Beatles
This song was written in 1965 by John Lennon and Paul McCartney of the highly acclaimed British rock band The Beatles. This song was number 1 in the US, UK, and Canad,a and according to some critics, it is very representative of the Beatles' musical style and message.

Before listening to the song, your teacher will prepare a written version of the lyrics with blanks left for some of the words. (The teacher could also assign students to prepare the written version with blanks.)

First, listen to the song without looking at the written version: https://www.youtube.com/watch?v=Qyclqo_AV2M
Now read through the written version your teacher (or classmates) has shared with you while you listen to the song again. Finally, listen a third time and check your answers.

Discuss
1. Do you think this song is only about a couple experiencing conflict in their love relationship?
2. What do you think about the song's message about settling conflicts? Are there both positive and negative elements in this message?
3. Have a listen to the version of the song performed by an Israeli Jew (Noa) and an Israeli Arab (Mira Awad) in 2002: http://www.youtube.com/watch?v=lFwRyaTvnYg. How does this version give you a different way of viewing the song?

    Explore on your own: This song has been recorded by dozens of artists in many different styles over the years (most recently a reggae version in 2009 by The Slackers). Explore other versions of this song on Youtube.

SELF-ASSESSMENT
Think about your learning. Complete a self-assessment for this chapter by using the template at the end of the text (p. 194).

> *Learning Tip: Maybe your progress in English feels slow. That's okay. Language learning is a lifetime project. Stay hopeful and optimistic about your learning. Take as your motto the refrain from the Beatles' song: "We can work it out!"*

Chapter 15 - Growing in Resilience

Get to Know Each Other Better

River of Life: At the beginning of this course, you drew your own river of life. You thought of your life as a river. The beginning of the river is like the early years of your life with your family. As the river flows, it moves through the different years of your life to the present.

Look again at the river that you drew. You probably showed some calm and peaceful times in your life. You may also have shown the hard times in your life, which flow like a violent and noisy river.

Now *add to your picture* people and events in your life that have made you a stronger person. What people and events helped you to grow in resilience?

Circle Sharing: When you are finished revising your picture, move the class into a circle and let everyone in the circle share one thing that has given them strength and courage in life. Follow the normal rules of circle sharing. If anyone does not want to share, that person may pass the talking piece to the next person in the circle.

Connect to the Topic

We all have people and events in our lives that have shaped us into who we are. As you have learned throughout this course, every member of the class has his or her personal interests, gifts, talents, and strengths. Everyone has made a positive contribution of some kind to the learning experience of the whole class. In this last chapter we consider how this course may have added to your personal resilience.

Look at the pictures:

1. Which caption goes the best with each picture below? First decide on your own. Then discuss your choices with the rest of the class. More than one right answer may be possible. Be ready to give reasons for your choices.

   A. "Resilient communities have resources to carry them through the deep waters of trauma and on toward healing."

   B. "The route from violence to healing is a long journey toward a brighter hope."

   C. "Resilient individuals and societies endure rough roads and hard climbs."

   D. "Traveler there is no path; we make the path by walking" (Antonio Machado, Spanish poet)

2. Which picture speaks the most powerfully to you? Why?

Shutterstock

READ

Develop your reading skills:
For this chapter, practice some of the important skills that you have learned in this course.
<u>**Before you read**</u>: (1) **Survey** the reading by looking at the title and the bold headings. (2) **Think about what you already know** about the topics referred to in the title and headings. (3) **Ask questions** related to each heading or (4) **Predict** what you think will be discussed in each section. (5) **Read the first and last paragraphs**.

<u>**While you read**</u>: (5) **Make connections** with what you have read before in this course or (6) **Make applications** of what you read to your own life. (7) **Identify the main idea** of each paragraph and (8) **Summarize** the main idea of each paragraph in one sentence as you go.

You're Already More Resilient!

(1)   When you began this course, you started by reflecting on your personal strengths. It has been the **intention** of this course that you grow even stronger. Your new strength comes from understanding more about suffering and trauma. Resilience is a meaningful concept only in the **context** of suffering. You are going to encounter hard times in life. You need knowledge and practical skills to face these hardships and survive. You want to grow strong enough so that you not only bounce back from traumatic experiences but **flourish**.

5

What you have learned about cycles of violence

(2)   You have learned that people spin in unending cycles of victim and aggressor for several reasons. When victims act out, they can become offenders. As aggressors, they **discharge** their trauma energy. But this trauma energy is not discharged in ways that bring them healing or completeness. Wreaking damage on the lives of others, they further traumatize themselves. When they take out their anger on others, they **violate** basic human values written deep within them.   There is a small voice within us all that questions the rightness of our actions and **nudges** us in healing directions. Sadly, we often ignore that voice. So we get trapped in the cycles of violence.

(3)   But does it have to be this way? No. As chapter 11 pointed out, "The cycles of violence can be repeated many times. But they can also be broken and **transformed**. First, people must become aware that they are trapped in a cycle. They must be aware that they do not have to continue harming themselves or others. They can choose to break free and begin walking the healing path."   The drive or need to "unfreeze" and heal stays with us no matter how long ago events happened. Individuals and groups can choose a healing path years later.

What you learned about the journey out of trauma

(4)   On the healing path, you work on addressing your own inner pain as well as on mending relationships with others. You become aware of your natural biological reactions to stress. You learn how to calm yourself and how to identify and talk about your emotions. You learn that some of the stress in your life comes from injustices in the larger society around you. Perhaps, it comes passed down to you from your **ancestors**.

(5)   You know the importance of getting to a safe place—physically, emotionally, or spiritually—in order for healing to begin. You realize that supportive and trusting relationships with other people are important. It is important to find a compassionate listener with whom to share your story. Your condition may be serious enough that the listener should be a professional counselor.

(6)   You must be **discerning** about the leadership that you trust. The way leaders (community officials, religious leaders, counselors, presidents) **interpret** events and frame what is happening might help individuals and groups to heal. Or these leaders could further **inflame** situations, keeping individuals and groups stuck in the cycles of violence. Positive leaders value freedom of speech and the ability to question. They separate **fantasy** from reality and **evaluate** dangers **realistically**. They help people reconnect to families and other groups because the leader is not the center of meaning for people in crisis.

(7)   Finally, in the previous four chapters, you learned about important stops you might make during the healing journey. You are ready to encounter the truth. You consider the risks of forgiving offenders. You remember that the truest justice is restorative. And you develop your creative problem-solving skills in order to build peace. Searching for answers and learning new skills will not only serve you in the future when you may be wounded in a traumatic event. These skills also help you build resilience and flourish in life under any **circumstances**.

You have choices to make

(8)   This path is not the same for every individual and it is not linear. The Spanish poet Antonio Machado (1875-1939) expressed it this way: "Traveler there is no path; we make the path by walking." As you deal with hardships in your life and perhaps face trauma, you may spend time at one or more of these stops on the healing path. After a time of recovery, you may find yourself suddenly back in the victim or the aggressor cycle. When that happens, however, you know there are **options**. Knowing what the choices are makes it easier for you to get back onto the path.

(9)   Individuals, communities, and societies can make the choice to transform great suffering into great wisdom. Trauma can be seen as an invitation to spiritual, emotional, and social transformation. If we say "yes" to this invitation, the resulting journey is "spiritual work of the deepest sort," says trauma expert Carolyn Yoder. "The journey leads into the depths of ourselves as individuals and groups. Here we come face to face with our own darkness. In this unlikely place, grace **abounds** and transformation and hope begin" (C. Yoder in *The Little Book of Trauma Healing*).

UNDERSTAND WHAT YOU READ

There are nine paragraphs in the reading above. Look at the reading again and match each topic with the number of the paragraph in which it is discussed. The first one has been done for you.

Topic	Paragraph number
People don't have to stay trapped; the cycles of violence can be broken	___
The path to healing is not straight and not the same for everyone	___
Leaders can play an important role for good or bad in the recovery from trauma	___
This course has been about growing more resilient	_1_
Understanding truth, forgiveness, justice and peace can bring healing & strength	___
Bad things happen when people get trapped in victim and aggressor cycles	___
Working through great pain and suffering, people can become wiser and better	___
Being safe and rebuilding trust are important in the recovery process	___
It's helpful to have personal awareness of where stress comes from and how one can cope	___

Pay attention to the details of the reading. If you need to read the text again, do so now. Then solve these riddles by matching the words on the right with the sentences.

1. ___ This idea only has meaning in relation to hardships in life.
2. ___ People who hurt other people experience this.
3. ___ This is where some stress in people's lives comes from.
4. ___ Positive leaders encourage this.
5. ___ People with serious trauma need this.
6. ___ This is essential for getting on the path to healing
7. ___ Having set out on the healing journey, a person can eventually get this.

a. injustice in society
b. asking questions
c. resilience
d. a trained counselor
e. trauma
f. wisdom
g. making a choice

Pay attention to important ideas in the reading. Match the correct ending with each sentence.

1. A small voice within us gently pushes us in healing directions ___
2. Even if traumatic events occurred years ago, ___
3. Bad leaders can keep their people stuck in cycles of violence ___
4. Separating real dangers from imaginary dangers, ___
5. When leaders are not the center of meaning for people in crisis, ___
6. If we slip back into the cycles of victim & aggressor, ___
7. We can experience change and begin to have hope for the future ___

a. positive leaders help their people to break free from cycles of violence.
b. because the healing journey leads us to face the darkness within ourselves,
c. they can help people reconnect to families and other groups.
d. as it questions the rightness of our actions.
e. by the way they explain events in the life of the community or nation.
f. people still feel a need to "unfreeze" and can choose a healing path.
g. we can more easily get back onto the healing path because we know what the choices are.

Discuss

1. Did you learn anything new from reading this text or was everything just a review of the previous chapters? In your opinion, what is the most important new idea in the text?
2. Paragraph 7 claims that the skills mentioned can help in all situations in life—not just in recovering from trauma. Can you give examples of how these skills are useful now and not just in the future when hardship may strike?
3. The last paragraph of this reading may represent the deepest thoughts in this book. Why does Carolyn Yoder (cited in the text) call the journey of healing a spiritual work? What does that mean to you? What does she mean by saying that bountiful (or overflowing) grace can be found in our inner darkness?

WORD STUDY

A. Define it yourself

ancestor _____
      (*hint*: use your knowledge of trauma passing from one generation to the next)

option _____
      (*hint*: compare with the next sentence; consider also the main topic of this paragraph)

transformation _____
      (*hint*: review the verb form of this word that you studied in chapter 9)

Word meanings

B. *Match each vocabulary item in columns 1 with the most appropriate meaning in column 2.*

New vocabulary	Line	Answers		Meanings
1. intention	2	___	a.	a small, gentle push or poke
2. context	3	___	b.	wise, knowing, deep understanding
3. flourish	6	___	c.	be plentiful, exist in great numbers, overflow
4. discharge	9	___	d.	break, go against, oppose, offend
5. violate	12	___	e.	explain, define, create meaning
6. nudge	13	___	f.	purpose, desire, goal
7. discerning	31	___	g.	dream, product of imagination
8. interpret	32	___	h.	do well, be successful, grow strong & healthy
9. inflame	33	___	i.	words, ideas, or facts in the surrounding area
10. fantasy	35	___	j.	in relation to the real facts & situation; not imagined or hoped for
11. evaluate	35	___		facts & situation
12. realistically	35	___	k.	let out, release, send out, relieve
13. circumstance	42	___	l.	condition or situation (that affects something else)
14. abound	54	___	m.	think carefully about and judge, decide the worth of something
			n.	cause great emotions or anger, make something worse

C. Fill in the blanks

Use vocabulary items number 1 through 7 to fill in the blanks. The sentences are part of a story.

1. Juan was feeling very tense because of some problems in his life. He got into an argument with his wife when she _____ him so that she could move past him out of the kitchen.
2. This event occurred in the _____ of a discussion they were having about money problems.
3. He became angry and said some unfair things that _____ her personal dignity.
4. It was never his _____ that he should say anything to hurt her feelings.
5. He wished that he had been more _____ in choosing his words.
6. Juan is sorry that he _____ his anger on his wife.
7. He wants to have a marriage that _____ and brings happiness to both him and his wife.

Use vocabulary items number 8 through 14 to fill in the blank. The sentences are part of a story.

8. Parts of the country _____ in energy resources like coal, oil, and natural gas. Experts have estimated these resources as being worth billions of dollars.
9. Unfortunately, the country's corrupt leaders only have _____ [plural] of increasing their personal wealth by selling the country's natural resources.
10. Ordinary citizens cannot _____ hope to see any benefits from these resources.
11. The global economic recession is causing increased suffering and has _____ people's opposition to the government.

12. Opponents of the government have begun to _____ the situation and are making a plan of action.

13. They believe that the _____ are right for creative nonviolent actions to force change in the government.

14. If they have _____ the situation correctly, nonviolent actions now could lead to positive changes.

D. Answer these questions using your new words in complete sentences. Then do the **give one/get one activity** with your classmates. Ask as many class members as you can to share two or more sentences with you.

1. What difficult circumstances did your ancestors face? How did your ancestors exhibit strength?

   _____

2. What intentions do you have after completing this course? What options will you have if you can get more education? or What options will you have if you move to a different community?

   _____

3. What is the best way for you to discharge the tensions that you feel building up in your body?

   _____

4. Who or what in your life nudges you to treat people respectfully? What things influence people to violate the rights or dignity of others?

   _____

5. How do leaders sometimes interpret events in ways that inflame conflict?

   _____

6. Dream for a minute about transformations that could take place in your country, community, family or personal life. What kinds of transformation are pure fantasy? What kinds of transformation could realistically occur?

   _____

7. What things are necessary in a community in order for people to abound and flourish?

   _____

8. When you are reading a challenging article, how do you use the context to help you discern the meaning of new words?

   _____

9. How do you evaluate the progress that you have made in this course? or How do you evaluate your own resilience?

   _____

Expression
take out (on someone or something) (verb) – This is a more informal (and normal) way of saying *discharge, let out,* or *release.* The two most common words that occur with *take out* in this meaning of the verb are *anger* and *frustration* (which means *feeling of disappointment, failure or defeat*). On whom do people usually *take out* their anger or frustration? Why do people *take out* their anger or frustration in this way?

Word Families

In chapter 9 you learned the verb *transform*, and in this chapter you met its noun form *transformation*. And in the previous chapter, you learned the word *reality*; now you study related words *realistic* and *realistically*. Study the examples in the left-hand column and make your own sentences in the right-hand column.

transform (verb) - this word is the action that someone or something does	
If we can reduce human violence, we will *transform* this community.	
transformation (noun) – this word refers to the **result** of action that has been done	
The *transformation* of the community will benefit many people.	
reality (noun) – we use this word to talk about the *real* circumstances in the world	
They accepted the *reality* that the new people brought different beliefs and customs into the community.	
realistic (adjective) - you already know the word **real.** If we say "His plan was *real*," that means he *really* had a plan; he had a *real* plan. But if we say, "His plan was *realistic*," then we mean that his plan was *sensible* or *reasonable*.	
Her plan was *realistic* because she considered all the circumstances related to the problem.	
realistically (adverb) - we change *realistic* to this form when we want to describe the action that someone is taking, often a mental process.	
She was thinking *realistically* when she made her plans.	

GRAMMAR STUDY

Pronoun usage: You will notice that this text uses a mixture of pronouns. The main pronoun forms are *you, we (us),* and *they.* Scan through the text quickly.
Which pronoun has been used the most frequently? _____

Look at paragraphs 4 through 7 for example. Why do you think the writer used *you* as the main subject of sentences throughout this passage? _____

_____

Now look carefully at paragraphs 2 and 3. Why do you think the writer has used a combination of *they* and *we* (*us*)? Notice especially where the use of *they* stops and the writer switches to *we*.

_____

_____

By changing pronouns, writers change their point of view.
a.   Sometimes writers want to address the reader directly in a pointed way.
b.   Other times they want to present information about others in an objective manner. In doing this, they might suggest that <u>those</u> people (or things) are different from you and me.
c.   And at still other times, writers want to include themselves together with their readers, saying something like "This is true for both the reader and for me, the writer."

Which pronoun will the writer use to express a. _____ , b. _____ and c. _____ ?

Practice with introductory clauses:
Introductory clauses help us to connect two or more ideas together. A comma goes after the introductory clause and signals to the reader that the main clause is coming up.

In a paragraph it is helpful to use introductory clauses as a way to connect smoothly the preceding ideas with the upcoming sentence. In paragraph 2 of the text above, there is a very good example of how introductory clauses serve to create a chain of ideas with each idea linking to the next one.

When victims act out, they can become <u>offenders</u>. <u>Acting as aggressors</u>, they discharge their <u>trauma energy</u>. But
offenders = aggressors   *key words are*

this <u>trauma energy</u> is not discharged in ways that bring them healing or completeness. <u>Wreaking damage on the</u>
repeated to connect the 2 sentences   *this clause explains further what*

<u>lives of others</u>, they further traumatize themselves. <u>When they take out their anger on others</u>, they violate basic
aggressors do   *this clause repeats and reinforces the previous intro clause*

human values written deep within them.
Notice how the main clause in this sentence & in the previous sentence contain <u>new</u> ideas.

You can use introductory clauses of two types. One type is represented by sentences 1a. and 2a. In these sentences, the introductory clauses begin with a subordinating conjunction (like *because, when, as, since,* etc.) include a subject (**bold**) and a verb (*italics*). The other type is represented in 1b . and 2b. In these sentences, the subordinating conjunction and subject are deleted and just the verb (*italics*) remains but in the –ing form.

Examples:
1a. Because **they** *separate* real dangers from imaginary ones, **positive leaders** help their people to break free from cycles of violence.
1b. *Separating* real dangers from imaginary dangers, positive leaders help their people to break free from cycles of violence.

2a. When **we** *know* what the choices are, **we** can more easily get back onto the healing path
2b. *Knowing* what the choices are, we can more easily get back onto the healing path

In order for the –ing form of the introductory clause to work, the subject of the introductory clause and the main clause must be <u>one and the same</u>. Sentence 3b. does not work.

3a. Because **the healing journey** *leads* us to face the darkness within ourselves, **we** can experience change and begin to have hope for the future
✗ 3b. *Leading* us to face the darkness within ourselves, we can experience change….

Now you try changing these introductory clauses to the second type (with an -ing verb).

4. When we slip back into the cycles of victim & aggressor, we can more easily get back onto the healing path because we know what the choices are.

187

5. When they explain events in the life of the community or nation in a certain way, leaders keep their people stuck in cycles of violence

_____

6. Because they are not the center of meaning for people in crisis, leaders can help people reconnect to families and other groups.

_____

7. As it questions the rightness of our actions, the small voice within us gently pushes us in healing directions.

_____

LIFE SKILLS
Story of Resilience

> **Develop your reading skills:**
> Practice some of the important skills that you have learned in this course.
> **Before you read:** (1) **Establish a purpose for reading.** You will remember that the second reading of the chapter usually provides a personal illustration of important ideas in the first part of the chapter. So your purpose for reading could be to see how the story of Neris Gonzalez illustrates growing resilience. Another way of deciding a purpose for reading might be for you to read the discussion questions that follow the reading. Then you could read in order to find answers to those questions. But you could also have a more personal purpose. For example, you could read for the purpose of comparing your own experiences with those of Neris.
> (2) **Connect with previous readings.** You will want to connect this reading with the ideas in chapter 15's first reading. What other readings will you want to connect with this one? (*Hint:* recall that chapter 2 was also about resilience). (3) **Determine what kind of text you are reading**. Is this a personal story told from the viewpoint of the one who experienced the events? Is it a story about another person? Does the story have setting, characters, and a clear series of events ordered by time? Or is this an opinion piece that expresses the writer's opinions on different topics? (4) **Skim.** You can determine the type of text by skimming. Read the bold headings, read quickly the first sentence of each paragraph, read the entire first and last paragraphs. Then go back and read the whole text more carefully. Before you go on, skim now.
>
> *While you read or after the first reading, while you read a second time*: (4) **Identify story elements** and (5) **Make a graphic organizer.** Make a graphic organizer to help you summarize the settings of this story, the characters (or people) involved in the story, and the sequence of events. (6) **Identify the story's main idea.** Do you know where to look for the main idea? What ideas are repeated in the first and last paragraphs? Try stating the main idea in your own words. Do the details of the story support this main idea?

A Resilient Worker for Peace & Justice
by Neris Amanda López González

Neris Gonzalez has endured horrors that most of us cannot imagine, but she has survived. Neris feels it is very important to tell her story. In fact, while she was in the United States, she worked very hard to learn English because she wanted to tell her story to American friends and neighbors, and even to the US government. It is a difficult story to read because of the strong emotions it raises. But Neris wants her story to be shared with others.

    I was a well-known person in the village of San Nicolas Lempa, El Salvador and the surrounding area. I worked to improve health care and education among the poor people of my area. Sadly, I also became well known to the Salvadoran military. They did not trust anyone who worked for justice for the poor. On December 26, 1979, I was out shopping in the market. Some National Guard soldiers seized me.

5   They took me to the basement of the National Guard house. There they kept me for two weeks. They raped me and used horrible methods of torture on my body. But what they did to my mind and spirit was even worse.

Life after torture

10   The torturer° lives inside of me. I fight against this memory of painful torture. ° Sometimes I am afraid to be with people whose personalities remind me of that trauma. So I find it difficult to sustain° relationships in my work and social life.

After torture, it was difficult to be with my family. I became shy with family members. I felt ashamed to be with children, close friends and loved ones. It was too shameful° to tell about the humiliating° things that happened to me.

15   I couldn't concentrate° mentally. I didn't like being alone. I jumped in fear in my sleep. I felt irritated,° worried, and panicky.° Torture is something that remains violent inside the body, causing pain and suffering. It breaks into daily life suddenly. In any given moment, I could be with friends and suddenly feel the heat of shame throughout my body.

20   For 15 years I cried alone and suffered more trauma as the war went on. After the war ended, I wanted to return to my normal daily life. I thought about continuing my education because I was not able to finish high school. But when I tried to study, I felt a struggle going on inside of me. I couldn't concentrate on my studies. I cried a lot and it was hard to steady my emotions. It was hard to find faith again and hope and the small piece of life that is called spirit.

Seeking help in another country

25   I left my country in search of treatment for torture survivors. At Kovler Center in Chicago in the United States I found help. Therapists at Kovler helped me through activities like massage, psychological treatment, and the therapy° of writing a book about my experiences.

While I was in Chicago, I started an organization called Ecovida. In Spanish *ecovida* means eco-life. This organization provided environmental° education. We started vegetable gardens in schools and communities. I worked with youth and adults in communities of Latino immigrants and other poor neighborhoods. This was another form of therapy for me. This work helped me to raise my self esteem, which torture had damaged. I saw children laughing. I watched youth become excited about wanting to understand science and act responsibly toward the environment. °

I also spent some time at places of spiritual retreat.° One was in the mountains of Montana and another at the house of the Sisters of Loretto in Kentucky. My spiritual guide Mennonite Sister Susan Classen helped me lift my self-esteem.° This spiritual therapy was so strong that it complemented° my physical activities. It helped me to connect again with spaces in my body that felt empty.

At home again

Now I am back in El Salvador. I am caring for my mother, who is almost 80 years old, and my special sister. I am working in a program of human rights with the El Salvador Ministry of Foreign Relations. I work for the commission for children who disappeared during the armed conflict. I feel very good about this work because I can identify with° the pain and suffering of the victims' families. This work is another way of re-filling my life with pride and dignity. I keep my goal of finishing my studies in social work, living a new life in the country that tortured me. My time in spiritual retreats filled my body and gave me strength to return to my violent country. I have faith and hope that I will be cared for. Angels are watching over me. I keep fighting against the trauma, and that helps to bring me healing.

In 1999 Neris joined a court case in the United States against two El Salvadoran military leaders who allowed the torture to happen. On July 23, 2002 the jury found the two military men responsible for the torture of Neris and two others. The court ordered the generals to pay more than 50 million US dollars to the three victims. After the trial, Neris said, "Without the case, my therapy would have been about words, not action. The case was the best therapy possible." For more information, see the following articles:

"Torture Victims Win Lawsuits Against Salvadoran Generals" by Manuel Roig-Franzia (Washington Post,

24 July 2002) and "Salvadoran General can be Deported from US for Aiding Torture" (Washington Post, 13 March 2015). Both articles are available online from www.washingtonpost.com

°torturer (n.) – someone who causes great pain to someone else
°torture (v.) – cause great pain to someone else over a period of time to punish or get information
°sustain (v.) – continue something or keep something going
°shameful (adj.) – causing one a lot of embarrassment or shame, shocking to others,
°humiliating (adj.) – making someone feel ashamed, stupid, or bad
°concentrate (v.) – put your mind on something, pay close attention to something
°irritated (v./adj.) – felt bothered, upset or angry
°panicky (adj.) – feeling scared, afraid, or worried
°therapy (n.) – healing treatment for a person who has an illness of the mind
°environmental (adj.) – having to do with the natural world, the air, sea, land, plants, animals & humans
°environment (n.) – the natural world, the air, sea, land, plants, animals & humans
°spiritual retreat (adj. + n.) – a quiet place where one goes to pray and think
°self-esteem (n.) – how a person feels about him- or herself; those with low self-esteem do not feel good about themselves
°complemented (v.) – went well together with something
°identify with (v.) – feel that you understand other people's ideas and feelings

A. *Six of the following sentences about this story are true. Which of the sentences are true and which are false? How would you change the false sentences to make them correct? Write T or F in the blanks.*

1. ___After being tortured, Neris found that she needed to spend time with family and friends.

2. ___Neris did not like to talk with others about what happened to her.

3. ___The hardships that she experienced made it very difficult for her to complete her education.

4. ___The trauma that she suffered affected her mind but not her body.

5. ___She could not find healing from her trauma until she left El Salvador and came to the US.

6. ___Neris felt better when she was working with young people and adults in community gardens.

7. ___She is not a religious person, so she did not get help from church people.

8. ___Neris now takes care of her mother and a sister.

9. ___Through different kinds of treatment, Neris feels safer, and she feels better about herself.

10. ___Neris is very afraid to return to her country.

B. *Discuss*
1. What signs of resilience or strength do you see in Neris? Where does Neris get her strength?
2. Were you surprised by anything in this story? What surprised you?
3. Since you know that Neris returned to El Salvador, what do you think the conditions are in that country today compared to 1979?
4. Neris mentioned getting help at the Kovler center in Chicago. What organizations exist in your country or neighboring countries to provide trauma-affected people with resources to heal and build resilience? Do an Internet search to find some of these resources.

EXTEND YOUR LEARNING
1. Journal
Write your answers to these questions in your journal.
What are some important choices that you have made to live life positively? How have those choices worked for you?

2. Music: Listen to "I Choose" by India Arie

India Arie is an African-American singer in the rhythm and blues tradition, sometimes also called "soul music." She was born in 1975, and since 2001 has won four Grammy awards and sold more than 3 million recordings. Her song "I Choose" comes from her album Testimony: Vol. 1, Life & Relationship which came out in 2006. Listen to the song and read the words at least twice. See the notes below about some of the language.
http://www.youtube.com/watch?v=rKDShRdJ3d4&feature=related

Notes on the lyrics:
There are several African-American dialect features in this song, as well as some features of informal English:
1. gonna – going to (= *will*)
2. gotta – got to (= *has to* or *must*)
3. get it off my chest – honestly tell your inner ideas or feelings to someone
4. let it go – stop keeping ideas or feelings inside, but letting them out
5. a fork in the road – a place where one road divides and the two new roads go in different directions
6. ain't nothing gonna happen – *ain't = is not* (the phrase means *nothing is going to happen*)
7. My past don't dictate – my past *doesn't* dictate
8. done been – have (already) been
9. chaotic circumstances – confusing situations: there doesn't seem to be any order or logic to what happens
10. gonna do what it do – going to do what it does

Discuss
1. Which words of this song can you connect with the story of Neris Gonzalez?
2. What connections can you make between this song and the main reading of this chapter?
3. Are you surprised that the song mentions *shame* (verse 2) and *guilt* (verse 3)? What do guilt and shame have to do with recovering from trauma?
4. The victim cycle in chapter 6 includes the label "helplessness," referring to the kind of helpless people sometimes learn through a traumatic experience. The reading in that chapter says, "They (trauma victims) lose their commitment to do anything to help themselves or to help others." In what ways does this song represent a contrast with the helplessness of a victim?

3. Movement
Create a dance or some motions to go with the song above. How will your movements communicate the ideas of active choosing and deciding?

4. Label the diagram
Think of a difficult situation that you experienced or a family member or friend experienced. Or think of some social situation that you know about. Label the blank snail model on the last page of the chapter to illustrate the stages that you (or the other people) went through. If you experienced any of the acting-in or acting-out reactions, fill those in, as well as any steps in the healing process. Don't worry about leaving out any stages that you did not experience.

Practice talking about your snail diagram with one other person in the class. Then share with the whole class using either formal presentations or the circle sharing method.

SELF-ASSESSMENT

Think about your learning. Complete the assessment using the template on page 194. Discuss your answers with the rest of the class. When you discuss your answers, notice how yours are like or different from your classmates' answers

After completing your self-assessment, use the questions below to think about the whole course.

1. What changes have you noticed in yourself as a learner? (You can look back over your self-assessments and see if you notice any patterns or changes.) Are you now willing to try some ways of learning that you avoided before? What ways of learning have been the best for you?

2. Which ideas in this course stand out the most in your mind? Which ideas have you found to be most related to your own life?

3. What does the future hold for you as a learner of English and as a person who is growing more resilient?

> *Learning Tip: Review your learning goals. How did you do at meeting your goals? Set some new goals for the next stage in your journey as a language learner. What can you plan to do on your own in the next four weeks? What can you plan to do in the next three months?*

Breaking Cycles of Violence • Building Resilience

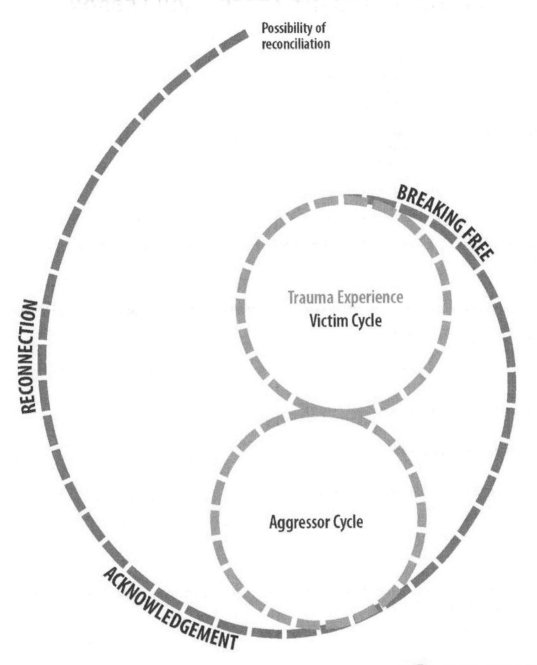

Possibility of reconciliation

BREAKING FREE

RECONNECTION

Trauma Experience
Victim Cycle

Aggressor Cycle

ACKNOWLEDGEMENT

© STAR Team at Eastern Mennonite University.
Adapted from Olga Botcharova's model © 1998. Published in
Forgiveness and Reconciliation, Templeton Foundation Press, 2001.

STAR
Strategies for Trauma Awareness and Resilience ®

Eastern Mennonite University STAR Program

Think about your learning. Use the form below to complete a self-assessment after each lesson. You may photocopy the form or answer the questions in your own notebook.

SELF-ASSESSMENT AFTER EACH LESSON

a. I felt most <u>engaged</u> with the

(choose one)
game
picture discussion
drawing/artwork
movement
circle sharing
music   activity because _____
drama/role play
reading
journal writing
other _____

_____.

b. What was the most important thing you learned from this chapter, and how did you learn it?

_____.

c. What was the most uncomfortable part of the lesson for you? How did you feel at that moment? Did your feelings help or hinder your learning? _____

_____

d. One thing that I want to practice more is _____

e. An idea that I want to explore more is _____

f. For me, the most unclear part of the chapter was _____

_____

Discuss your answers with the rest of the class. When you discuss your answers, notice how yours are like or different from your classmates' answers.

Vocabulary Reference List

The words in this list are organized alphabetically. All words followed by the number 1 are from the first reading in each chapter. Those followed by 2 are from the second reading. The chapter number in which the word is featured is at the far right of each column.

n = noun   np = noun phrase   v = verb   vp = verb phrase
adj = adjective   adv = adverb   p = preposition   pp = prepositional phrase

	Reading		Chapter		Reading		Chapter
abounds	1	v	15	bitterness	1	n	12
abuse	1	n	3	blurt	2	v	6
academic dean	2	np	1	bottle up	1	v	7
access	1	n	14	bounce back	1	v	2
accommodate	1	v	14	bouquet	2	n	8
account for	2	v	1	boycott	1	n & v	14
accumulate	1	v	9	break free	1	v	11
accurate	1	adj	7	break out	1	v	11
accusation	2	n	14	break the silence	1	vp	11
accuse	2	v	7	brief	1	adj	7
achieve	1	v	12	bring back	1	v	7
acknowledge	1	v	7	build bridges	1	vp	8
acupoint	2	n	7	buy into	1	v	10
acute trauma	1	np	4	cadet	2	n	6
adequate	1	adj	14	calm	1	adj	2
affection	2	n	9	calmness	1	n	7
affirm	1	v	8	catch off guard	1	vp	6
aggression	1	n	10	chaplain	1	n	12
aggressive	1	adj	10	charge	2	v	14
aggressor	1	n	10	chosen trauma	1	np	10
agonizing	2	adj	6	chronic	1	adj	6
agricultural	2	np	1	circumstances	1	n	15
cooperative				collapse	2	v	13
alert	1	adj	8	collar	2	n	6
ancestor	1	n	10	colleague	2	n	7
angina	2	n	6	collective resilience	1	np	2
anxiety	1	n	4	collective trauma	1	np	4
anxious	1	adj	9	commission	2	n	11
appeal	2	v	11	commitment	1	n	6
appetite	1	n	9	communal	2	adj	11
approach	1	v	10	communicate	1	v	1, 8
arrest	2	v	9	communicative	1	np	1
at the expense of	1	pp	11	language teaching			
atmosphere	1	n	10, 11	community	1	n	2
authentic	2	adj	8	compassion	1	n	8
authorities	1	n	12	compatriot	2	n	11
avoid	1	v	6	complement	2	v	2
aware	1	adj	5, 7, 11	complex	1	adj	11
axis	1	n	10	complexity	1	n	11
be present for	1	vp	8	complicated	1	adj	11
be the target of	1	vp	3	component	1	n	13

compulsive	1	adj	9
comrade	2	n	11
concentrate	2	v	2
concentrate	1	v	6
confidence	1	n	2
confront	1	v	11
connection	1	n	7
contact	1	n	5
content	1	n	1
content-based instruction	1	np	1
context	1	n	6, 7, 14
cooperate	1	v	14
cope with	1	v	9
correctional facility	2	n	13
corrupt	2	adj	5
corruption	2	n	5
counselor	1	n	4
counter	1	n	14
counter-violence	1	n	14
creative	1	adj	2
creative writing workshop	2	np	13
criminal	1	n	9
crisis	1	n	7, 10
critical	2	adj	9
criticize	1	v	7
dash	1	v	5
decidedly	2	d	13
defy	1	v	14
dehumanize	1	v	10
delight	2	v	9
demonize	1	v	10
depression	1	n	9
diminish	1	v	6
diplomatic	2	adj	6
disaster	1	n	3
discharge	1	v	15
discomfort	1	n	8
disheveled	2	adj	9
disorder	1	n	9
display	2	v	9
dispute	2	n	14
distress	1	n	4
disturb	1	v	7
domestic	2	adj	8
drugged out	2	adj	12
earthquake	1	n	3
economic recession	2	np	4
elderly	2	adj	8
elderly	1	adj	4
eliminate	1	v	7
embody	2	v	8

embrace	2	v	1
empathy	1	n	8
energy	1	n	5
engage	1	v	7
enormous	1	adj	3
ensure	1	v	13
environment	2	n	2
environmental	2	adj	2
equality	1	n	12
essential	1	adj	11
estimated	1	adj	13
eternal	2	adj	12
ethnic	1	adj	10, 13
evaluate	1	v	15
eventually	1	adv	10
evil	1	n & adj	10
execute	1	v	13
exhibit	1	v	5, 6
explore	1	v	2
expose	1	v	9
extract	2	v	5
extreme	1	adj	3
fantasy	1	n	6, 15
fed up	2	adj	14
felt terrible	2	vp	3
financial	1	adj	9
financially	1	adv	9
first aid	1	np	7
flash backs	1	n	6
flee	2	v	3
flee	1	v	5
flexible	1	adj	2
flight	1	n	5
flourish	1	v	15
frequent	1	adj	6
frustration	2	n	14
fulfillment	2	n	13
generation	1	n	4
generosity	1	n	12
generous	2	adj	11
genocide	1	n	13
glance	2	n	13
gloomy	2	adj	9
goosebumps	2	n	6
grace	1	n	12
gracious	2	adj	11
graze	1	v	5
grieve	1	v	11
ground rules	1	np	8
guilt	1	n	7
hardship	1	n	2
harm	1	n	3
harmony	1	n	7

have issues	2	idom	13
healthy	1	adj	2
hearing	2	n	11
humiliating	2	adj	2
humiliating	1	adj	15
humiliation	1	n	10
hurricane	1	n	3
hypervigilant	1	adj	6
identify	1	v	12
identify with	2	v	2
identity	1	n	10, 12
ignore	1	v	9
illustrate	1	v	13
imagine	1	v	7
immediate future	2	np	12
in the long run	1	pp	5
in the name of	1	pp	10
indicate	1	v	14
indication	1	n	8
inequality	2	n	3
inequality	1	n	13
inflame	1	v	15
inflict	2	v	11
inhuman	1	adj	10
initial	1	adj	6
injustice	1	n	13
insecurity	2	n	5
inspirational	2	adj	14
inspire	2	v	14
instinctively	1	d	5
instruction	1	n	1
insult	1	n	3
intense	1	adj	4
intensive English program	2	np	1
intention	1	n	15
interfere	1	v	5
interpret	1	v	15
interrupt	1	v	8
investigate	2	v	5
irritable	1	adj	9
irritated	2	adj	2
isolate	1	v	6
Jacob wrestling with God	2	allusion	12
JROTC	2	n	4
justice	1	n	11
justify	1	v	10
keep in mind	1	vp	4
knot	2	n	7
labor camp	2	n	9
liaison	2	n	4
liberate	1	v	14
light	2	adj	13
linear	1	adj	6
literally	1	adv	5
livestock	1	n	13
lose track of	2	v	8
machete	2	n	14
madness	2	n	14
major	2	n	5
mass	1	n	8
massacre	2	n	11
massage	2	n	8
memorial	1	n	11
memorialize	1	v	11
mercy	1	n	11
mingle	2	v	14
mini-rage	2	n	12
miserable	2	adj	6
mood	1	n	9
motionless	1	adj	5
motivation	1	n	2
mourn	1	v	11
multiple	1	adj	11
mutual	1	adj	8
name-calling	1	n	3
narrative	1	n	10
national guard	2	n	3
natural resource	1	np	3
neglect	1	v	4
nonexistent	1	adj	14
nonviolence	1	n	14
nonviolent	1	adj	14
nonviolently	1	adv	14
nudge	1	v	15
numb	1	adj	6
observe	2	v	5
of course	1	pp	12
offender	1	n	11
ongoing	1	adj	4
open-ended questions	1	np	8
option	1	n	15
original	1	adj	4
orphanage	2	n	9
overwhelm	1	v	3
panicky	2	adj	2
parallel	1	adj	14
parole violation	2	n	13
participant	2	n	14
participate	2	v	14
participatory trauma	1	np	4

partriotic	1	adj	10
passively	1	adv	14
pay attention to	1	vp	7
peacebuilding	2	n	1
penalty	1	n	13
perceive	1	v	10
performance	1	n	1
persist	1	v	4
persistently	1	adv	14
perspective	2	n	13
pharmaceutical company	2	np	4
physical	1	adj	3
physically	1	adv	3
pick up	2	v	13
pin	2	v	14
policy	1	n	14
pose	1	n	14
positive	1	adj	5
post traumatic stress disorder	1	np	4
prefer	1	v	14
prejudice	1	n	3
preserve	1	v	9
principle	1	n	8
process	2	n	8
process	1	n	7
prohibit	1	v	14
project	1	v	10
promote	1	v	7
protest	1	v	12
psychological	2	adj	2
psychological	1	adj	7
pursue	1	v	13
put an end to	1	vp	10
ransom	2	n	6
rare	1	adj	8
reaction	1	n	4
realistically	1	d	15
reality	1	n	14
reassurance	1	n	7
recession	1	n	10
reconcile	2	v	11
reconciliation	2	n	11
recount	2	v	13
recover	1	v	2
redemptive	1	adj	10
reflect	1	v	8
reflective listening	1	np	8
release	1	v	5
rescue	1	v	4
residential	2	adj	13
resilience	1	n	2
resilient	1	adj	2
resist	1	v	14
resolving	1	v	8
respond	1	v	2
restoration	1	n	11
restorative justice	1	np	13
retributive justice	1	np	13
revenge	1	n	6
risky	1	adj	9
ritual	1	n	11
roar	1	n & v	5
ruin	1	v	9
rumor	2	n	7, 13
sacred	2	adj	8
sacrifices	2	n	4
savage	1	adj	10
scold	2	v	9
secondary trauma	1	np	4
secure	1	adj	10
security	2	n	5
security	1	n	10
self-disciplined	2	adj	9
self-esteem	2	n	2
sense of defeat	1	np	8
sentence	1	v	13
serve a sentence	2	vp	13
set out (on)	1	v	11
shake off	1	v	5
shame	1	n	3
shameful	2	adj	2
shatter	1	v	6
sheath	2	n	14
shock	1	n	3
shortcoming	1	n	10
show up	1	v	6
similar	1	adj	4
simmer	2	v	12
sit-in	1	n	14
slump	2	v	12
snail diagram	2	np	12
social movement	2	n	5
spend time	1	vp	8
spiritual retreat	2	n	2
spree	2	n	12
spring	1	v	5
stabilize	1	v	13
stay on guard	1	vp	6
stirring	2	adj	13
stressed	1	adj	2
strip	1	v	10
structural	1	adj	3
structured	1	adj	13
suicidal	2	adj	7

suppression	1	n	11
surreal	2	adj	12
survivor	1	n	7
suspect	2	v	5
suspect	1	v	13
suspicious	2	adj	5
sustain	2	v	2
sway	1	v	2
symbol	2	n	8
sympathize	1	v	6
sympathy	1	n	8
take out on	1	v	15
take___ a step further	1	vp	12
tampered	2	v	14
target	1	n	3
technical	1	adj	4
technique	2	n	7
tempt	1	v	12
tension	1	n	14
terribly	2	adverb	3
testimony	2	n	11
therapeutic	2	adj	13
therapist	2	n	8
therapy	2	n	2, 13
threat	1	n	3, 5
threaten	1	v	5
throw off track	2	v	5
tolerant	1	adj	9
tornado	1	n	3
torture	2	v	2
torturer	2	n	2
transfer	1	v	9

transform	1	v	9
transformation	1	n	15
trap	1	v	11
trauma	2	n	2
trauma	1	n	3
traumatic	1	adj	3
tremble	1	v	5
trigger	1	v	6
try	1	v	13
tsunami	1	n	3
ultimately	1	adv	12
unbearable	2	adj	14
undocumented	2	adj	4
unspeakable	2	adj	13
urban	1	adj	14
urine	2	n	14
vague	2	adj	9
vehicle	2	n	5
versus	1	p	10
veterinarian	2	n	4
victim	1	n	6
violate	1	v	15
violence	1	n	3
violent	1	adj	3
vivid	1	adj	6
vodka	2	n	9
vomiting	1	n	6
vulnerability	2	n	14
wallow	2	v	12
wand	2	n	11
wreak havoc	1	vp	5
ya gotta beef	2	idiom	12
zone	2	n	3

Index

Keep in mind that you can search for information in this book by using several different tools. For the main topics covered, use the table of contents. For specific reading skills, language functions, grammar structures, and life skills, use the Scope and Sequence chart in the front of the book to help you find the chapters you are looking for. For featured vocabulary words, use the list preceding this index. In searching for other kinds of information, use this index.

About the Author

    R. Michael Medley has taught English to speakers of other languages and provided training for pre- and in-service English language teachers for 30 years in Pakistan and the United States. For 10 years he directed the Intensive English Program at Eastern Mennonite University, and since 2013 has chaired the Department of Language and Literature, where he coordinates the minor in teaching English to speakers of other languages and teaches courses in linguistics, grammar, second language teaching, writing, and public speaking. He specializes in language and culture, English grammar, and methods of language teaching. He also serves as adviser for international students in EMU's Bridge Program and faculty liaison for visiting scholars from China.

    Medley has published in *TESOL Journal, SPELT Journal, CELEA News, College Teaching, Christian Scholar's Review, Global Issues in Language Education*, and the *International Journal of Christianity and English Language Teaching*. He is co-author and editor of a popular teacher resource manual *How to Teach English: A Survival Kit for Teachers of English at the Early Stages*, which was published in Pakistan (1994) where he and his family lived and worked from 1983-94.

    His current research interests include the second language acquisition experiences of trauma-affected learners and strategies for teaching such learners; teaching culture and intercultural communication as a means of peacebuilding; and scaffolding English language learners' access to academic language in complex texts using tools provided by systemic functional linguistics. Many of these interests come together in this textbook for high intermediate and advanced learners of English.